The Caddo Chiefdoms

Indians of the Southeast

Series Editors

Theda Perdue
University of Kentucky

Michael D. Green
University of Kentucky

Advisory Editors

Leland Ferguson
University of South Carolina

Mary Young
University of Rochester

The CADDO CHIEFDOMS

CADDO ECONOMICS AND POLITICS, 700–1835

David La Vere

University of Nebraska Press

Lincoln & London

⊚ The paper in this book meets the minimum requirements
of American National Standard for Information Sciences—
Permanence of Paper for Printed Library Materials, ANSI
Z39.48-1984.

Library of Congress Cataloging-in-Publication Data
La Vere, David.
    The Caddo chiefdoms : Caddo economics and politics,
700–1835 / David La Vere.
        p.   cm.
    Includes bibliographical references and index.
    ISBN 0-8032-2927-5 (cloth : alk. paper)
    1. Caddo Indians—History. 2. Caddo Indians—Politics
and government. 3. Caddo Indians—Economic conditions.
4. Chiefdoms—Louisiana—History.   I. Title.
E99.C12L3   1998   98-13860
976.3'004979—dc21   CIP

For Andrea Kalas

Contents

Series Editors' Introduction

I N the burgeoning literature on chiefdoms, scholars, mostly archaeologists, have taught us much about the political and social organization of Southeastern Indians prior to the arrival of European explorers, traders, and settlers. This scholarship has broadened our understanding of the roles of kinship, exchange, reciprocity, and religion in the development of Mississippian societies. These and other analytical models have become central to our understanding of Mississippian chiefdoms.

Until recently, few ethnohistorians used the work of archaeologists to inform their interpretations of post-contact Native societies. In this new history of the Caddos, David LaVere builds on the scholarship of Mississippian chiefdoms. With roots clearly identifiable in the Mississippian world and with political institutions that conform to our understanding of chiefdoms, Caddo history in the eighteenth and early nineteenth centuries becomes, to LaVere, a continuation of that ancient past. Caddo elites filled leadership positions, found spiritual guidance for political actions, and through control of trade in foreign goods exercised social and political power, much as their Mississippian ancestors had done. LaVere's use of an archaeological paradigm to explain historical events represents the best of ethnohistory. We therefore welcome this important new book to the Indians of the Southeast series.

THEDA PERDUE

MICHAEL D. GREEN

Preface

W HEN I first began researching the Caddos, so little had been published on them that I was torn between writing a traditional political history and taking a more thematic approach. Fortunately, this decision was taken out of my hands, as within the last few years several excellent books on the Caddos have been published. These include Timothy Perttula's *The Caddo Nation*, F. Todd Smith's *The Caddo Indians: Tribes at Convergence of Empire*, and Cecile Carter's *Caddo Indians: Where We Come From*. Because Smith and Carter did such fine jobs chronicling Caddo–Euro-American relations, there was no need to repeat what they had already covered so well. This allowed me to indulge my curiosity and examine themes that show how Caddo society went from powerful, highly ceremonial chiefdoms arising in the eighth century to being forced by the United States to cede their land in Louisiana in 1835.[1]

Since my subject is not Caddo-European relations, I have tried to avoid the traditional method of dividing the Caddos' history into French, Spanish, and American periods and the use of year-by-year chronicling. Having been fortunate to get to know several Caddo people while researching this book, I quickly realized that the Caddos, like so many other Indian peoples, had different concepts of historical periodization than did Euro-Americans. They put little emphasis on events and dates, and rarely think of Caddo history as divided into periods named for and by others. Rather, they seem more concerned with activities and relationships. Caddo relationships, occupations, endeavors, and changes in their society spanned all these "periods." Though a chronological thread runs through the book, each chapter deals mainly with a particular theme: the rise of the Caddo people and the establishment of their Mississippian chiefdom political organization; the Caddos' roles as producers and consumers in the horse-and-hide-for-gun trade, and how the use of kinship made this a particularly lucrative exchange for the Caddos; the many changes that took place in Caddo society from their close association with Europeans and their participation in the hide-and-horse trade; the Osage and Choctaw raids that dissolved some of the old chiefdoms while giving more power to the ancient Kadohadacho chiefdom and the increasing Caddo reliance on European kinsmen; and finally the shattering of the Kadohadacho chiefdom as Americans appropriated Caddo land.

My decision to use a thematic approach was also influenced by the availability of records. Naturally, there were no written documents that detail the rise of the Caddo chiefdoms prior to the sixteenth century, so I had to rely on archaeological and anthropological sources, and a handful of the very earliest firsthand accounts of European contact with the Caddos. Even with the creation of French and Spanish outposts and settlements among the Caddos, the records are sparse. A search through France's Archives des Colonies revealed few important documents relating to the Caddos. Even the Natchitoches Parish Court House, in Natchitoches, Louisiana, the oldest Euro-American settlement in the Louisiana Purchase and the main eighteenth-century outpost among the Caddos, houses only a few records from the French years in Louisiana.

Fortunately, the Spanish were much better about keeping complete records. In Texas, the Béxar Archives provided a more thorough look at the Spanish relations with the Caddos, particularly the communities of the Hasinai chiefdom. Even better, hundreds of unpublished documents relating to the Caddos during the second half of the eighteenth century were found at the Natchitoches Parish Court House, and also among the Papeles Procedentes de Cuba, at the Archivo General de Indias, in Seville, Spain.

The Americans wrote extensively about the Caddos. Because there are few American documents relating to the Caddos during the first half of the eighteenth century yet so many from the second half, a strict chronological approach would be inherently uneven and would short-change the early Caddo-French connection. I hope a thematic approach will alleviate this.

Acknowledgments

While my name appears on the cover of this book as author, it could not have been written without the assistance of a whole army of friends and colleagues. Two men to whom I owe an extremely large debt of gratitude are Gary Clayton Anderson and Michael Green. I do not really believe either of them realizes how much they influenced my thinking, my career, and my life. Gary taught me to broaden my thinking about Indian peoples and drilled into my head that the quality of history you write depends on the questions you ask. Mike showed me how to write about Indian peoples, constantly reminding me to keep the Indians at center stage.

Hard on their heels come people like Harold Livesay, Cynthia Bouton, Theda Perdue, Marietta Le Breton, Pete Gregory, Larry Yarak, Lee Cronk, Butch and Dayna Lee, Loretta Price, Brian Hosmer, Jacob Sulzbach, the late John Impson, Cynthia Vail, and Andrea Kalas. They listened to my ideas, answered my questions, criticized my writing, assisted my translations, allowed me to pester them while continually keeping their good humor, and generally kept my spirits up. Pieces of all of them are in this book, and it would never have been finished without them.

Then there are special people at the universities, libraries, archives, and museums around the world who went far beyond their normal duties in assisting me. Many thanks are due Larry Hill and the Department of History, at Texas A&M University; Bill Page and Susan Pullen, at the Sterling Evans Library, Texas A&M; Henry Hill and Phil Pearson, at Blinn College, College Station, Texas; Mary Lynn Wernet, at the archives at Northwestern State University, in Natchitoches, Louisiana; Randy Lucky, former assistant clerk of court at the Natchitoches Parish Courthouse; and to all the people at the Archivo General de Indias in Seville, Spain, who helped me despite the way I mangled their language.

A word of thanks goes to all my colleagues at the University of North Carolina, Wilmington, for all their indulgence. UNCW provided a summer stipend and a grant from the Moseley Award to help complete the research for this book. A special nod of appreciation goes to Andrew Clark,

Kathleen Berkeley, Michael Seidman, and Larry Cable. I am truly indebted to William Harris, of Earth Sciences, for help with the map.

None of this could have been possible without the support of my family. I owe to my father and mother, Dick and Ann La Vere, debts of all sorts that I can never repay. Thanks also to my sisters, Rhonda and Tracy La Vere. The one sad part in all this was that my father and my grandmother, Sarah Osborne, did not live to see the publication of this book.

Finally, thanks to the Caddo people. Tribal Chairman Vernon Hunter, Buntin Williams, Thurman Parton, Cecile Carter, Roscoe Shemayme, Randelett Edmonds, Phil Newkumet, and Mike Meeks welcomed me with open arms and open hearts. I found that fictive kinship is practiced even to this day. Talking with them provided insights that could not be found in books. They are truly a great people.

The Caddo Chiefdoms

1 // Introduction

> On one of the banks of the [Neches River], which flows near the
> village of the Navedachos, one sees a little mound, which their an-
> cestors erected in order to build on its summit a temple, which
> commanded the nearby village, and in which they worshipped
> their gods. It is rather a monument to the multitude than to the in-
> dustry of its individuals.
>
> ATHANASE DE MÉZIÈRES, 1779,
> in *Athanase De Mézières*
> *and the Louisiana-Texas Frontier,*
> *1768-1780,* 2:263

As Athanase De Mézières gazed at that ancient Caddo temple mound on the Neches River in what is today eastern
Texas, like so many Euro-Americans before him, and
many more after, he misread much of what he saw. He was right about
one thing, however. Long before Europeans arrived, the Caddo peoples
were a great multitude. Prior to the sixteenth century, perhaps hundreds of thousands of Caddo people made their home in an area
stretching from the upper reaches of what today are known as the Red,
Sabine, Angelina, and Neches Rivers in northwestern Louisiana and
northeastern Texas to the Arkansas River in southwestern Arkansas
and southeastern Oklahoma. The Caddos lived in permanent towns
and villages; scratched out fields to grow maize, beans, and squash;
worked the deep, slow-moving rivers for fish and stalked deer through
the woods and meadows. The forests of hardwoods and pines, home to
hundreds of thousands of white-tailed deer and black bears, provided
food, clothing, and the materials for a host of utensils for Indian families. Sometimes Caddo hunters trudged out to the prairies and plains to
the west where, on foot, they hunted buffalo and returned with dried
meat and hides.

By the time the first Europeans arrived among the Caddos, members
of Hernando de Soto's expedition in 1542, Caddo culture had been
thriving for over eight hundred years. Over these centuries the Caddos
had developed powerful political, religious, and economic traditions.

Unfortunately, since the practice of history has usually been confined to what can be found in written records, Southeastern American Indian history usually only begins with the arrival of Soto. This period of Caddo history is often overlooked. By starting Caddo history in 1542, with Soto's expedition, or in 1686, with Sieur de La Salle's lost Texas colony, many of their tactics and actions make little sense—Caddos merely react to the Europeans and become victims of progress.

In reality, traditions developed in the many centuries prior to the coming of the Spanish and French gave the Caddos structures and systems that allowed them to take advantage of the Europeans and adapt to the many changes this meeting brought to their society. So it was ironic that De Mézières would discount the industriousness of the Caddos. Had De Mézières wanted to, he could have found scores of temple mounds throughout the Caddo area. The last mounds had been built during the fourteenth century, but it had taken thousands of highly organized workers under the careful direction of powerful priest-chiefs years to build them. During the Mississippian cultural tradition, which began around A.D. 700, Caddo society depended on maize for survival and prosperity. Because of this, some family leaders gained prestige by their apparent proficiency in controlling the elements that made the maize the grow. As their prestige increased, they were able to call on their extensive kinship relations, and through this became more powerful and further solidified their leadership over their individual community. These chiefs came to wield powerful political and religious authority in their communities, or chiefdoms.

While each Caddo community was a chiefdom in its own right, some of these community priest-chiefs, as they became more powerful and influential, through force and/or diplomacy, drew other Caddo communities and weaker chiefs under their authority. The priest-chiefs also used religious rituals and ceremonies to bolster their prestige and power. For many of these rituals to be effective, the chief needed commodities such as copper and seashells that could only be found outside Caddo territory. With the Caddo priest-chiefs' need for ceremonial goods to validate their authority and because of the Caddos' fortunate geographic location on the margins of the woodlands, prairies, and plains, these powerful Caddo chiefs began to dominate the regional economy.

From the west came Wichita buffalo hides and meat, as well as Pueblo turquoise, cotton, and pottery. From other Mississippian chiefdoms to the east came pottery, seashells, copper, galena, and a variety of valuable stones and minerals. Caddo artisans transformed many of these goods into items that increased the prestige and power of the chiefs, not only among the Caddos but also with other peoples east and west. For example, during the twelfth and thirteenth centuries Caddo artisans at the great chiefdom of Spiro on the Arkansas River produced intricately engraved conch shells and copper sheets, beautifully stylized pottery jars and bottles, sculpted statues of clay and stone, and a variety of other ritual goods. Some of these were destined for the graves of their chiefs, others were put back into the exchange networks for use by other peoples as religious and ceremonial items and as reminders of their chiefs' power. Caddos also provided bois d'arc wood (for bows), hides, salt, maize, and other foodstuffs, but just as important were the news, information, and ideas they circulated. Essentially, the Caddos functioned as a door between the peoples of the Plains and Southwest and those of the Southeast. This ability to be a people "in between" would become a familiar role and one that only added to Caddo authority.[1]

The Caddos' constant demand for commodities brought them into contact with a host of different peoples, many of whom had control over the items the Caddos wanted. To ensure a steady supply of goods, the Caddos had established a system of gifts, reciprocity, and kinships. Strangers were brought into Caddo society by marriage, or they became fictive kin through ritual adoption. Kinspeople had a variety of duties, one of which was to provide generously for their family through the giving of gifts. Adopted kin were expected to give gifts of, among other things, those commodities from their native area that the Caddos needed or wanted.

Through these extended kinships chiefs increased their prestige and influence, but the major multicommunity chiefdoms themselves were never permanent. Over the centuries, various chiefdoms rose and fell. In the fourteenth century, for example, a very long drought made many of the priest-chiefs unable to ensure bountiful harvests, and as famine loomed, the great Caddo chiefdom at Spiro, in present-day eastern Oklahoma, broke apart, scattering many of its survivors south to the remaining Caddo chiefdoms along the Red, Sabine, Angelina, and Neches Rivers. The drought brought an end to mound building throughout the area, and the production of highly stylized religious items also declined. To cope with the hard times brought by the drought, the Caddos came to rely even more heavily on trade with the peoples to their east and west.

By the mid–sixteenth century the great Caddo chiefdom of Naguatex had risen at the great bend of the Red River and had subjugated the nearby communities of Amaye and Macanac. Although he ruled over only a few communities, the chief of Naguatex possessed an influence that stretched across wide ranges of both space and time. In east Texas were the smaller, independent Caddo community chiefdoms of the Nisohone, Nondacao, Lancane, Hais, Soacatino, Guasco, Naquiscoza, and Nazacahoz. From Naguatex to Nazacahoz, all these Caddo chiefdoms continued their exchanges with the Plains Indians and Pueblos, but the rising Apache power in the southern plains began to disrupt the Pueblo connection. Then, in 1542, from the east came the Spanish conquistador Luis Moscoso, leading the survivors of Hernando de Soto's southeastern expedition. The Spanish cut through the Caddo chiefdoms, destroyed and pillaged the villages, and left behind diseases that reduced the Caddo population and disrupted the chiefdoms.[2]

By the end of the seventeenth century several new, large chiefdoms had been formed. The old Naguatex chiefdom had been replaced by a Kadohadacho chief. Eclipsing the Naguatex, later called the Natchitoches, was the Cadodacho community, whose chief ruled three subchiefdoms and whose community gave its name to the entire Kadohadacho chiefdom. The Kadohadacho chief enjoyed tremendous prestige not only among his own peoples but also among the Caddo chiefdoms and peoples in Texas and with the Wichita peoples further west. In Texas, the priest-chief of the Hais community expanded his power into the Hasinai chiefdom and pulled nine other subchiefdoms under his authority. A few small, independent Caddo chiefdoms, such as the Petit Caddos, Yatasís, Lower Natchitoches, Adaes, and Ais, had been settled along the Red River and into east Texas. Just as they always had, the Caddo peoples of these chiefdom communities controlled the regional economy, still exchanging maize, salt, pottery, and bois d'arc wood for hides, meat, and horses, which were beginning to appear on the margins of Caddo territory.

When the Spanish and French arrived in Caddo country, in the last years of the seventeenth century, the Caddos found that their political and economic traditions allowed them to take an active role in shaping European needs to their advantage. These Europeans were quickly pulled into the Caddo kinship system and were expected by their Caddo kin to provide valuable firearms, musket balls, kettles, cloth, beads, and a host of manufactured goods. Although the chiefs tried to control the flow and distribution of these European wares, any Caddo individuals who could acquire and distribute these goods found their own prestige enhanced. Since the wealth and prosperity of these Frenchmen and Spaniards, and their colonies of Louisiana and Texas, respectively, depended on hides and horses from the Caddos, these Europeans realized that they had better form kinships with the Caddos. Many French traders married Caddo women and thus secured a spot in Caddo society. The Caddos adopted others, making them "fictive" kinspeople. Once they became kin, the Europeans found that they were expected to uphold and abide by a host of social obligations. These included being generous with their new kinspeople by sharing with them valuable gifts of manufactured goods, providing good counsel, and helping them against their enemies. In turn, these European kinspeople received places in Caddo families that ensured them a wife, food, deerskins, horses, and protection—all things the Europeans sought. As long as Europeans upheld their kinship obligations, the Caddos had no need to manufacture these goods themselves as their new kinsmen would supply the goods for them.[3]

The Caddos also took advantage of their position between Spanish Texas and French Louisiana by playing one European empire's colony against the other. Also, French and Spanish settlements in Caddo territory were isolated from other European communities—it was a long way to New Spain and New Orleans—so European settlers in east Texas and along the Red River depended on the Caddos for food and military support, as well as for the hides and horses needed to propel European mercantile capitalism.

They may not have wanted to admit it, but the Spanish and French in the area soon found themselves reliant on the Caddos. The Caddos, drawing on their ancient trade networks, dominated the deer-hide and horse trade. At the same time, to the west, the Caddos managed to thwart their Apache rivals by forming alliances with the Wichitas and Comanches, who were moving onto the southern plains and pushing the Apaches before them. The Caddos brought the Comanches into their trade network by supplying European goods in return for hides and slaves. They maintained such a good relationship with the Comanches that the Spanish eventually begged the Caddos to help arrange a peace between the two. The French and Spanish relied heavily on the Caddos not only as suppliers of deer hides and horses but also as military allies and as diplomats to help keep peace between the many Indians of the area and themselves. To keep the Caddos satisfied and allied, officials from both Spain and France showered them with gifts and exchanged vast amounts of manufactured goods for hides and horses, which garnered for the Caddo chiefs and principal men even more power, authority, and control over the regional economy.

The Caddos developed especially strong kinship bonds with French Louisiana traders and officials, who gladly provided manufactured goods in gifts and trade. But as the Caddos developed a certain dependence on European goods, they manipulated their kinships with the Europeans to their advantage. At the same time, French traders found themselves having to balance the obligations of reciprocity with the need to make a profit from the hide and horse trades. Despite this, the Caddos' desire for manufactured goods and the French need for hides and horse complemented each other, and these kinship bonds that developed between the Caddos and the French citizens of the outpost at Natchitoches remained strong even after Spain received the Louisiana Territory from France in 1762.

Still, while European kinships and manufactured goods could bolster the prestige and power of both individuals and the chiefdoms themselves, these did not come without severe consequences. European diseases devastated Caddo populations to the point where they could no longer function as a viable community and the survivors of some stricken communities were absorbed into other communities. Again, the Caddos turned to old structures to provide a means of dealing with these calamities. As the Hasinai chiefdom broke into its component communities during the middle years of the eighteenth century, for example, the ancient and respected Kadohadacho chiefdom expanded, again with the Cadodacho chief at its head, extending his influence all the way to the communities of the old Hasinai chiefdom. European manufactured goods flooded into Caddo villages, bringing changes in wealth and status but also a dependence on firearms and metal-edged weapons. Essentially, an arms race began, with all the Indian peoples of the area trying to acquire these valuable items. The Caddos' centuries-old exchange networks allowed them not only to acquire the weapons but even to pass some on to their Plains allies, which further cemented alliances.

The wealth the hide and horse trades produced for the Caddos, as well as the constant need of all Indians for firearms, eventually made the Caddos targets of rival Indian exchange networks. Osages from the Arkansas River valley raided Caddo villages for horses and hides, which they exchanged with rival traders from France, Spain, and England. Similarly, after Spain acquired Louisiana in 1762 and England's American colonial border reached the east bank of the Mississippi River, Spanish officials invited Indian peoples living east of the Mississippi, such as the Choctaws, to move west to help form a barrier against Anglo-American encroachment. As the Choctaws moved into Caddo territory, they also raided Caddo villages, hunted on Caddo hunting grounds, and tried to usurp the Caddos' exchange relations with Euro-Americans. Exacerbating these raids were the frequent shortages of European firearms and manufactured goods that often developed because of European wars or from colonial rivalries in North America.

Despite all this, the "great chiefs" of the Kadohadachos, as the Europeans called them, still possessed tremendous power, and the Spanish found them to be formidable figures to deal with, as well as necessary political, military, and economic allies. But by the early years of the nineteenth century the Caddo chiefs had to deal with a much more dangerous problem, namely, the arrival of a people who had little desire to make kinship with the Caddos. With the Louisiana Purchase, in 1803, the Caddos found themselves back in their familiar intermediary position, this time with Spanish Texas on one side and United States' Louisiana on the other. The rivalry between the Spanish and the Americans and the need of each for Caddo allies played into Caddo hands, and by 1815 the Great Chief of the Kadohadachos, as spokesman for all Caddos, reached the zenith of prestige and power.

This soon faded, as American settlers moved into the Caddo area.

Rather than for plying the hide or horse trade, American settlers and local officials wanted to own Caddo land for farming. They saw no reason to form kinships with the Caddos. Also, by the 1820s, after the Mexican Revolution, the Americans came to see Texas as less of a threat, so there was little need for Caddo allies. With few Americans willing to make kinships, Caddo power dwindled, the prestige of the Great Chief declined, and the Caddos in Louisiana found themselves pushed off their lands. In 1835, two years after the death of Dehahuit, the last Great Chief of the Kadohadachos, and under pressure from the United States government, the Caddos ceded their land in Louisiana and moved to Texas.

The amazing thing is not that the Caddos lost their lands—after all the 1830s was the decade of Indian removal—but that after 150 years of sustained contact with the Europeans and Americans they managed to hang on to it as long as they did. Additionally, to the very end, the Caddos retained much of their ancient Mississippian culture. The powerful hereditary Great Chief of Kadohadachos linked the Caddos to these ancient Mississippian traditions and ways of life. In turn, bolstered by the prestige and status accorded him by his descent from the Mississippian chiefs, the Great Chief expanded his own power, created important new kinship bonds, dominated a regional economy, and forced the Europeans to work within the Caddo system of gifts, reciprocity, and kinship, all the while protecting and providing for the welfare of the Caddo people. The death of the Great Chief Dehahuit, in 1833, broke the Cadodacho community's hold on the Great Chief lineage and thereby severed a major link to the once mighty Caddo Mississippian cultural tradition. Only with this and the Caddo land cession of 1835 did the Caddos find themselves having to come to grips with a wholly new world.

Preston Holder, in *The Hoe and the Horse on the Plains,* expressed his belief that the Caddos and Osages, by holding on to old ways, were unable to deal with the changes brought by Europeans, such as horses, guns, diseases, the market economy, Euro-American intruders, and the horse-riding peoples of the plains who raided them. Willard Rollings, in *The Osages,* pointed out that the Osages did change: they expanded their territory at a time when other Indians were losing it, and they even adapted to the European political and economic system. The Caddos of the late eighteenth and early nineteenth centuries fit neither of these patterns. They adapted to the use of horses, guns, and manufactured goods, but within a Caddo society shaped and molded by its Mississippian cultural tradition. Out of the Mississippian years, the Caddo peoples developed the sense of a magnificent history, which provided them with a cultural unity, a reliance on a powerful chiefdom political system, the ability to control a regional economy, and a flexible kinship system that allowed them to embrace wealthy strangers with valuable commodities. Essentially, then, the Caddos' long success stemmed from their ability to incorporate new peoples, commodities, and ideas within their ancient framework. Only when the last important links to these traditions were severed did the Caddos find their power diminished and themselves pushed from their ancient lands. But even at the end of the twentieth century, Caddos still remember that they were once a great and mighty people.[4]

2 // The Ancient Caddo Chiefdoms

[The Hasinai are] a populous nation of people, and so extensive that those who give detailed reports of them do not know where it ends. . . . [They] live under an organized government, congregated in their pueblos, and governed by a cacique who is named by the Great Lord, as they call the one who rules them all.

BISHOP OF GUADALAJARA, 1676;
quoted in Kelley, "Juan Sabeata and Diffusion
in Aboriginal Texas," 989

Y EARS ago, according to the story, the Caddo people lived underground in a village they called Old-Home-in-the-Darkness. Here, thousands of Caddos lived for ages immemorial, growing crops that the "first man" gave them. The "first man," whom the Caddos named Neesh or Moon, also told the Caddos that they should choose one wise and able man to be their *caddí* or chief, that they should do whatever the caddí commanded, and that they should consider him to be a great father. The Caddo people met in council and chose Neesh to be their caddí.

Neesh told the people they were going to leave Old-Home-in-the-Darkness for a new land. The people should divide themselves into groups and each group should select a leader. Once this was done and the people were ready to go, Neesh told the leaders that they must beat their drums and sing as they traveled. Above all, he commanded, no one should look back, because if anyone did, the remaining people would have to stay in darkness.

Neesh led all the people toward the west and they came out of the ground. Some Caddos say they came out at a cave near the confluence of the Bah'-hat-te-no and the Bah'-ha Sah-sin, or what eventually came to be called the Red and the Mississippi Rivers. Others say it was on the banks of Soto Lake, in western Louisiana. Wherever it was, problems soon arose. Coyote came out of the ground early in the procession, and when only half the people had managed to make it out of the ground, Coyote looked back. So one half of the Caddo people continued west while the other half turned back to live in darkness. This place came to be called the Cha-cah-nee-nah, or the "place of crying."

The Caddos who made it out carried corn and pumpkin seeds, pipes, flints—all things to help them in their new world, where they saw the sun for the first time. The Caddos settled along rivers such as the Bah'-hat-te-no, or Red; the upper Cooh'-cooh-ah-tsi-yo, or Sabine; the Nah-cha-wi, or Angelina; and the upper Cah-ye-tsi, or Neches. One of the most important places for these Caddo peoples was a place called "Tall-timber-on-top-of-the-hill," near present-day Caddo Lake, Louisiana. Here Neesh called all the Caddo people in the new world to assemble for the first time. As these people settled in villages along the rivers, Neesh began to make mountains, and from the top of one mountain he saw that some of the people had not followed him but had scattered in all directions. When the people came out of the ground they all spoke Caddoan, but after they scattered into different groups they all began to speak different languages.[1]

Caddo people tell this story to explain their origins and how they came to their traditional homeland in northwest Louisiana, northeast Texas, southeast Oklahoma, and southwest Arkansas. No one can say how long ago this happened. While hunting and gathering peoples lived in this area for over ten thousand years, the Caddo culture emerged in the area between the Arkansas River and the middle reaches of the Neches, Angelina, Sabine, and Red Rivers between A.D. 700 and 800. Though horticulture always had played some role in the subsistence of these early peoples, maize came into their society about this time and helped the Caddo culture to blossom. Maize, beans, and squash—the "three sisters"—became the backbone of Caddo agriculture. While men still hunted and women still gathered, agriculture provided much more food and better nutrition than did hunting and gathering. As settled agricultural communities formed, maize and its two other "sisters" brought a Caddo population explosion, out of which developed a theocratic chiefdom, essentially a political and social system based on rank and status in which the chief possessed both political and religious authority. Since agriculture became the mainstay of Caddo society, the Caddos developed religious rituals, ceremonies, and activities, such as sun worship and mound building, that "ensured" successful crops and increased the authority of the chief, thus shoring up this ranked system. Because the rituals often required goods not found in the Caddo area, the Caddos' participation in long-range and large-scale exchange networks took on a new significance.[2]

During the eighth and ninth centuries this change from hunting and gathering to more complex forms of social organization based on maize agriculture also occurred among peoples living in the Southeast and the Midwest. After 700 the peoples of southeastern North America entered a period that archaeologists call the Mississippian cultural tradition. Caddo culture formed the westernmost part of the Mississippian tradition, and the Caddos may have been instrumental in passing on many Mississippian traditions to the southeastern peoples.[3]

As Caddo culture blossomed after 700, two related but separate Caddo societies developed. One was south of the Ouachita Mountains, mainly along the Red River, in northwest Louisiana, northeast Texas, southeast Oklahoma, and southwest Arkansas; the other was north of the Ouachita Mountains, along the Arkansas River basin in western Arkansas and eastern Oklahoma.[4]

One of the earliest southern sites recognized as Caddo is the George Davis site, between Alto and Nacogdoches, Texas, which began about 780. Here the Caddos built a village of round, thatched houses and a ceremonial center, complete with a conical burial mound and two platform temple mounds. In the north some of the earliest Caddo sites were found along the Arkansas River; one on Plum Bayou, in central Arkansas, and the other near present-day Spiro, Oklahoma, on the Arkansas River near the border of Oklahoma and Arkansas. Between these two major concentrations and radiating out from them, Caddos lived in small, dispersed villages and hamlets along the area's rivers and streams.[5]

Among the Caddos, two types of population centers formed: large, well-populated, centralized towns and ceremonial centers with temple mounds, and more dispersed rural hamlets surrounded by corn fields but with no mounds among them.[6] Together, a ceremonial center with its central town and temple mound surrounded by several dispersed outlying hamlets created a single community, such as the Cadodacho, Nadaco, Natchitoches, and Petit Caddo "tribes" the Europeans saw in the late 1600s. In reality, because of their political system, these individual Caddo communities were small chiefdoms in their own right. In some instances a community chief might increase his power, enlarge his territory, and, either peaceably or through force, pull several nearby communities under his political and religious leadership to form a single major chiefdom. Essentially, then, these were all separate and individual but culturally and linguistically similar Caddo communities, each led by a chief, and with some of them tied together under the leadership of a more powerful priest-chief. For example, when Europeans first made sustained contact with the Caddos, in the late 1600s, they found the Hasinai chiefdom, in eastern Texas, composed of ten communities, or subchiefdoms; the Kadohadacho chiefdom, at the great bend of the Red River, comprising four separate subchiefdoms; and several independent Caddo community chiefdoms south of the Kadohadacho and east of the Hasinai.

Because agriculture became so vital to these communities, most, especially the mound centers, formed along major rivers and streams; the rural hamlets without mounds were usually located on sandy ridges or terraces above small streams. The town, with its temple, became an important hub for the surrounding area, as the priest-chief lived and performed the essential religious ceremonies there. Dispersed about the town, anywhere from a half-mile to several miles away, were the smaller, rural, family-oriented hamlets. These hamlets depended on the town for religious and chiefly leadership. In return, they provided warriors, workers, and additional food and other goods for the town's chiefs, nobles, and commoners. A community's area, incorporating its town and hamlets, depending on the prestige and power of its chief and the amount of arable land, might stretch anywhere from ten to eighty miles. In 1716 the Spanish reported that the territory of the Hasinai chiefdom's Nacogdoche community, in eastern Texas, consisted of a main village and twenty-one hamlets, which the Spanish called *rancherías*. Together they covered a distance of about twenty-five miles from north to south. Similarly, the territory of the Ais community was home to seventy families settled into eight *rancherías* scattered over a distance of five miles.[7]

Despite the differences in size and social rankings between the central town and the outlying hamlets, residents in both relied heavily on the farming of maize, beans, and squash, and to a lesser extent on hunting. The amount of arable land played an important role in determining the physical size and prosperity of the village or hamlet. Between 700 and 1550 hundreds of Caddo towns, villages, and hamlets dotted the area between the Arkansas and Red, Sabine, Angelina, and Trinity Rivers. According to archaeologist Timothy Perttula, precontact Caddos lived in an area that supported a large number of people, possibly as many as 250,000.[8]

Like other Mississippian peoples in the Southeast and Midwest, the Caddos developed a political system based on chiefly authority. Chiefdoms possessed marked degrees of social rankings in which there was inherent inequality and that were led by high-status individuals who inherited their positions. At the top of Caddo society was the chief and his or her close relatives. People in the community were given their social rank according to how close their genealogy lay to the chief. Chiefs wielded greater authority, controlled resources, and could coerce community members into complying with their edicts.[9]

A Caddo chief's authority came from being the head of a lineage considered to be descended from the sun. In essence a Caddo chiefdom was a theocracy, with the chief serving not only as political leader but also as the religious high priest. When the Spanish missionaries arrived at the Hasinai chiefdom, in the 1690s, they found the priest-chief, called the *xinesí,* ruling like a king; he was considered the most influential and powerful individual in the area. The xinesí ruled several nearby communities, lived in the town of the chiefdom's main community, performed no manual labor, built neither his own house nor temples, and neither personally planted, harvested, nor hunted. In minor chiefdoms independent of any major chiefdom, the role of xinesí might be included with that of community chief.[10]

As the religious and political leaders of possibly two or more communities, the xinesís performed a number of duties, especially in their role as the chiefdom's high priest. The xinesí, whose person was considered sacred, either led or participated in the special rites and ceremonies that maintained the people's proper relationship to the gods. Some of the xinesís' most important spiritual duties included guarding the sacred fire, consecrating the sowing and the harvests, and officiating over the first-fruits and naming ceremonies. The important political decisions for the chiefdom, such as those determining peace and war, also fell to the xinesís. They also assembled the leaders of individual communities of their chiefdoms to demand tributes, oaths, and promises in order to appease the gods. Through their moral authority, the xinesís controlled much of the labor of their subjects.[11]

The xinesís ruled by virtue of their descent from the sun. The Caddos recognized the sun as essential for agriculture, and the xinesí, who served as the sun's representative on earth, became instrumental in performing the rituals to ensure agricultural success. This close relationship between the xinesí and the sun can be seen in the building of platform mounds and the placement of temples on top of these mounds. Sometimes the xinesí's residence would be built atop these mounds, all of which placed him higher and therefore closer to his celestial kinsman. The xinesí also maintained the sacred fire, which was considered a piece of the holy sun on earth. When xinesís died, they were buried in the temples floors or in conical burial mounds surrounded by sumptuous grave goods.[12]

Among his subjects, the xinesí wielded considerable but circumscribed power. The Caddo people accorded him tremendous respect and tried to supply him with whatever he needed. The xinesí could sentence lawbreakers to punishments ranging from minor whippings to death for crimes against chiefs or their families. Still, the authority of the xinesí was limited, as he was required to meet with a council of nobles and other high-ranking men to listen to their advice when making certain decisions. The successful leadership of the xinesí and other Caddo governing elites depended largely on the leader's wisdom, charisma, and generosity. A leader ruled more by example than by sanction, with compromise and consensus essential. Much of the leader's actual power came from generously redistributing the wealth and tributes that his position earned him. The xinesí gave gifts, sponsored feasts, provisioned war parties and construction details, and doled out food to subjects hit by hard times. This generosity gained the xinesí, as well as other local leaders, even greater status and power through the creation of reciprocal obligations—to accept a xinesí's generosity was to create a debt.[13]

While the xinesí sat at the pinnacle of a Caddo chiefdom's society, below him existed a set of Caddo nobles and functionaries who wielded power in their individual communities, towns, and hamlets and acted as subchiefs and advisors to the priest-chief. Below the xinesí was the caddí, who also inherited his position and possessed some religious authority but served as the chief of a single Caddo community. While the xinesí ruled a large, multicommunity chiefdom, each separate community of the chiefdom was governed by a caddí, who presided over the smaller community temple but mainly handled the affairs of everyday community life and decision making. In those Mississippian Caddo communities not connected to a larger chiefdom, the caddí acted as both the political and religious leader for community.[14]

The position of caddí was very prestigious. Father Francisco Casañas, a Spanish Franciscan missionary in eastern Texas and one of the first Europeans the Caddos encountered on a sustained basis, wrote in 1691 that in "each tribe there is a caddí. He is like a governor ruling and commanding his people. . . . Each caddí rules within the section of country occupied by his tribe, no matter whether it be large or small."[15]

The caddí was required to handle a wide range of duties. To assist him and to serve as his advisory council were the *canahas,* the representatives from the outlying rural hamlets scattered around the community's main town. The canahas were mainly elders and were probably the patriarchs of lineages, as most hamlets were lineage-based. The canahas, sometimes referred to as "principal men," not only were close advisors but also might be used on diplomatic missions. Though the caddí exercised power, he still required consensus for many decisions. According to Father Casañas, "If the caddí wants to do anything, he calls the old men together, listens to each of their views, and then decides to do what he thinks best, explaining his view to some of the men and urging agreement. So all go away satisfied and of the same opinion."[16]

With the assistance of his advisory council, the caddí met with his counterparts from other communities to settle disputes between them and assembled the canahas to advise him on some decision that would affect the whole community. The caddí judged, punished, and sometimes expelled lawbreakers. It also fell to the caddí and the canahas to conduct the councils that planned the seasonal buffalo hunts. At these councils they also planned raids on enemies, selected the leader of the war party, and then hosted the victory ceremony. Around the community the caddí and canahas set the dates for the building of houses, hosted the occasional community feasts, and provided food and other goods for them. They also sponsored and officiated at the planting and harvest ceremonies. When emissaries or foreign visitors arrived in a community, the caddí and canahas formed the official village reception committee, conducted the calumet ceremony, presented gifts to the emissaries, received the gifts given by them, and then distributed the gifts among the community's populace.[17]

The high status and prestige of the xinesís and other governing elites even affected how the Caddos reckoned heredity and descent. Unlike other Southeastern Muskhogean peoples, most of whom were matrilineal, the Caddos utilized a unique bilineal system based on the rank of the father and the mother. When a child was born, if the mother was of a higher rank than the father, then children of both sexes traced their descent through the mother's lineage. If the father was of a higher rank, the sons belonged the father's lineage and the daughters belonged to the mother's. The xinesís, caddís, and canahas all inherited their positions from their fathers. In 1691 Father Francisco Casañas reported that "the office of caddí also descends through the direct [that is, male] line of blood relationship." Father Isidro Espinosa noted in 1722 that "all these people have their principal captains. His office is perpetual and one of his sons or relatives inherits it when he dies. There is no controversy or litigation in this arrangement. If the chief captain dies, leaving only a small son, the Indians recognize him as their head and, during his minority, they furnish him a counsel [*sic*] composed of *caziques* who supply the place of chief and carry him to all the meetings . . . [and] assign to him the highest seat."[18]

The caddís, and possibly even the xinesís, did not always have to be male. Spanish missionary Gaspar Solís, who visited the Hasinai chiefdom's Nabedache community during the mid–eighteenth century, reported "there is an Indian woman of great authority and following, whom they call Santa Adíva which means 'great lady' or 'principal lady.' Her house is very large and has many rooms. The rest of the Nation brings presents and gifts to her. She has many Indian men and women in her service called tammas conas, and these are like priests and captains among them. She is married to five Indian men. In short she is like a queen among them." A woman caddí may not have been uncommon during the Mississippian cultural tradition, as other peoples in the Southeast possessed female chiefs as well.[19]

Below the xinesís, caddís, and canahas existed a hierarchy of minor functionaries, who, though important, did not partake in the community decision-making process. *Tammas* and *chayas,* who also inherited their positions, carried out the decisions made by the caddí and canahas, with the tammas responsible to the caddí and the chayas subordinate to the canahas. It was the tammas who actually directed community work projects. They also collected the first harvests of various plants and took them to the caddí for use in ceremonies. The tammas and chayas tended to act as town criers, making sure the villagers were informed of assembly decisions and then ensuring the decisions were carried out.[20]

The village *conna,* or medicine man, though not involved in the political decisions of the community, was considered a very important person in Caddo society. He handled the medicine and curing of the people, utilizing herbal medicine as well as prayer, rituals, and divination. The position of conna could be precarious as he might be killed by village or family members if a person was not cured of an illness. Constant failure to cure might bring a charge of witchcraft upon the conna, which could lead to execution.[21]

While elites inherited most Caddo political offices, some commoners rose to nonhereditary elected or appointed governing positions, such as that of war chief. The war chief, and warriors themselves, occupied an important and honored position and contributed to the chiefdom's and community's decision-making process. Warriors who achieved a victory could add the term *amayxoya* to their names, which meant "great man." When strangers approached a Caddo town, the war chief at the head of a party of warriors met the strangers and escorted them to the caddí.[22]

Despite the need for consensus, the xinesís, caddís, and canahas wielded considerable power over the general population. The construction of large platform temple mounds required the ability to raise and direct an enormous number of workers over long periods of time. At the community level the caddí could deploy and control labor for building houses or planting and harvesting. According to Father Espinosa, who lived among the Hasinai chiefdom in 1722, when a person needed a new house, he contacted the caddí or canaha. The caddí chose the day for construction and then directed the tamma to announce the date among the people. The tamma spread the word and ordered the men of the households to bring poles to create the frame of the house, while women brought the thatch for making the roof and walls. On the day of construction the people arrived with their poles and thatch and, at the caddí's signal, construction began. Latecomers received five or six strokes from a switch from the tamma, but according to Espinosa, no one was offended by this punishment.[23]

The caddí also deployed labor at planting time. The women were told the date that planting was to begin so they could gather and prepare food for those involved. On the designated day, those chosen to actually till the soil, using hoes of seasoned walnut or buffalo shoulder blades, worked the fields of the xinesí first, then the fields of the caddí, and then, in turn, those of the other political and religious officials. While this crew did the heavy work of turning the soil to a depth of several inches, members of each household planted the seeds. According to Father Casañas, during the period of planting "the caddíces work like the rest, but the grand xinesí never goes out of the house for anything except to take a walk or to make certain visits."[24]

While Caddo people might have been divided between leaders with high rank and commoners without significant rank, it would be more appropriate to say that the typical Caddo community was divided between leadership households and commoner households. People from the elite households governed the towns and hamlets while commoners provided work and service.[25]

For Caddos, kinship played an extremely important role as each individual was enveloped from birth inside a web of kin relationships. Unlike Caddo nobles, whose descent would be determined by the rank of the father and the mother, Caddo commoners lived within a matrilineal kinship system and were born into a matrilineal clan. The Kadohadacho chiefdom communities recognized at least eight clans: Sun, Thunder, Beaver, Eagle, Raccoon, Otter, Wolf, and Panther. According to Father Juan Morfí, the Hasinai Caddos said that some of them were "descended from bears, others from dogs, beavers, coyotes, etc." Unfortunately, this is all that is known about Caddo clans, and since so little information about them exists, it is impossible to discuss with any certainty the rules that governed clans and their members. The Caddo clan system has not survived into the late twentieth century; the

Caddo people do not remember their clans, nor do individual Caddos consider themselves members of any particular clan.[26]

If Caddo clans were similar to other Southeastern Indian matrilineal clans, then individuals were expected to marry outside their clans. Marriage was a rather simple affair to arrange for those Caddos not born into the governing elite. Most Caddos married at the age of eighteen or nineteen. Men had to prove they could support a wife by at least being able to kill a deer. A brave man personally asked the woman's parents for her hand; those a little more timid sent an old man, or maybe a relative or a friend, to ask for them. The prospective groom brought presents to the woman's parents. If the woman's family did not like her suitor, they could reject him. If they agreed, they accepted the presents. According to anthropologist John Swanton, who studied the Caddos during the early twentieth century, marriages for commoners tended to be matrilocal, meaning a Caddo man usually went to live with his wife's family. As in all matrilineal societies, the couple's children reckoned descent from and belonged to the family and clan of the mother.[27]

In matrilineal societies, the mother's eldest brother played an important role in the education and discipline of children, especially his nephews, since he was in the same clan as them, unlike the father, who was in a different clan. Maternal uncles disciplined their nephews, and the boys listened to these uncles even more closely than to their biological fathers. Politeness toward maternal uncles and fathers was essential, and no child, of whatever age, talked back, especially if these men were governing officials, connas, or warriors. With age and seniority being one of the dividers of a Caddo community and household, this politeness carried over to most seniors. People never referred to their elders by name; instead they used terms of respect for older men and women—*tsa* for men, *sa* for women.[28]

Still, boys mainly learned from their maternal uncles all that they needed to know to become Caddo men, warriors, and husbands. Maternal uncles taught their nephews Caddo traditions and history, as well as how to hunt, make war, and conduct the many ceremonies and rituals they needed to know. Caddo society was divided by gender, and girls, though they respected their maternal uncles, remained under the supervision of their mothers, aunts, and other women of the clan. From them the girls learned how to farm, cook, sew, tan hides, and conduct the rituals and ceremonies they needed to know to become Caddo women, wives, and mothers.

In day-to-day Caddo life, men and women lived in different worlds. The men fished or hunted deer, bear, and small game. The bow and arrow had been developed around A.D. 400, so Caddo men had long been proficient in its use. In fact, the Caddos became known for their fine bows made of the pliable bois d'arc, or Osage orange, wood. While men hunted, women managed the household and gathered hazelnuts, figs, berries, grapes, and tuna cactus (prickly pear) fruit. Women also participated in festivals and public ceremonies.

There were also times when men and women worked together. When it came time to till the soil, all members of the town or hamlet turned out, with the men breaking the soil while the women planted the seeds of corn, beans, melons, and other vegetables. In the fall, many members of a community made trips on foot to the prairies and plains to hunt buffalo. Before the Caddos acquired horses, this was a time-consuming job, with men killing the buffalo and women dressing the meat and hides. Only a few buffalos could be butchered since without horses, everything had to carried back to the community on the shoulders of the men, women, children, and dogs. For this reason, during these early Caddo years, deer were always more important to Caddo subsistence than buffalo. In the wintertime, when they were not hunting, the men spent the cold days making bows, arrows, moccasins, and hoes while the women dressed deerskins and buffalo hides, wove reed mats for bedding, and made earthen pots and cane baskets.[29]

Caddo families lived in large, thirty-foot-diameter, dome-shaped houses made of cane, wattle, or straw, which, from afar, looked like a large beehive or haystack. Inside these huts lived three generations of families related by blood or marriage. A Caddo commoner household contained ten to twenty persons led by a middle-aged woman. She controlled the house and the fields around it. The older generation occupying the house consisted of the woman who "owned" the house and her husband. If her mother was dead, some of her unmarried or widowed sisters of approximately the same age might live with her. The next generation consisted of her daughters and their husbands, if they had married, as well as unmarried sons. Finally, the third generation comprised the children of the middle generation. The matriarch of the household had much influence over what happened in her house and became involved in the activities and personal lives of the household's members. Conversely, the domestic authority of the matriarch's husband was limited to his responsibilities for his sister's children, who lived in another house in the community. While ties between parents and children were strong, there was an especially strong bond between grandparents and grandchildren.[30]

The Caddos possessed close kinship ties among themselves, but they also developed close relations with other, more distant peoples. The Caddo peoples of the Mississippian cultural tradition, like all peoples in eastern North America of that time, did not live in isolation. Rather, they participated in dynamic, long-distance exchanges that brought them into contact with a variety of different peoples and cultures and in which a wide array of subsistence and ceremonial goods changed hands. Some of these exchanges took place peacefully, as gift-givings and trade, some violently, as raids. It was not unusual for the Caddos and other eastern peoples to make very long journeys, sometimes over a thousand miles, usually on trading expeditions, but sometimes on raids and attacks.[31]

The Caddos built on ancient exchange systems and networks already in place by A.D. 700. For example, peoples living in the Caddo area between A.D. 1 and 600 often interacted with peoples living along the Mississippi River to the east and with other peoples living in northeastern Oklahoma. Sometimes these interactions could be violent, as can be seen in some burials found in southern Oklahoma dated between 400 and 600. Archaeologists have found the skeletons of nine individuals, killed by arrows, that still contained several large dart points stuck in their bones. The type of rock used to make the points and the style in which they were fashioned indicate that these people were killed by outsiders raiding the area. Similar sites abound. In fact, skeletal remains in eastern Oklahoma and northern Texas dated prior to the rise of the Caddo culture show high levels of violent injuries, indicating fierce conflicts between groups. These raids and hostilities between peoples in different regions coincided with the expansion of ranked societies and chiefdoms in the area.[32]

Whether it was to raid or to trade, Indian peoples used a web of trails that connected different regions and cultures of North America. A southern east–west route originating on the Atlantic coast near present-day Saint Augustine, Florida, became one of the most important trails. It passed along the Gulf coast, crossed the Mississippi River near Natchez, continued west, and reached the Red River among the villages of the Natchitoches Caddo community near the present-day town of the same name, in Louisiana. Several north–south routes crossed this major east–west trail, thus connecting it to the peoples of northeastern North America. From the villages of the Natchitoches Caddos, the trail continued west through the Caddo communities in eastern Texas, crossing the Angelina, Neches, Trinity, and Brazos Rivers; these communities would eventually form the Hasinai chiefdom. From there the trail passed through present-day San Antonio, Texas, on its way to Chihuahua and Casas Grandes (a major Pueblo trade center during the thirteenth century), and then south into the Valley of Mexico.[33]

The Natchitoches Caddo villages along the Red River formed at an important crossroads for four major trails. The first was the major southern St. Augustine–Casas Grandes trade route. The second was a more northerly route from the Natchitoches Caddos up the Red River to the communities of the Caddo chiefdom on the great bend of the Red River, near present-day Texarkana, Texas, where the Kadohadacho chiefdom would eventually form. From there the trail followed the Red River to the Wichita Indian villages, eventually crossing the southern plains and connecting to the Pueblo towns around Santa Fe. While this second route was used by the more southerly Caddos to reach the Pueblos, prior to the fifteenth century the more northern Caddo communities along the Arkansas River reached the Pueblos by following the Arkansas and Canadian Rivers. A third route ran northeast from both the Natchitoches and Kadohadacho communities, linking them to the communities of the northern Caddo chiefdom at Spiro and to the great mound-building chiefdom and population center at Cahokia, east of St. Louis. The fourth was a southwestern extension of the third route, going from the Kadohadacho communities at the great bend of the Red River, through the Hasinai communities in the Neches and Angelina River valleys, and finally connecting to the major southern trade route on its way to the Casa Grandes.[34]

The ability of the Caddos to control the crossroads of these important trails, as well as to maintain their geographical position in the area where the southeastern woodlands met the western prairies and Great Plains, allowed them to tap into exchange networks across the continent. Though Indian peoples raided each other, they also peacefully exchanged a much greater quantity of goods. These items usually fell into two categories: subsistence goods and ceremonial goods. Subsistence goods included such things as corn, beans, deer or buffalo meat, salt, and wood for bows. Ceremonial goods, which raised the status of a Caddo individual, might include such items as sea shells, nuggets of copper or turquoise, galena, pipes, and even certain forms of pottery.[35]

For these peaceful exchanges to take place, the participants had to produce something the other needed or wanted. This "mutualistic exchange" involved critical resources. One society traded certain special goods for things that only another society could provide, like corn for buffalo meat, or bois d'arc wood for tuna cactus fruit or pottery jars. Most of the people in these societies were able to participate in this exchange, and everyone benefited. The problem with this type of exchange was that it had the potential to create a degree of dependency on the goods or services of the other group.[36]

Although it is difficult to track the exchange of subsistence goods during the years prior to the eighteenth century, the Caddo peoples along the Red and Arkansas Rivers probably exchanged corn, beans, squash, and other products with the Wichitas and other peoples to the west for bison meat. Salt from saline springs near the Red River became a major commodity Caddos provided to southeastern peoples who needed it to bolster their primarily agricultural diet. Since bois d'arc wood grew abundantly in the Caddo area, the Caddos earned reputations as being some of the finest bow makers, and Caddo traders exchanged bows and bois d'arc wood for a variety of goods with peoples living in all directions.

Status-producing ceremonial goods are much easier to track, and the Caddos, especially the great Spiro chiefdom on the Arkansas River, controlled a large number of them. Many of these ceremonial goods—sea shells from the Florida Gulf coast; copper from the Great Lakes; mica, flint, marble, and greenstone from the Appalachian Mountains; flint from the Ouachita Mountains; and galena and flint from the Ozark

Mountains—wound up in Spiro, indicating the robust trade and exchange that took place with the Caddos. Spiro craftspeople often reworked these raw materials, which were of ceremonial value even in unworked form, into virtual works of art, which then might be reexchanged or buried as grave goods with Spiro chiefs in large earthen mounds. Besides these raw materials, Spiro also received a large quantity of already processed ceremonial goods, such as intricately engraved shells, worked copper, chipped stone, and wonderfully designed and crafted ceramics. Most of these goods, which were created at other sites in the East, became grave goods for Spiro and other Caddo regional elites. The burials at Spiro contained hundreds of pounds of shells and beads, engraved conch shells, copper plates, and carved-stone ceremonial items such as pipes, as well as feather cloaks, woven mats, and blankets. There were more of these ceremonial Mississippian tradition items found at Spiro than at any other major southeastern ceremonial center. Not all these went into graves, and the chiefs at Spiro redistributed many of these ceremonial goods. They also added some of their own crafts, such as flint knives and points, copper-coated wooden pins, effigy pipes, and shells etched with such motifs as winged snakes, spiders, large cats, and many almost individualistic human figures engaged in all sorts of activities, from playing games to hunting. Besides these ceremonial goods, the Spiro peoples also received such mundane items as buffalo wool and rabbit-hair yarn.[37]

Prior to the fifteenth century, Caddos elites controlled most of this ceremonial goods exchange since the goods were to be used in religious rituals, with most eventually winding up in the graves of chiefs. In fact, the ability to control trade helped create status and bolstered the creation of the hierarchical chiefdom theocracy. A Caddo lineage leader would be in a position to dominate regional exchange connections through his ability to control the labor of his kinspeople, upon whom he could prevail to produce items for exchange. The lineage head might request labor or goods from his kin in order to sponsor a feast or a special ritual. Those community members who benefited from the feast or ritual found themselves obligated to reciprocate and provide the lineage head with labor or goods. The lineage leader could generously redistribute these goods to create an even greater cycle of debt and reciprocity, called buffering exchange, through which he or she gained even greater status. The person who acquired and controlled the goods needed to perform religious ceremonies that ensured successful harvests and prosperous times, and who had a number of kinspeople already in his or her debt, gained additional followers and power. During the eighth century some Caddo lineage heads, through control of the ceremonial goods trade and buffering exchange, gained enough power to establish themselves and their lineages above the rest to become the lineages that produced caddís, with a few rising even higher to become the producers of xinesís. As will be seen, the Cadodacho community at the great bend of the Red River seemed to be especially adept at providing high-status, powerful Caddo chiefs.[38]

Spiro elites used these ceremonial goods to consolidate their power by parceling out some of these goods to regional Caddo communities controlled or allied to the Spiro chiefdom. These ceremonial goods, by the religious and spiritual power imparted to them, helped place those who controlled them at the top of the Spiro social pyramid, but they also gave power to the Spiro chiefdom in the Caddo region. As archaeologist Dennis Peterson determined, Spiro elites' "position and the right to wield power were represented by conspicuous wealth like engraved copper and shells. These exotic items may have made the leaders of the Spiro society feel they could control or influence the natural elements."[39]

The Caddo chiefdoms also participated in the Southern Ceremonial Complex, a religious movement that swept the Southeast from about 1250 to 1450. Though regional diversity existed, certain motifs characterize the Southern Ceremonial Complex and are often seen inscribed on pottery, effigies, pipes, gorgets, and shells found in Caddo burials. These motifs include bilobed arrows, striped poles, batons and maces, fringed aprons, effigies of men playing the game *chunkey,* circles with crosses inside of them, forked human eyes, long-nosed masks, and human hands with eyes or beads at the wrist. The human figures engraved on many of these goods wear ear spools, necklaces with pendants, hair knots on the back of their heads, and tasseled belts.[40]

The Caddos, like those at Spiro, may well have been the prime exporters of the Southern Ceremonial Complex religion, as Caddo ceremonial goods have been found not only in the Southeast but also on the plains to the west. Mississippian cultural tradition trade items, such as shell gorgets and copper earspools, have been uncovered at sites on both the southern and northern plains. Gulf coast shells and a Caddo "weeping eye" pipe have been found in Harlan County, Nebraska. Caddo pottery and a marine-shell, long-nosed god mask have been found in Woodbury County, Iowa. Other Caddo pottery and pieces of a Caddo pipe from southeastern Oklahoma and from Louisiana have been found in Saline County, Kansas. Shell gorgets with weeping-eye motifs have been found in Wells County in eastern North Dakota, and in Burleigh County in southeastern North Dakota. Caddo Mississippian tradition influences have also been found among the peoples living at that time along the upper Republican River.[41]

Besides tangible subsistence and ceremonial commodities, contact with other peoples also brought information and new ideas that influenced agriculture, religion, and the culture in general. Participation in exchange systems may have provided the Caddos with influences from Mesoamerica, which in turn may well have brought about the characteristics associated with the Mississippian cultural tradition and the Southern Ceremonial Complex. These Mesoamerican influences came through the Gilmore Corridor about A.D. 500. According to anthropologist Alex Krieger, this corridor was a belt of prairie running diagonally across Texas from the Rio Grande to the piney woods of eastern Texas. Through this corridor passed the major southern trade route, going southeast from the Caddo communities on the Red River and eastern Texas all the way to the Valley of Mexico. The corridor was easy to travel because it was open grassland, and the many rivers and streams cutting through it were narrow and not choked with undergrowth. Ample game, fish, birds, and plants provided sustenance for any travelers.[42]

Exactly to what extent Mesoamerica influenced the southeastern part of North America and whether Mesoamerican peoples actually brought maize to North America is hotly debated by scholars. Krieger believed that the Gilmore Corridor was used only for communication and not so much to introduce tangible Mesoamerican products, like maize plants. None of the foreign peoples who used the corridor stayed in it long enough for them to influence directly the cultures of the people living on the Caddo side of it. It was probably used by traders, travelers, and migrating peoples, and they passed through the corridor rather quickly. "If small groups passed along it more than once in a century or so, we should expect to find much more material evidence of it," Krieger wrote. Instead of tangibles, the peoples moving through it passed on concepts and information associated with Mesoamerica. The Davis Site, located between Alto and Nacogdoches, Texas, was one of the earliest truly Caddo culture sites. It sits at the top of the Gilmore Corridor in eastern Texas and may well be the place where Mississippian cultural tradition characteristics, concepts brought by Mesoamerican traders, originated and then spread throughout the Southeast.[43]

There is no doubt, though, that the Caddo cultural characteristics of the Mississippian tradition appear similar to those found in Mesoamerica of that time. Historian Francis Jennings believed that one of the best indicators of this influence was the change in mound construction that took place throughout southeastern North America around 800. The shift from conical burial mounds to flat-topped platform mounds on which temples and houses for the chiefs were placed indicated an intrusion of Mexican ideas into Louisiana. Jennings believes the Southeast suffered an actual physical invasion of Mexicans, with a Mexican ruling class imposing their will and religion on the area peoples and creating the platform mound complexes, especially the great mound complex at Cahokia, Illinois.[44]

Although it is not apparent that a Mexican ruling class was imposed on Caddo commoners, a small, copper, long-nosed mask from about 1200 found in the Gahagan Mound, in northwestern Louisiana, is tangible evidence of Mesoamerican influence on the Caddos, if not actual exchange. The mask was three inches tall and two inches wide with a long, seven-inch copper strip for the nose. Long-nosed masks have been found throughout eastern North America, including sites in Wisconsin, Missouri, Florida, Oklahoma, Tennessee, and Alabama, and they cut across cultural traditions of the Southeast. The mask found at the Gahagan Mound, which was actually used as an ear ornament, was not manufactured by the Caddos but more than likely was created elsewhere and traded to them. Anthropologist Charles Hudson believes these long-nosed masks indicate a definite Mesoamerican connection through traveling Aztec traders, called *pochtecas,* who may have ventured into the Southeast. The god of these Aztecs, named Yacatecuhtli, was often portrayed with a long nose.[45]

Between 800 and 1350 the Caddos reached an incredibly high level of political and social complexity, as indicated by their political chiefdoms, stratified society, ceremonial centers with temples and large earthen mounds, extensive trade routes delivering exotic goods, and sumptuous graves for the elites. Then, after about 1350, Caddo society faced a series of crises that forced it to become less dramatically ceremonial. After 1350 the Caddos stopped building the great earthen temple and burial mounds. During this time the great Spiro chiefdom broke apart. Burials became less elaborate, and rather than conducting mass burials, Caddos began to bury their dead in individual graves. These crises (identified below) also forced the Caddos to increase their trade with the plains and Pueblo peoples, and soon stone arrowpoints and knives, bison bone tools, and new pottery styles came to predominate in Caddo society.[46]

The most likely cause for this shift came from long-term climatic changes that brought a decrease in rainfall to the central plains and prairies. This drought eventually affected all the Caddo communities, but it hit the Spiro chiefdom in the Arkansas River valley especially hard. Maize agriculture became precarious as decreasing and less predictable rainfall made the growing of corn and other crops less reliable. Soon the land could not support the large, highly organized population and hierarchical social system. Building such large earthen mounds needed a huge population, as well as a political system that could organize such a work. This required plenty of food, which in turn created pressures on the surrounding arable land. As food shortages developed, the priest-chiefs along the Arkansas River valley, now obviously unable to control the elements, faced more difficulty in preserving order and harmony. By 1450, with its economic support gone, the large chiefdom at Spiro collapsed and these Caddos moved away into smaller villages and hamlets in order to take advantage of isolated arable lands. Many of these people moved further south and joined the Caddos living along the Red River and in eastern Texas, who had also quit building large, temple mounds during this time. By 1550, though most Spiro villages and hamlets in the Arkansas River basin had been abandoned and the building of mounds had ceased throughout Caddo country, the Caddo chiefdoms, along with their ceremonial centers and stratified societies, remained entrenched among the Red River and eastern

Texas Caddos, though on a less ceremonial scale than previously.[47]

This climatic change forced the remaining Red River and eastern Texas Caddo peoples to find new ways to live. Up to this time most Caddo trade had been with the Mississippian tradition peoples to east and southeast. Now, during the first half of the fifteenth century, without giving up their connection to the Southeast, the southern Caddos greatly expanded their exchange networks to the west, eventually reaching the Pueblo peoples west of the Great Plains. Because of their geographical location on the edges of the woodlands, prairies, and plains, the Caddo communities along the Red River and in eastern Texas came to dominate the regional economy between the Mississippian Southeast and the Puebloan Southwest, acting as trade middlemen between the two regions.[48]

One of the first western exchange links these southern Caddo communities made was with the southernmost bands of the Wichita peoples, such as the Teyas, who lived in semipermanent villages along the rivers and springs in the Texas panhandle and southern Oklahoma. The Teyas were a plains-dwelling, Caddoan-speaking Wichita people who lived in small semisedentary villages along the upper Brazos, upper Red, and upper Canadian Rivers. After 1350 the Teyas created a mutualistic exchange with the Pueblo peoples, such as those around what would become known as Galisteo and Santa Fe. In the early years of this exchange the Teyas and other plains peoples provided bison meat and hides to the Pueblo peoples and received corn in return. The Pueblo people wanted bison meat to supplement their corn diets but found it difficult to get enough buffalo meat as the climatic change pushed the buffalo further into the lusher grasses of the east. In return the Teyas and other southern plains peoples, who had access to plenty of buffalo, needed more corn to help when crop failures due to drought caused shortages.[49]

With trade connections now more open between the Wichitas and the Pueblos, the Caddo traders from the southern communities moved to participate in and take advantage of this exchange. These Caddo traders visited the Wichitas, usually carrying pottery, bois d'arc wood, and salt. Shards of pottery from the Caddo communities at the great bend of the Red River have been found at numerous sites that were occupied by the Wichitas and at Pueblo sites as well. The Wichitas might have used some of these Caddo goods themselves or exchanged some of them with the Pueblo peoples. From the Pueblos, the Wichitas received corn, but also pottery, turquoise, and cotton cloth, and they put these into the exchange network going back east. Fragments of Pueblo pottery has been found at Red River Caddo sites in northeast Texas.[50]

While the Teyas and other Wichitas may have been the major link between the southern Caddos and the Pueblos, as this cross-plains trade picked up momentum, more direct contact developed between the Caddos and Pueblos. The Red River was a natural travel artery to the Pueblo villages of New Mexico. The Sanders site, in Lamar County in northeastern Texas, the western-most site of Caddo mound building, provides good evidence of the vitality of this trade. Peoples moving up and down the Red River frequently visited the site, leaving behind the pieces of their broken utensils and wares. The site abounds with pottery shards from other places. For example, the remains of Caddo jars that were mainly used as trade items have been found there. Also found were conch-shell gorgets and beads of *olivella* shells, as well as awl sharpeners of Catahoula sandstone, which were carried to the site from southeastern Texas or southwestern Louisiana. Other evidence of direct Pueblo-Caddo interactions has been found at the Moore site in Major County, Oklahoma. Here archaeologists found 310 turquoise beads, a turquoise pendant, and 210 *olivella* shell beads in the grave of a person who may have been one of the Pueblo traders or ambassadors who periodically visited the area between 1400 and 1600.[51]

As this direct Caddo-Pueblo exchange solidified, another crisis arose between 1450 and 1500 that disrupted this trade, namely, the arrival of the Athapaskan peoples on the southern plains. While their arrival did not sever the exchange relations between the Caddos and Pueblos, it forced the Caddos to develop other routes, linkages, and types of exchange with the Pueblos and the peoples of the southern plains. These northern Athapaskan peoples had been migrating south out of present-day Canada by following the expansion of the tall grasses in the central plains. As these hunting and gathering peoples, who came to be called Apaches, expanded into the southern plains along the eastern frontier of the Pueblos, they formed new alliances with the Pueblo farmers of the Galisteo basin and Pecos River valley. This changed the overall Caddo-Wichita-Pueblo exchange system.

Apache newcomers began to squeeze out the Wichitas as the main suppliers of bison meat and hides to the Pueblos, and suddenly the Caddos and Wichitas found themselves in competition with the Apaches for Pueblo commodities. This trade rivalry led to conflict between the Caddo-Wichita alliance and the Apaches, which remained sharp up through the early nineteenth century.[52]

By 1500 the Apaches took over most of the Pueblo trade and halted the Caddos' exchange across the southern plains. The Apache wedge forced them to forge new trade routes further south with such peoples as the Jumanos and Coahuiltecans. Still, the Caddos and Wichitas did not disappear from the Pueblos. Francisco Coronado, during his sojourn at the Pecos Pueblos in 1541, found two Caddoan-speaking Indians, one of whom the Spaniards called the Turk, who was a priest and was possibly an ambassador to the Pueblos.[53]

While the Caddos were adjusting to the Apache intrusion a more serious crisis appeared from the east in the mid-1540s that brought tremendous destruction to the Caddos, as it did to most Indian peoples of the Southeast: Spanish troops, led by the conquistador Hernando de Soto, landed in Florida in 1539. In his search for gold, Soto cut a swath of fire and blood through almost every major southeastern chiefdom. Soto's successor, Luis Moscoso, finally reached the Caddo chiefdoms in 1542, as the Spanish expedition tried to escape the Southeast through the Gilmore Corridor.

In July 1542 the Caddo communities of Amaye, Macanac, and Naguatex, located at the great bend of the Red River, found themselves confronted by Moscoso's army. Moscoso had learned that each community was ruled by a chief, but that the chief of Naguatex governed all, with the chiefs of Amaye and Macanac his vassals. Undoubtedly hearing of the Spaniards' trail of destruction throughout the Southeast, the chief of the Naguatex ordered a surprise attack, but the Spanish stood firm and Caddo warriors suffered great losses in defeat. The Spanish marched into the main village of Naguatex, where they spent two weeks appropriating food, supplies, and slaves, then burned the town before crossing the Red River and entering the lands of the eastern Texas Caddos.[54]

The Caddo communities of eastern Texas, many with names strikingly similar to those the Spanish would again encounter in the late

1600s, now became casualties of war. At the chiefdom of Nisohone the Spanish entered one of the outlying hamlets, describing it as "a town of four or five houses, belonging to the cacique of that miserable province, called Nisohone. It was a poorly populated region and had little maize." Unhappy with the lack of supplies at Nisohone, the Spanish continued their march, finally approaching the chiefdom of Nondacao, which they described as "a very populous region and the houses scattered about one from another as is customary in mountains, and that there was abundance of maize." The chief of Nondacao immediately submitted; he and his principal men appeared before Moscoso "weeping like those of Naguatex, that being their custom in token of obedience." Other Caddo chiefdoms fell before the Spanish, including the Lancane, the Hais, the Soacatino, the Guasco, the Naquiscoza, and the Nazacahoz. Of the eastern Texas chiefdoms only the Hais put up any resistance, battling the Spanish for an entire day before being defeated. Among the Guasco the Spanish found cotton shawls and chunks of turquoise from the Pueblos. Unfortunately for the Caddos, the Spanish realized that supplies became more meager as they traveled further west, so they turned around and again looted the communities of supplies before moving on out of Caddo territory to the northeast and then down the Mississippi River.[55]

Besides death and destruction, the Spanish also left disease among the Caddos and all Indian peoples throughout the Southeast. At Chaguate on the Ouachita River, near present-day Arkadelphia, Arkansas, a sick Spaniard decided to desert the expedition and live with the Caddos. There is no report of the man's illness, but whatever it was, if it was a viral infection, it could easily have spread throughout the Caddos, who had no immunities to European diseases. This was not the only Spaniard to desert and live among the Caddos.[56]

Soon after the incursions of Soto and Moscoso, diseases began to kill off the people of the Southeast. The population of the Caddo area went from as many as 250,000 to as low as 8,000–40,000 in the late 1600s. Diseases brought both human and cultural loss. Among many of the southeastern peoples, the epidemics wiped out entire populations, often so fast that ancestral traditions were lost. In fact, because of the diseases that swept through the southeastern Indians, archaeologists and historians have been able to study only the smallest fragments of the knowledge, philosophy, religions, and artistic symbolism that was in existence at the time of Soto. Besides decimating populations, disease also decreased the labor force and took out religious lore, traditions, and essential knowledge. It killed off workers, leaders, specialists, and other people essential to the continuation of that society: interpreters, craftspeople, medicine people, hunters, foragers, singers, dancers, and a host of others. The Soto-Moscoso expedition forced many Indian societies of the Southeast to reorganize, including the Caddos.[57]

Because of this decline, large Caddo population concentrations now began to be restricted to areas along the Red River and the other major waterways. By the last quarter of the seventeenth century, the Caddo people lived in a much smaller area than they had at the height of the Mississippian cultural tradition, in 1250. But the chiefdom political system remained, and when the French and Spanish arrived among the Caddos, in the 1680s, the Caddos had coalesced into three regions, with only two major, multicommunity chiefdoms remaining. Just west of the great bend of the Red River, the Kadohadacho chiefdom formed out of the remnants of the Naguatex chiefdom. It comprised four smaller communities stretching along the river: the Cadodachos; the Upper Natchitoches, or probably the once formidable Naguatex; the Upper Nasonis; and the Nanatsohos. In all likelihood, with their defeat by Moscoso, the Naguatex, now called the Natchitoches, had split. An upper group remained at the great bend and part of the Kadohadacho chiefdom, while a southern group moved further downriver, near the present-day town of Natchitoches, Louisiana. The chiefly power of the Naguatex also transferred to the Cadodacho community, which eventually gave its name to the entire Kadohadacho chiefdom. The chief of the Cadodacho community and leader of the entire Kadohadacho chiefdom took on greater importance and exercised his power throughout all Caddo communities. The Cadodacho community came to be held in high respect by all the Caddo peoples and was deemed the progenitor of the entire Caddo people.[58]

The other remaining major Caddo chiefdom was the Hasinai, located southwest of the Kadohadacho along the upper and middle reaches of the Angelina, Neches, and Sabine Rivers, in eastern Texas. Out of the disruptions left by Moscoso in 1542, the chief of the Hais, or

Hainai, expanded his power to create the large Hasinai chiefdom, which possessed a larger population and more subject communities than did the Kadohadacho. The Hasinai chiefdom consisted of ten communities: the Hainai, Nabedache, Nacogdoche, Lower Nasoni, Nadaco, Neches, Nacono, Nechauis, Nacao, and Nabiti.[59]

A third cluster of Caddo communities lived east of the Hasinai and southeast of the Kadohadacho along the Red River and in western Louisiana and eastern Texas. These peoples were either the remnants of a former chiefdom in the area or had broken away from one of the remaining chiefdoms, probably the Kadohadacho, and had over the decades been bolstered by other Caddo peoples. Near present-day Natchitoches lived the Caddo communities of the Natchitoches, Ouachita, and Doustioni nations. These Lower Natchitoches had undoubtedly split from the Naguatex and migrated downriver from the Kadohadacho. Later, the Ouachita and the Doustioni Caddos from eastern and southern Arkansas joined the Natchitoches to create a single community. North of the Natchitoches on the Red River, between them and the Kadohadacho, lived the Yatasís. In the same area lived a group called the Petit Caddos, who tended to center around Soto Lake in western Louisiana. To the west of the Natchitoches, between them and the Hasinai, lived the Adaes and Ais, probably the Caddo peoples who had lived in the area the longest. Sometimes these various entities remained at peace with each other, and sometimes they warred against each other. For example, in 1690, when French explorer Henri de Tonty reached the Red River in his search for the survivors of La Salle's expedition, Yatasí guides refused to lead him to the Kadohadacho chiefdom because they had just killed three Kadohadacho ambassadors and feared retaliation.[60]

To the west of these Caddos lived the Caddoan-speaking Wichitas. Distantly related to the Caddos, politically they were peripheral to the Caddo peoples but still maintained a close economic and exchange relationship with the Hasinai and Kadohadacho chiefdoms. The Wichitas, whom the Spanish often called the Panis, included the Taovayas, who lived on the upper Red and upper Brazos Rivers, west of the Kadohadacho and Hasinai. To the southeast of the Taovayas, on the Brazos and Trinity Rivers, lived the Tawakonis, Yscanis, and Wacos. Between the Wichitas and the Kadohadacho chiefdom lived the Kichais, a Wichita people who migrated back and forth between the Kadohadacho communities and those of the Wichitas further to the west.[61]

Despite the devastation brought by Moscoso, Caddo exchange with peoples of the southern plains and Pueblos only increased. The coming of the Spanish to the Southwest and the creation of the Spanish province of New Mexico, in the late 1500s, did not halt this cross-plains exchange and in fact contributed to its vitality by introducing guns, metalware, horses, beads, and other types of European goods into the exchange networks. During the 1600s, southern plains peoples such as the Jumanos and the Coahuiltecans became instrumental in connecting the communities of the Kadohadacho and Hasinai chiefdoms with the Spaniards of New Mexico.[62]

The name "Jumano" is applied to a large number of southern plains Indians in southwestern Texas and northern Mexico. They were mainly nomadic hunter-gatherers of the southern plains. Their linguistic affiliation is not clear and has variously been described as Athabascan, Uto-Aztecan, Tanoan, and Caddoan. They are best known as sixteenth-century Indian traders of the southern plains. Prior to the eighteenth century they were allies of the eastern Texas Caddos and became allies of the Spanish when those Europeans arrived, but by 1700 the Jumanos had been absorbed by the southern Apaches. The Jumanos occupied the Concho River area of Texas as early as 1583 and had their trade connections with the Caddos to the east and the Pueblos to the west in place by that time.[63]

Around 1600 the Jumanos began holding trade fairs on the rivers of central Texas, which Caddos from the Kadohadacho and Hasinai chiefdoms attended. Trade fairs had always been important to the Caddos. Now, during the 1600s, trade fairs funneled Spanish and Puebloan goods, songs, folktales, and dances into the Caddo communities. Trade fairs also could in some ways be detrimental to the Caddos. The Spanish in New Mexico also held fairs in order to acquire Indian slaves. Plains Apaches raided Caddo and Wichita villages, took captives, then carried them back to New Mexico, where they became Spanish slaves.[64]

By the mid-1600s long-range exchange networks across the southern plains had become solidified between the Caddos, the Jumanos, and other Indian peoples. Sign language facilitated these exchanges of goods and ideas. Travel from the Jumano winter communities around La Junta to the Hasinai communities took only about twelve days. During the spring, when the trees began to bud, the Caddos began the trading season, often welcoming their Jumano exchange partners or sending out Caddo traders. This trade continued through the summer and early autumn. When the leaves began to fall, the Jumanos left and the Caddos, as well as other Indian peoples, then journeyed out to the plains to hunt buffalo.[65]

While tangible commodities such as bison products, salt, bows and arrows, turquoise, cotton, feathers, shells, and, after the late 1500s, European metalware all became important items in the southern plains trade networks, the exchange of news and information was still significant. The Caddos learned about the arrival of the Spanish in New Mexico from their Jumano exchange partners. When the French first arrived among the Hasinai communities, in the spring and summer of 1686, they reported finding Jumano traders there. The Jumano traders told the French about the Spanish to the west and then took news of the French presence to the Spaniards in Mexico. Later, in 1690, Spanish missionaries among the Hasinai often sent correspondence to the Spanish missions in Mexico and New Mexico by the Jumano traders.[66]

The Spanish in Mexico first received news of the Caddos through the Jumanos and Coahuiltecans, and the first eastern Texas Caddos seen by the Spanish were two individuals who came with Jumano chief and trader Juan Sabeata to El Paso del Norte in October 1683. Sabeata told the Spanish he wanted a missionary to come to his people's home on the Concho River, as there were thirty-three nations in Texas that wanted baptism and Spanish ambassadors. To further entice the Spanish, Sabeata told how during a battle with other Indians a cross had appeared that helped them win the battle without bloodshed. Later, the Spanish found out that this was a lie concocted by the Hasinai Indians that were traveling with Sabeata from their villages in the east. Now the Hasinai Caddos wanted to go home, but they would have to pass through Apache territory, with whom their people were at war. Because of this, they feared they could not safely make it alone. So the Hasinais and Juan Sabeata realized that if Spanish priests came with them to their home, they would be accompanied by a bodyguard of Spanish soldiers to escort them through Apache territory. Sabeata went on to tell the Spanish of thirty-six Indian nations, "including the great kingdom of the Texas," that had exchange relations with the Jumanos and who wanted to receive ministers from the Spanish. The Hasinai Caddos, called Tejas or Texas by the Jumanos and the Spanish, reported that other Europeans, whom they thought were Spaniards, were visiting the eastern Caddos by water. It is unclear who these Europeans were, as Robert Cavelier, Sieur de La Salle, did not enter Texas for another two years, but they may have been some long-forgotten French-Canadian *coureurs de bois*.[67]

In the last decades of the seventeenth century, as European powers gathered around them, the Caddo people remained tied together culturally while keeping intact the basic political and religious framework of the chiefdom as well as their hierarchical societies. Priest-chiefs continued to conduct religious ceremonies and rituals in the plazas and temples of villages, but no new temple mounds had been erected for well over two hundred years. While some elite burials still took place, they were not in mounds but in extended family cemeteries with grave goods for each individual. These priest-chiefs continued wielding extraordinary power and prestige.[68] In 1676 the Spanish Bishop of Guadalajara in Coahuila wrote a description of the Hasinai chiefdom, or Tejas, which he got from Coahuiltecan Indian traders. He described it as

> a populous nation of people, and so extensive that those who give detailed reports of them do not know where it ends. These [who give the reports] are many, through having communicated with the people of that nation, which they call Texas, and who, they maintain, live under an organized government, congregated in their pueblos, and governed by a cacique who is named by the Great Lord, as they call the one who rules them all, and who, they say, resides in the interior. They have houses made of wood, cultivate the soil, plant maize and other crops, wear clothes and punish misdemeanors, especially theft. The Coahuiles do not give more detailed reports of the Texas because, they say, they are allowed to go only to the first pueblos of the border, since the Great Lord of the Texas does not permit foreign nations to enter the interior of his country. There are many of these Coahuiles who give these reports, and who say that they got them through having aided the Texas in their wars against the Pauit, another very warlike nation.[69]

The Caddos proved themselves highly capable of adapting to or overcoming adverse circumstances. To cope with the great droughts and climatic change of the fourteenth century, which forced them to abandon certain geographical areas as well as mound building, the Caddos expanded trade in both the Southeast and the Southwest. When the Athapaskan peoples interrupted this trade with the Southwest, the Caddos moved their trade routes further south and continued a vigorous exchange with peoples of the southern plains and the Pueblos of New Mexico. Similarly, as the Comanche peoples moved onto the southern plains, around 1700, the Caddos pulled them into their exchange networks. When the Spanish expeditions of Moscoso cut through Caddo territory, bringing devastation, disease, and depopulation, the Caddos managed to weather the crisis by relying on their chiefdom political system, though some communities, like the Yatasís, did manage to break away and achieve a measure of independence.

As these Caddos of the Mississippian cultural tradition came into sustained contact with the Spanish and French in the late seventeenth and early eighteenth centuries, they found their chiefdom political system and their centuries of involvement in long-distance exchange gave them a tremendous advantage. When Europeans arrived wanting to exchange firearms and other manufactured goods for hides, horses, and food, the Caddos quickly agreed. As this trading gained momentum, European mercantile capitalism collided with the Caddo kin-ordered mode of production and the powerful chiefs who had long been used to controlling the regional economy.

3 // The Horse, Gun, and Deerskin Trades

The Tama or chief of [the Nabedaches] said that . . . the French from Nachitos [sic] brought them everything by means of the Caudachos in exchange for deer hides, buffalo hides, bear tallow, horses, and mules.

JOACHÍN DE OROBIO BAZTERRA,
1 October 1745, Reel 8, Béxar Archives

WHEN the Spanish from Mexico and the French from the Mississippi River valley entered Caddo territory in the 1680s, they brought with them commodities that the Caddos found valuable. These included such items as firearms, gunpowder, musket balls, metal hoes, knives and axes, needles, beads, bells, cloth and clothing, mirrors, kettles—all things the Caddos greatly desired but could not manufacture themselves. It did not take long for the Caddos to realize that European items not only helped them to increase their yield of deer hides, corn, and other field and forest products but also made them more formidable warriors. Because of the value inherent in these manufactured goods, they produced status, wealth, and power for the Caddo individual fortunate enough to acquire them. With this in mind the Caddos quickly moved to draw these Europeans inside their kinship systems and trade networks, while at the same time they tried to control the flow of European goods to other Indian peoples.

After the Spanish and French arrived, the Caddos became producers of Indian goods for the Europeans. They now exchanged with Europeans hides, horses, bear's oil, and food, which they either procured and processed themselves or acquired from other Indian peoples and which had long been part of their own economy. They also became both consumers and "suppliers" of the European manufactured goods that they acquired from the Europeans either as gifts or through trade. As consumers they used these goods themselves, as either subsistence or status-producing commodities. As suppliers they acquired these goods from the Europeans and then exchanged them to other Indian peoples for horses and hides, which enabled them to acquire even more European goods. Essentially, then, the Caddos became consumers of European goods, exchange middlemen between the Europeans and other Indian peoples, and producers of raw materials—hides and horses—for European mercantile capitalism.

History and geography also worked in favor of the Caddos. Their chiefdoms' illustrious lineage gave them a strong influence among all the different Indians of the area, and their ancient exchange networks and their location between Spanish Texas and French Louisiana allowed the Caddos to continue to dominate the area economy. This made both the Europeans and other Indian peoples reliant on them.

The horse and hide trade that produced these European goods added a new dynamic and a new intensity to traditional Caddo exchange relations. While kinship-based mutualistic and buffering exchange remained important, direct trade became much more common, with the Caddos becoming concerned with prices, quality, and quantity of goods. Hunting and raiding patterns changed in order to produce more goods. With the large amount of wealth entering and passing through Caddo villages, caddís found they could expand their power if they could control the movement of these goods, and individual Caddos also understood they could increase their own personal status within the community by acquiring them. To do this, the Caddos used both gift exchange and trade. In gift exchange the Caddos utilized an inclusive system of exchange relations based on reciprocity and kinship. The first step in creating kinship was through the giving of gifts. Gift giving initially produced a friendly feeling between the people involved. From there they established social ties that cemented the two parties into a fictive or ritualized kin relationship. This kinship created social obligations that each of the parties was required to uphold. One party essentially adopted the other into its society and family. Henri de Tonty, who explored parts of Caddo territory in 1690 while searching for survivors of Robert Cavelier, Sieur de La Salle's ill-fated Texas colony, understood this when he explained that the giving of gifts bound the two parties "as by oath to a strict alliance that hereafter they should live as brothers."[1]

In Caddo society the bonds of kinship obligated "brothers" not only to give gifts but also to receive them. Gift giving created obligations of reciprocity from which the giver might receive, among other things, a spouse, food, and other various forms of assistance, trade items, even military allies. In this context, gifts became something other than charity. Without an offering of gifts, relationships often failed to materialize, and without some type of kinship bond, parties became "strangers" or "nonkin," and therefore subject to confrontation and violence. Trust needed to be established before trade could take place, so the Caddos and most of these new European strangers laid down their weapons, exchanged gifts, and became kinspeople, some through adoptions, some in marriage, and some in blood.[2]

Gift giving can also be considered buffering exchange. It became a form of insurance to reduce risk, especially the risk associated with fluctuating supplies. An individual gave a gift and continued giving gifts over time to keep the relationship strong, but, more importantly, through this, he or she stored up a supply of favors. Later the recipient of the gifts was obligated to reciprocate with food, assistance, or material goods when these things were needed by the original giver. For some Indian peoples the idea that an individual could starve to death while others around them had food seemed incredible, as they believed that if a person was hungry, he or she could always go share a kinsperson's meal.[3]

For the Caddos, these obligations of reciprocity were a key element in what anthropologist Eric Wolf classified as a "kin-ordered mode of production." Gifts created both affinal, or marriage, kinships and fictive kinships, those made through adoption. Kinspeople were expected to maintain their kinship bonds through continual gift exchange. Above all they were to be generous in their giving, because after all, they thought, who could comprehend the ingratitude of a rich brother who would not share his wealth with his family?

Gift giving also brought rare and valuable commodities into the society, even more so once European manufactured goods entered the exchange networks. As opposed to capitalism, where money is used to purchase wanted goods, these goods came through reciprocal gift giving. As long as the Europeans upheld their reciprocal obligations to provide for and help their kinspeople, then the Caddos could expect to receive firearms, powder, kettles, beads, and such from their new kin. These manufactured goods would then filter down through continual exchange to all levels of Caddo society, from the xinesí and caddí to a hamlet's women and children. The Caddos reciprocated by providing gifts of food, wives or sexual partners, protection, deerskins, horses, and bear's oil. Even more than providing goods, reciprocity demanded that kin be loyal to their new family and provide sage advice, counsel, and assistance when called on. The Caddos took these obligations seriously, and they expected individuals to fulfill their duty to their new kin.[4]

Though Caddo society was highly structured, with the positions of xinesí and caddí being hereditary, individuals gained status, favor, and political advantage by the generous distribution of goods and presents. In this way the chiefs and other nobles retained their authority, but it also allowed some people outside the hereditary elite to increase their status and power through their ability to acquire and redistribute the desired goods. A good Caddo hunter who could acquire a quantity of deer hides and then exchange them for manufactured goods, which he might then give away as gifts, would earn high esteem and dedicated supporters. While everyone in a Caddo community utilized small-scale gift giving and reciprocity, the xinesís and caddís controlled most large-scale exchanges and the redistribution of the rare and uncommon goods that came into the community. Domingo Ramón, during his expedition to reestablish the Spanish Texas missions in 1716, gave gifts of cloth, blankets, hats, and tobacco to a group of Hasinai Caddos. Ramón wrote of how amazed he was that a certain few Hasinai "captains" took the goods he gave them and redistributed them to individual Caddos until the captains had nothing for themselves. The captains, Ramón noted, remained as happy as if they had received all of the goods themselves. Ramón may have understood their happiness more if he had realized that although these principal men might not actually possess the manufactured goods, by giving them away they had gained prestige, status, and power and created obligations of reciprocity among their people.[5]

In fact, almost every area of a Caddo's life involved some aspect of giving and receiving. Marriages and fictive kinships began with the giving of a gift. Return gifts then came, and these new kin strengthened their relationship by the continual exchange of presents. A distinct difference existed between gift exchange and trade, and the power of kinship should not be underestimated. Kinship produced strict obligations of reciprocity that each party had to uphold or risk dissolution of the kinship and possibly violence. The Caddos had a word for such kin, especially men who had fought together: *tesha*. *Tesha* meant "brother," although a tesha relationship could also be established between women. Among Caddo men and women, if their tesha were in danger, then obligations called for them to stand by their brother, even unto death. If a person's tesha asked him for any certain possession then he was bound to give it. If the request was refused, the relationship was broken on the spot.[6]

Because the Caddos wanted to make strong kin relationships with Europeans who could ensure a steady supply of manufactured goods, when survivors of La Salle's disastrous Texas expedition arrived among the Hasinai Caddos, in 1687, the Hasinais urged the French to remain among them and become kin. Some French did stay and quickly assimilated into Caddo society. Two French sailors remained behind, married Hasinai women, and became warriors. Pierre Talon, a boy who also remained behind with the Caddos, admitted that the Hasinai treated him extremely well, even tattooing him as if he had been born a Hasinai child.[7]

As La Salle's survivors passed through the Hasinai villages during their attempt to find their way back to the Mississippi River and Canada, the Caddos continually tried to forge affinal and fictive kinship ties with them. Henri Joutel recorded that one night while he was in bed, an old man brought a "young maid" and told him she was to be his wife. Wanting only to get back to Canada, Joutel ignored her for hours until the woman got bored with his indifference and left. Hasinai women amazed the French by their willingness to go to bed with them. Later, as Joutel and the other Frenchmen prepared to leave, the Hasinais begged them not to go, "promising us wives, plenty of provisions; representing to us the immense dangers, as well from enemies who surrounded them, and from the bad and impassable ways and the many woods and rivers we were to pass."[8]

Unfortunately, Joutel and his companions totally misunderstood the actions of these Caddos and saw lewdness where they should have seen generous gift giving. Caddo society did not think of a woman's sexual activities in the same restrictive way as Europeans did. Joutel believed Hasinai women were always ready to have sex with a Frenchman in order to acquire needles, knives, and especially strings of beads. He found, much to his relief, that the husbands of these women rarely showed jealousy. Most all of the early French and Spanish descriptions of the Caddos mention the ease with which a woman could divorce her husband and take up with another man. What they did not understand was that the woman's—or her husband's or father's or mother's brother's—gifts to them included work, food preparation, and children, as well as sexual gratification. For these gifts she and her family definitely expected something in return, like blankets, meats, hides, and, in the case of the French, manufactured goods. Not only did Caddo women expect something tangible, in the case of powerful foreigners they also hoped to acquire some of the man's power through sexual intercourse, which in seventeenth-century Caddo society had few of the taboos found among Europeans.[9]

If kinships through marriage could not be formed, the Caddos were just as happy to form fictive kinships through adoption, considered equally as powerful in creating reciprocal social obligations. Just as with marriages, Caddos created fictive kinships by the giving of gifts, often done in association with the ritual smoking of the calumet. The calumet ceremony involved smoking tobacco and possibly other herbs in a long-stemmed pipe adorned with feathers. According to historian Francis Jennings the calumet ceremony was a "pledge of sincerity and an instrument of diplomacy" and was often used to conclude peace between peoples and communities. It was common among most Indian peoples of North America and may actually have entered Indian society by way of the Caddos, spreading from them throughout the Southeast. Among the Caddos, once the pipe was lit, the caddí drew on it and blew the smoke in puffs to the Indians' six cardinal points: the first puff was up toward the heavens, the second puff to the east, the third to the west, the fourth the north, the fifth to the south, and the sixth to earth.[10]

The calumet as an adoption ceremony can best be seen in Joutel's description of the ceremony the Hasinais performed with La Salle's surviving brother, Jean Cavelier. After presenting gifts and smoking the calumet pipe while singing and chanting, the Hasinai chief "brought two maids . . . [and] made them sit down on each side of Monsieur Cavelier, in such a posture that they looked one upon the other, their legs extended and intermixed, on which . . . [the chief] laid Monsieur Cavelier's legs, in such a way that they lay uppermost and across those of the two maids." The calumet ceremony often took three days to complete, and in the case of Jean Cavelier, once the ritual ended, the Hasinai assured him that "he might pass through all the nations that were allied to them by virtue of that token of peace, and should be everywhere well received." Time and time again over the next century, French traders and soldiers described their ritual adoption into Indian society in much the same way.[11]

When the Spanish and French began to establish missions and outposts among the Caddos in the late seventeenth and early eighteenth centuries, they found it necessary to adopt this kin-ordered mode of production, in which kinships and gift exchange played such central roles. On an official, diplomatic level the French and Spanish governments provided regular distribution of gifts of European goods to the Caddos, who, in return, provided military and economic assistance. Pierre Talon advised that giving gifts was the best way to win the Caddos' friendship. He recognized the power of gifts and reciprocity, and the problems that could develop when a kinsperson did not uphold the expected reciprocal obligations:

> As for trade among them [the Hasinais], nothing appeared easier . . . [and] nothing is easier than winning their friendship: a hatchet, a knife, a pair of scissors, a pin, a needle, a necklace or bracelet or glass, wampum, or some other such trinkets being ordinarily the price, because they love passionately all sorts of knickknacks and baubles that are useful or ornamental. But also, as they give voluntarily of what they have, they do not like to be refused. And, while they are never aggressors, neither do they ever forget the pride of honor in their vengeance.[12]

The Caddos expected these diplomatic gifts; in fact, they demanded them because diplomatic gifts created kinship ties between European leaders and Caddo chiefs. It was not naiveté that caused the Indians to address their Euro-American allies as "brothers" or "fathers," or the king and president as "Great Father," and to call themselves his "children." Kinship terms like *brother, father,* and *children* can be found throughout the French and Spanish documents. These were not mere euphemisms, figures of speech, or baby talk. To the Caddos, and to Europeans who understood them, these were terms of actual kinship and constant reminders of the obligations one owed to one's family. These obligations required the European "fathers" and "brothers" to provide for the welfare of their Caddo "children," and the best way to do this was by giving them gifts of manufactured goods and other forms of assistance. In return, the European "brothers" and "fathers" could expect their Caddo "brothers" and "children" to provide them with gifts: hospitality, hides, horses, and assistance, as well as all the associated reciprocal obligations of kinship.[13]

The French and the Spanish quickly learned the importance of providing gifts to the Indian peoples. In 1717 French Louisiana's commissioner of finance and commerce criticized the colonial governor for not sending merchandise to Louis Juchereau de St. Denis, who commanded Fort St. Jean Baptiste on the lower Red River among the Natchitoches Caddo. As he explained it, all the Indians in that area, even the most remote, went to Natchitoches, where they expected the commandant to provide them with presents. "That is what keeps these nations on our side. Deprived of these little attentions, they are less disposed in our favor. That makes them think that the French are beggars and slaves. . . . That alienates them and takes from them all good will." The Caddo leaders expected these gifts, and to uphold their obligations the French and Spanish annually distributed a quantity of manufactured goods. Commandants of French and Spanish outposts in Caddo territory also tried to ensure they always had a supply of manufactured goods on hand to give as gifts when parties of Caddos might suddenly visit.[14]

Once European manufactured goods began arriving in their communities, the Caddos immediately tried to control their distribution. One way they did this was by having Caddo parties, and in some instances whole villages, pick up and move to the immediate proximity of European outposts. In 1700 Frenchman Louis Juchereau de St. Denis, along with his cousin Jean-Baptiste Le Moyne, commonly known as Bienville, visited the Natchitoches Caddos and the Kadohadacho chiefdom along Red River. They gave gifts to the Caddos while the Caddos sang the calumet ceremony and made fictive kinships with them. St. Denis visited them again in 1705 and told the Caddos of the French set-

tlements in southern Louisiana. To be nearer the source of French manufactured goods, a large contingent of Natchitoches Caddos moved
about 250 miles southeast, to an area near Lake Pontchartrain. Moving
to facilitate the acquisition of goods had long been a Caddo tactic.
When Caddo peoples found an area that provided the commodities
they wanted, they formed exchange groups and sent them to go live
near the peoples providing those commodities. There this group set up
a small village to facilitate this trade and send goods back to their main
communities. The Petit Caddos and Yatasís became known for shifting
their villages between the Lower Natchitoches and the Kadohadacho
communities, places where the French eventually built outposts. While
in southern Louisiana, the Natchitoches became closely associated and
intermingled with the Acolapissa Indians. In 1713, once St. Denis established Fort St. Jean Baptiste des Natchitoches up the Red River in Caddo
country, the Natchitoches Caddos decided to move back to their home
country to be nearer that outpost. Unfortunately for the Natchitoches,
the Acolapissas also wanted to control the distribution of goods. As the
Natchitoches prepared to move back north to Red River, the Acolapissas, realizing they were being cut out of the trade network, attacked
the Natchitoches to prevent their leaving. The Natchitoches had to
fight their way out of southern Louisiana, losing many of their people
in order to return to the Red River.[15]

In reality the Caddos did not have to move very far, because the advantages of Caddo territory brought both Europeans and Indians to
them. Their large, settled communities, which produced enormous
quantities of corn, salt, hides, and horses, attracted both the Spanish
and the French. For the French, the Red River, with its head of nav-
igation at the Natchitoches Caddo villages, provided a natural distribution point. Also, the southern St. Augustine–Casas Grandes trail passed
through the Natchitoches villages and further facilitated exchange east
and west. Further up the Red River the Kadohadacho chiefdom, consisting of the Cadodacho, Upper Natchitoches, Nanatsoho, and Nasoni
communities, lay at the crossroads of three major trade routes that
connected them to the Natchitoches villages downriver, southwest to
the Hasinai communities in eastern Texas, northwest to the Quapaws
and Osages, east to the Chickasaws and Choctaws, and west to the
Wichitas and Comanches.[16]

Because their location and the exchange activities brought them into contact with so many different peoples, the Caddos became masters of Mobilian, the southeastern trade language. A derivative of Chickasaw, Mobilian used a wide mix of western Muskhogean grammar and Indian and European words and patterns of speech. Spoken by most all people involved in the Louisiana horse and hide trade—Indians, Africans, French, Spaniards, and even Anglos—it became so common around Natchitoches that it could still be heard as late as the mid–nineteenth century. Le Page du Pratz, in the 1720s, reported that the Natchitoches and other Caddo peoples "have a peculiar language; however, there is not a village in either of the nations, nor indeed in any nation of Louisiana, where there are not some who can speak the Chickasaw language, which is called the vulgar tongue, and is the same here as the Lingua Franca is in the Levant."[17]

As the French and Spanish arrived in Caddo territory, the Indians heartily welcomed them. When Spanish missionaries and soldiers first arrived at the Hasinai chiefdom in the late 1680s searching for survivors of La Salle's expedition, the Caddos rapidly agreed to the erecting of missions and presidios among their communities. Much to the disappointment of the Spanish, the Caddos had no desire to live at the missions, become Christians, or serve as unpaid laborers. In fact, not one Caddo convert was ever recorded at any of the eastern Texas missions. The crop of souls was so bad that these seventeenth-century missions closed after just two years. Six missions and a few presidios were later reestablished, in the early eighteenth century, but they fared no better. Spain abandoned half of them in 1729, leaving only three weak and almost deserted missions among the Caddos, as well as the presidio Los Adaes, fifteen miles west of Natchitoches. Spain erected one more presidio, near the mission at Nacogdoches, but this was in 1774. While the Caddos refused Christianity, they saw the missions and presidios as distribution points of European merchandise. Unfortunately for the Caddos and the Spanish, these eastern Texas outposts existed far from the main Spanish population centers of Mexico, New Mexico, and southern Texas. It was thus difficult for Spain to deliver the amount of merchandise the Caddos wanted. This Spanish presence and authority among the Caddos remained weak and rather ineffectual.[18]

The French fared much better. They had no wish to Christianize the Caddos but instead wanted them as trade partners and political and military allies. In 1713 Louis Juchereau de St. Denis built Fort St. Jean Baptiste among the Natchitoches Caddos, where the present-day town of Natchitoches stands on the lower Red River. In 1720 Bénard de La Harpe built the Nassonite Post, later renamed Fort St. Louis de Cadodacho, at that important village of the Kadohadacho chiefdom near the great bend of the Red River. The French had a much easier time bringing goods up the Red River from New Orleans, and so quickly outpaced Spain in providing merchandise to the Caddos. Because of this the Caddos made much closer exchange relations and kinships with the French than with the Spanish. It was not long before French traders established permanent residences among the communities of the Cadodachos, Petit Caddos, and Yatasís, thus making it even easier for the Caddos to acquire merchandise. As Louisiana Caddo communities filled with manufactured goods, they attracted other Caddos and Indians, especially those living in Spanish Texas, who came to trade with both the Caddos and the French traders living among them.[19]

Frenchmen who lived among the Caddos were usually adopted into the community, often marrying Caddo women and having children. Not much is known about the control Caddo leaders exerted over resident traders, but probably as long as intermarried French traders lived at these villages, Caddo leaders could regulate what was exchanged and to whom while enjoying economic advantages and increased influence and power. Visiting bands of Wichitas, Hasinai Caddos, and other Indians, especially during the early years of French occupation, came to these Louisiana Caddo villages, paid respects to the chiefs, and then made exchange relations with the Caddo's French kinspeople, who depended on the Caddo host families for food, protection, and many other obligations. While the French trader might provide manufactured goods to the various Indian peoples arriving at the Caddo village to trade with him, the village leaders undoubtedly regulated what goods were traded, and so essentially continued controlling the distribution of these goods. The trade, though, created its own dynamic, and by the mid–eighteenth century the Caddos could not prevent traders from passing through their villages on the way to the Wichitas and Comanches further west. Still, as French traders used the Cadodacho,

Petit Caddo, and Yatasí villages as jumping-off areas for trade expeditions into Texas, Caddo leaders often provided the traders with reliable escorts and assistants who not only guided, helped, and interpreted for the Frenchmen but also acted as informants for the Caddo leaders, enabling them to control the distribution of goods from afar. Even better for the Caddos, French traders venturing beyond the pale and protection of the Kadohadacho chiefdom often found themselves at the mercy of the Wichitas and Comanches, who demanded more goods for fewer commodities. So while French traders might venture out to the western nations, for some it was much safer to remain among their Cadodacho, Petit Caddo, and Yatasí kinspeople, trade with them, and allow Caddo traders to handle most of the exchanges, or at least be protected by the Caddos when other Indian peoples came to them to trade.

Caddo women desired kettles, knives, axes, and needles that lightened the drudgery of their daily work; Caddo men mainly wanted guns, gunpowder, ammunition, and metal with which to edge their hand-held weapons. It was the potential of these weapons that made the Caddos understand the need to control the trade. Drawing on their ancient exchange relations and the influence their chiefdoms' illustrious histories gave them with the Indians to the west, the Caddos passed firearms on to their Wichita and Comanche trade partners, realizing this would cement alliances with them and bring additional hides and horses to their communities. Conversely, the Spanish, at least in the early years of contact with the Caddos, tried to prohibit the introduction of firearms among the Caddos and other Indians, believing Indians with firearms would be a threat to Texas missions, outposts, and ranches. They correctly realized that if they gave the Caddos firearms, many of these weapons would eventually wind up in the hands of enemy Comanches and Wichitas. So during their early years in Texas, the Spanish, when they gave gifts or participated in trade, rarely if ever provided firearms.[20]

This proved no obstacle to the Caddos, as the French were more than willing to provide firearms both as gifts and in trade. Since the French saw the Caddos as trade partners and military allies, the introduction of firearms could only make the Caddos better producers of hides and horses and more effective allies. Also, as the French trading system required individual traders to venture out to Indian villages and often live among the Caddos, French traders, needing to acquire as many hides or horses as possible to pay off the debts they incurred in purchasing trade goods, found it very difficult to resist the demands of their Caddo kinspeople who insisted on firearms and ammunition in exchange for their deer hides. The trader's predicament of being caught between the obligations of kinship and the demands of mercantile capitalism made it extraordinarily difficult for the French and Spanish to control the acquisition of firearms among the Caddos and other Indians.

From their very first contact with Europeans, the Caddos had seen the potential of firearms, and they wanted them. When Joutel and the other survivors of La Salle's expedition arrived among the Hasinai communities with their guns, the Hasinais urged those Europeans to join them in an attack on their enemies. The Caddos were already capable warriors, often battling with the Karankawas on the Gulf coast to the south, the Lipan Apaches to the west, the Chickasaws to the east, and even with other Caddo communities, often riding long distances to attack. Two of Joutel's French compatriots went on a raid with Hasinai warriors against the Cannohatinos in which, according to Joutel, their weapons proved decisive, killing several Cannohatinos and helping the Hasinais bring back two female captives. Once back at their village, the Hasinais scalped one woman alive, gave her a charge of gunpowder and a musket ball, then sent her home to her people as a warning that now the Hasinais possessed a new weapon and would not hesitate to use it against them again.[21]

Almost immediately after St. Denis founded Fort St. Jean Baptiste among the Natchitoches Caddo, in 1713, French traders began regularly to provide the Caddos with guns, or fusils, as they were called. As early as 1716, when Captain Domingo Ramón reestablished the Spanish presence in eastern Texas, he found the Caddos had more guns than his soldiers. On 27 June of that year a party of 25 Hasinai warriors on horseback, most of them principal men carrying nine French shotguns, greeted Ramón's party. Two days later Ramón met another delegation, of 150 Hasinais, again with most carrying French guns. In 1718, when Martín de Alarcón and his troops visited the Hainai chiefdom, he found his entire command out-gunned by the village's honor guard alone.

Not only did the French supply the firearms, the traders also taught the Caddos how to load, aim, and fire them. Since firearms were point-and-shoot weapons, like bows and arrows, it did not take long for the Caddos to become as proficient with them as the Europeans.[22]

Soon almost all Indian peoples of western Louisiana and eastern Texas had access to French firearms. The Nabedache Caddos reported that the French came to the Kadohadacho chiefdom and other Caddo peoples in eastern Texas every summer to trade guns, powder, bullets, and a host of other goods in exchange for deer hides, buffalo hides, and horses. By 1724 Spanish officials found the Caddos well supplied with French guns, powder, and shot. This frustrated the Spanish, and they complained that French firearms made the Caddos formidable adversaries fully able to avoid subjugation and missionization.[23]

The Caddos received some of their weapons from the French in direct trade, exchanging deer and buffalo hides and horses for guns. They also received fusils as gifts. As Spanish lieutenant Don Manuel Antonio Lozoia explained to his superiors, the Caddos had a very close relationship with the French, especially with St. Denis and his son of the same name. In one instance, Lozoia recounted, the younger St. Denis had "obtained a larger supply than usual of guns, powder, bullets, *bayetas,* breechcloths, vermillion and other effects which he gave liberally to the aforesaid [Caddo] Indians, by which means he had so endeared himself to them that they idolized him so much that the deponent believed that, if it were possible, they would undergo a thousand torments for the sake of pleasing him."[24]

Although the Caddos might be well armed and highly competent with the guns they received, the firearms themselves were not of a very high quality. These flintlock trade fusils were flimsily manufactured and often broke with very little use. Because of this the Caddos constantly needed more fusils, as well as gunsmiths to visit their villages to repair the broken ones. So by the 1740s the French traders living at the Caddo villages, such as Alexis Grappe and his family, not only traded with the Caddos and other Indians who visited that village, they also acted as gunsmiths.[25]

Still, firearms did not totally replace traditional Caddo weapons. While the fusil might be excellent for hunting deer when the hunter had time to sit, wait for his quarry, take careful aim, and then fire, it was not so good for hunting buffalo from horseback or for making war. It was almost impossible to reload a flintlock fusil while on horseback, so when they did hunt buffalo with flintlock firearms, they did it on foot. As for war, the lethality of firearms in the hands of Indian bands in the eighteenth century has been greatly overestimated by historians. Firearms gave those who possessed them a psychological advantage over their enemies: a fusil created lots of smoke and noise; the ball flew faster than an arrow, unseen, and could not be dodged; and if the ball did hit home, its penetrating power created a horrendous, sometimes fatal wound. In reality fusils were not very reliable and were notoriously inaccurate even for professional European armies of the eighteenth century. The gap between the size of the barrel and the size of the ball, the lack of barrel lands and grooves, undercharging, bad flints, rain, humidity, and other defects and problems made trade fusils highly unreliable. In warfare between Indian bands the attackers might be able to get off one round before the fight developed into a hand-to-hand melee with the participants depending much more on bows and arrows, tomahawks, hatchets, axes, knives, and lances.

Because of all these defects, as well as the fusil's tendency to break, the Caddos remained largely dependent on the bow and arrow and other hand-held weapons. Metal tomahawks, knives, axes, and hatchets remained important goods provided to them by the European traders. Caddos often broke up useless fusil barrels to make projectile points and to edge their weapons. As late as 1830, Jean Berlandier reported that the Caddos and others Indians of what is now Texas "make most of their own weapons, with the exception of the blade of their lance, which is generally the blade of a Spanish sword. All the rest is of their own handiwork. In the villages they buy iron barrel hoops which they cut and work into heads for their arrows. But the bow, the quiver, the shield, the war club, and the saddles for their horses are the product of their own industry."[26]

Despite the fusil's unreliability, the Caddos and other Indian peoples tried to acquire as many of them as possible because of the psychological advantage it gave them in war and because it increased their hunting productivity. Unfortunately, there were never as many firearms available as the Caddos and other Indians wanted. Still, with the demand by the various Indian peoples in Texas for fusils and other man-

ufactured goods, the Caddos once again found themselves in their age-
old position of trade middlemen.

Ever since the rise of their culture, in the eighth century, the Caddos
had served as middlemen between the peoples of the plains to the west
and the southeastern peoples to the east. With the arrival of European
merchandise in their villages, the Caddos directed these manufactured
goods west to the Wichitas and Comanches, accepting hides, horses,
and Indian slaves in return to exchange with the French and Spanish
for more and newer goods. In all likelihood Caddo traders and exchange partners probably passed used merchandise to other Indians.
Older guns, kettles, knives, and such went into the Indian trade networks, while Caddo individuals kept the newer merchandise supplied
by their European kinspeople for themselves, passing it on again when
it became worn and new merchandise appeared. In fact, the decline of
grave goods placed in eighteenth- and nineteenth-century Caddo burials can be attributed to the fact that by then the Caddos tended to pass
these used goods on to other Indian peoples instead of burying them
with their dead.[27]

Spanish Texas governor Joachín de Orobio Bazterra reported on this
kind of Indian-to-Indian trade in 1745. In that year the chief of the Nabedache Caddo explained to him that the Cadodachos and several
eastern Hasinai communities acquired European merchandise from the
French at Natchitoches. This merchandise was then passed on to the
Nabedaches; in fact, they received most of their French goods "by
means of the Caudachos [Cadodachos] in exchange for deer hides, buffalo hides, bear tallow, horses, and mules." Fifty years later the Spanish
still found that the Indians of Texas often received their weapons
through trade with other Indian peoples.[28]

As the Caddos sent firearms and other weapons to the Wichitas and
Comanches, the Spanish in Texas became considerably agitated. Their
firearms and their access to a reliable supply of them made the Caddos,
Wichitas, and Comanches arrogant in their dealings with the Spanish.
Well armed, they attacked and raided Spanish outposts, missions, and
ranches deep inside Texas. The most celebrated incident occurred in
1758, when a large band of Wichitas, Comanches, and Hasinai Caddos,
armed with French weapons, attacked the Apache mission at San Sabá
and killed eight Spaniards. The Spanish tried to retaliate the next year

and sent a large force to the Taovaya Wichita village on the upper Red River, which they found palisaded with a French flag waving over it. Wichita, Caddo, and Comanche warriors carrying French firearms sortied out and mauled the Spanish expedition, sending it retreating in panic back to San Antonio. The warriors also captured the expedition's two cannons, which remained in Indian hands for almost twenty years.[29]

The Spanish blamed the French in Louisiana for supplying the weapons used by these Indians, but Louisiana governor Louis Billouart de Kerlérec explained it was the Caddos themselves, not the French, who actually controlled the Indian trade. In a scathing letter to the Spanish, Kerlérec explained that the Natchitoches Caddos often supplied weapons and goods to the Hainais and Nadacos, who in turn provided weapons to other Indians. "The circulation of goods becomes infallible in view of the evident ties that exist among the neutral [Natchitoches] Indians and your new enemies [Wichitas and Comanches]."[30]

The Spanish investigated Kerlérec's claims, and to their dismay found that most of the firearms used by the Comanches and Wichitas against San Sabá had been supplied by the Yatasís and Cadodachos. Just as bad, in Spanish opinion, they found that former Texas governor Jacinto de Barrios had also supplied firearms and ammunition to the Caddos and other Texas Indians.[31]

This situation caused some Spanish officials in Texas to conclude that they should also provide firearms to the Indians in Texas. As long as these Indians received weapons from the French they would never come to live in the missions. Instead they would become bolder, more aggressive, and produce more horses and hides to exchange with the French for more guns. If the Spanish did not provide weapons, they would lose their Indian allies, provoke more raids against Spanish outposts, and hurt their own traders, who needed to supply hides and horses to towns in southern Texas and New Spain. So Spanish officials approved giving firearms and ammunition to the Caddos and other Indian peoples. Texas officials hoped that supplying the guns would stop the deadly attacks on Texas outposts and ranches. Then, once the Indians came to rely on them for the guns, the Spanish could cut off the supply if the Indians did not adhere to Spanish policy.[32]

When Spain took control of Louisiana in the late 1760s, after the end of the French and Indian War, they began providing a few firearms to the Caddos but intended to limit the quantities. In 1770, soon after they actually took possession of the Natchitoches outpost, the Spanish distributed a large quantity of gifts to the Cadodachos, the Petit Caddos, the Natchitoches, and the Yatasís. The gifts for the Cadodachos included twenty pounds of gunpowder, forty pounds of musket balls, two hundred flints, but only two guns. The Petit Caddos received ten pounds of powder, twenty pounds of fine shot and balls, one hundred flints, and only one gun. The Natchitoches received four pounds of powder, eight pounds of fine shot and balls, fifty flints, and one gun. The Yatasís received six pounds of powder, twelve pounds of shot and balls, fifty flints, also only one gun. Other lists of Spanish gifts for the Caddos included much the same: firearms, gunpowder, musket balls, assorted firearm accoutrements, and metal-edged weapons.[33]

While Spanish policy limited the number of firearms traded to the Caddos and other Indians, official Spanish traders, many of them the same Frenchmen who had done business with the Caddos during the French administration, found they had to provide more weapons than Spanish authorities wanted. Spanish Natchitoches commandant Athanase De Mézières, a former French soldier and Indian trader, son-in-law of St. Denis, and Caddo by adoption, authorized Natchitoches merchant Juan Piseros to send three traders to the Cadodacho, Petit Caddo, and Yatasí villages, carrying with them one year's supply of goods, which they would exchange for deer and buffalo hides. Among these goods slated for exchange were forty fusils and four hundred pounds of French gun powder for the Cadodachos; thirty fusils and two hundred pounds of powder for the Petit Caddos; and fifteen fusils and two hundred pounds of powder for the Yatasís. Also included for the three villages were numerous gun flints, steels, worm screws, knives, axes, tomahawks, and nails. Eventually the Spanish Natchitoches commandant promised that he would provide a fusil and two ells (about ninety inches) of broadcloth to any Caddo who arrested and brought in to him any unlicensed trader found living among their villages.[34]

The amount of firearms and weapons provided to the Caddos by Spanish-licensed traders only increased over time. In September 1774, among the usual trade goods, the Petit Caddos received 40 fusils, 494 pounds of gunpowder, and 1,043 musket balls. In 1776 merchant Joseph Pavie shipped from New Orleans 40 fusils, 1,500 gun flints, 450 pounds of powder, 900 pounds of balls, 10 sabers, and a large assortment of metal-edged weapons for the Caddo trade. In November 1781 Cadodacho chief Tinhiouen the Younger, the most important chief among all the Caddos at that time, received 18 fusils, 150 pounds of powder and balls, and 200 gun flints in trade. In 1784 the new Spanish commandant at Fort Miro, on the Ouachita River in eastern Louisiana, invited Brave Cachou, the chief of the Petit Caddos, to come trade at that post, where he could receive "fusils at 25 pots" (of bear's oil), as well as powder, balls, hatchets, picks, knives, razors, and tomahawk pipes.[35]

Spain's plan to force the Caddos and other Indians to stop raiding in Texas by limiting firearms came to naught. Though Spanish authorities might threaten to cut off gifts of firearms to the Wichitas and Comanches, the Caddo middlemen proved too strong to be stopped. Spain's weakness stemmed from her being caught between the pincers of two trade networks originating in Louisiana. The first was the Caddo-Wichita-Comanche network. By the early 1700s, as La Harpe discovered, the Caddo communities in Louisiana and Texas had developed extensive trade partnerships to the west with the Wichitas and Comanches. The other network was further south and connected the Attakapas, Tonkawas, and Apaches. Just as France's Natchitoches post served the Caddo network, the French post of Opelousas served the Attakapas network. From these two settlements French traders provided guns and other merchandise to their Indian trade partners while exporting a large quantity of hides and horses. Although extremely profitable for all involved, these two networks existed in complete separation from each other.[36]

The existence of these separate exchange networks helps to explain some of the raiding the Spanish experienced in Texas. As Comanches entered the southern plains during the late seventeenth and early eighteenth centuries, they vied with the plains Apaches for control of large expanses of western Texas, eastern New Mexico, and northern Mexico. This competition for territorial supremacy and access to European goods meant the Comanches possessed few, if any, kinship ties with the Apaches, and vice versa. Viewing each other as nonkin meant they launched raids and revenge killings against each other. This also meant both the Comanches and Apaches needed a constant, sure supply of firearms and other weapons. While some of these goods might be found in western Texas and New Mexico, the surest and most plentiful supply came through the Louisiana trade networks.

In order to ensure a reliable supply of guns and merchandise, and because trade partners rarely made war on each other, the Comanches and Apaches made peace, kinships, and trade partnerships with the peoples east of them. Therefore the Comanches and Apaches raided Spanish settlements and each other's camps for slaves, horses, and hides. The Comanches exchanged these items with the Wichitas, who passed these goods on to the Caddos for guns and merchandise. The Apaches turned to the Tonkawas and Attakapas. Because the trade networks demanded that gifts be given, kinships made, and obligations upheld, the participants along these networks rarely made relationships with members of the other trade network.[37]

The Spaniards in Texas found themselves caught between these two trade networks and at the mercy of Comanche and Apache raids. Spain's attempts to appease both failed as gifts and assistance to one were considered a sign of disloyalty by the other. After all, if gifts made kin and established close relationships, the gifts given by the Spanish to the Apaches to stop their raids only angered the Comanches, Wichitas, and Caddos, who saw this as breaking the kinship bonds they had forged with the Spanish. Those Spaniards providing the Apaches with gifts were considered nonkin by these peoples and subject to attack. This reasoning by the Comanches, Wichitas, and Caddos is what brought on their 1758 attack against the San Sabá mission, which had been established for the Apaches.[38]

Even when Spain acquired Louisiana, after the French and Indian War, she had no luck in breaking these trade networks. While the new Spanish trade regulations briefly caused a dearth of European merchandise among the Wichitas and Comanches, the Kadohadachos and Hasinai Caddos quickly made up the shortage through their kinship ties with unlicensed French creole traders around Natchitoches who were willing to ignore Spanish law in their quest for profits. Raids by gun-wielding Comanches and Wichitas became so serious that in the early 1780s, Texas governor Domingo Cabello begged Spanish Louisiana officials—to no avail—to halt the flow of firearms to the Ais, Yatasís, Hainais, Nacogdoches, and other Hasinai communities, because the weapons eventually wound up in the hands of enemy Indians further west.[39]

If the Spanish authorities in both Texas and Louisiana had had their way, they would have severely limited the number of firearms given to the Caddos. But laws stipulating that firearms and ammunition for the Caddos and other Indians could only be supplied by traders authorized by Spanish officials proved impossible to enforce. The Caddos, who possessed extensive kinship relations with the French and French creoles living around Natchitoches, continued demanding firearms and other goods from their kinspeople. They could continue to acquire these firearms from these French-turned-Spanish citizens because of the cut-throat competition among the various traders for the horses, hides, slaves, and bear's oil that the Caddo supplied. Despite Spanish laws that ordered all traders to be bonded and supervised by the Natchitoches commandant, the Caddos easily found traders, usually their European kinspeople, willing to ignore the law and trade firearms and other merchandise to profit from the goods the Caddos supplied.[40]

From their very earliest contact with the Europeans, the commodities the Caddos could provide to the French and Spanish gave them the upper hand in the trade. While the Caddos wanted and needed firearms, metalware, and other goods, mercantile capitalism equally needed to be fueled by hides, horses, and slaves—things only the Indians could supply in quantity but which the Caddos controlled in that part of Louisiana and Texas. As suppliers of these goods the Caddos acted both as primary producers and as middlemen who acquired some of these goods from other Indians and in turn exchanged them with the French and Spanish.

As primary producers the Natchitoches, Yatasís, Hasinais, and other nearby Caddo peoples supplied corn, beans, pottery plates, jars, jugs, and bottles, often created in a European style, to the French and Spanish. In fact, those Spaniards and Frenchmen who moved to Caddo territory found themselves dependent on the Caddos for both their physical and economic survival. The Spanish missions and presidios of eastern Texas were far from the main Spanish population centers of southern Texas and Mexico. The French in northwestern Louisiana also found themselves isolated from the main French population along the lower Mississippi River valley. Natchitoches was twenty-five days' travel by boat from New Orleans. Now the old Caddo tactic of mutualistic exchange came into play with the Caddos providing food and other goods to both the Spanish and French in return for manufactured goods. As early as 1715 the Nasonis, Yatasís, Natchitoches, and Hasinai Caddos were providing corn to the French and Spanish settlements in their areas.[41]

Horses became one of the major commodities the Caddos supplied to French Louisiana. In some instances Caddo men captured horses on the prairies and plains for exchange with Europeans; in others they acquired these from the Wichitas and Comanches and then later exchanged them with the French. The Caddos probably acquired their first horses during the 1670s or early 1680s. When Joutel and the La Salle survivors passed through the Caddo communities in the late 1680s they found that the Caddos already possessed many horses. The Caddo ascribed high status to the horses and those who possessed them. At the Fish Hatchery site, an early-eighteenth-century Caddo village on Cane River near present-day Natchitoches, Louisiana, over one hundred Caddo burials have been found complete with pottery, shells, glass beads, and metal objects. Nearby but buried separately were the skeletons of two horses, each with a large earthen bowl placed near the head. The absence of any human remains with the horse burials indicated that they were not funeral sacrifices. Rather, the Caddos esteemed the horses enough to give them a burial of their own. At other historic Caddo sites along the Red River, small clay figurines of horses have been unearthed.[42]

Henri de Tonty, during his 1690 search for La Salle, reported that one Caddo community he visited possessed thirty horses, which they called *cavali,* a term similar to the Spanish word for horse, *caballo.* The Nabedaches had many more, he noticed, with each house owning four or five and many of these branded with the Spanish king's symbol of an R and a crown. According to Tonty the Caddos used their horses for both hunting and war, and rode with "pointed saddles, wooden stirrups, and body-coverings of several skins, one over the other, as a protection from arrows. They arm the breast of their horses with the same material, a proof that they are not very far from the Spaniards." In reality, the Caddos got the idea for covering their horses not from their contact with the Spanish, which was infrequent at this time, but from their continual wars with the plains Apaches, who armored their horses with stiff hides.[43]

Caddo peoples participated in the horse culture and possessed horses long before the peoples of either the northern plains or the southeastern woodlands. Once acquired, horses rapidly became important trade items for the Caddos. Pierre Talon believed the Hasinai possessed so many horses that the Europeans could acquire them for only a few hatchets, knives, or other goods. Joutel managed to do exactly this, receiving one horse for some metal knives and an axe. The Caddos exchanged horses not only with Europeans and neighboring Indians peoples, but also with peoples great distances away. In 1711 French travelers on the Mississippi River found the Illinois Indians grazing horses that they said they obtained from the Caddos.[44]

Fortunately for the Caddos, their territory proved excellent for horses. These "mustangs," the feral descendants of the Andalusian stock brought by the Spanish during the early conquest of New Spain, were small, fast, ideally suited to the area, and rather easy to tame. By the end of the eighteenth century perhaps two million of them grazed between the Arkansas River and the Rio Grande. Bénard de La Harpe, who visited the Kadohadacho chiefdom in 1719, reported that the land was filled with animals, was very fertile, and "furnished a quantity of horses that could be fed at little expense." He went on to report that the Caddos and Wichitas captured these "very beautiful horses which they esteemed very much, for they could not be without them for hunting or war." While horses added greatly to the Caddos' ability to hunt, they also made them much more formidable warriors. As the Marquis de Altamira wrote in 1744, the Caddos and other Indians were "more bellicose and daring" due to their proficiency on horseback, which stemmed from "their natural aptitude and agility, and because they use them frequently, in hunting buffaloes, deer, bears, and other animals that abound in their area." Horses increased the Caddos' mobility and speed, widened their range of hunting and warfare, made them better hunters and more fearsome enemies, and expanded their trade networks. Caddo traders could now carry more goods over longer distances. Possession of horses came to symbolize wealth, and thereby they became a commodity to acquire, exchange, and trade in order to build more status, prestige, and power.[45]

Once the French arrived along the Red River the Natchitoches and other Caddo communities began supplying horses and cattle. By the early 1720s the French reported that the Natchitoches Caddos possessed twenty-five horses, while the French settlers around the fort there owned forty-two horses, along with twelve head of cattle. Though French officials in New Orleans did not approve of it, several French traders paid their taxes with horses received from the Caddos.[46]

Natchitoches quickly became the channel through which horses from Texas spread into Louisiana and the English colonies further east. In 1726 St. Denis sold 13 horses at New Orleans for 2,600 livres. Throughout the rest of the eighteenth and into the nineteenth century, the number of horses flowing into Louisiana continued to grow. Louisiana governor Bienville complained in 1737 that the French could easily acquire over 200 horses from Texas, but that it was difficult to move them to the population centers in Louisiana. Still, the next year, Bienville planned to send 400 Caddo horses to French Illinois. In February 1776 French residents of Spain's Natchitoches jurisdiction possessed 1,258 horses, and between March 1775 and February 1776 they exported over 1,000 horses and about 100 mules. As late as 1802, John Sibley reported that in that year alone, over 7,300 horses from Texas passed through western Louisiana.[47]

Spanish authorities took a dim view of the Caddo horse trade with the French because of the violence it instigated. With horses in such high demand by Euro-Americans, the Comanches, Wichitas, and Apaches raided Spanish missions and settlements and other Indian peoples to acquire horses, leaving the Spanish Tejanos clamoring for government protection. Even Caddos sometimes participated in these horse raids. According to one witness, the Nabedaches became enraged at the governor of Texas because he demanded that they, whom the Spanish determined lived under their jurisdiction, stop welcoming to their villages the French traders from Natchitoches. To express their anger, the Nabedaches went to the Texas capital at San Antonio and drove off a herd of about four hundred horses. Spanish soldiers gave chase and while on the trail were ambushed by the Nabedaches, who stole an additional 150 horses from the troops. The gun-for-horse trade, the Spanish determined, caused most of the problems for Texas and its settlements, and officials constantly complained that unlicensed French creole traders, called *contrabandistas,* slipped across the border to Hasinai villages to acquire horses and mules.[48]

In Texas and on the southern plains the gun-for-horse trade created a vicious cycle in which horses were turned into guns and guns were turned into horses. Though Spain, especially after the acquisition of Louisiana, tried to stop the Caddo horse trade by making it illegal for traders to exchange goods for horses, this proved just as unsuccessful as so many other prohibitions on the Indian trade. Just as guns increased horse production through raids, so did it stimulate slave and hide production. Caddo, Comanche, Wichita, Apache, and Tonkawa warriors mounted on mustangs and carrying trade fusils became more aggressive and successful in their raids against the Spanish in Texas and against other Indian peoples not in their respective trade networks.[49]

Slaves had long been one of the spoils of raids made by the Caddos. When Joutel and the other La Salle survivors passed through their villages, the Caddos persuaded some Frenchmen to assist in a raid on the Cannohatinos, from which they brought back several children as captives. When La Harpe visited the communities along the upper Red River in 1720, among the gifts he received from the various Indian peoples was a young Apache slave. One of the chiefs apologized for not being able to give him more slaves; if he had arrived a month earlier, the chief said, they could have given him seventeen, but all the captives had since been killed and eaten.[50]

Prior to the arrival of the French, captives had been a by-product of Caddo warfare, but now because slaves constituted a source of labor and wealth for the French in northwest Louisiana, the Caddos and other Indian peoples began making war for the purpose of acquiring them. This demand by the French for Indian slaves altered the way the Caddos treated prisoners of war. The Caddos normally tortured male captives to death, sometimes ritually eating parts of the body in order to acquire the prisoner's power. Still, not all were killed, and some, especially women and children, became slaves and eventually incorporated into families of the community. After the coming of the Europeans, the Caddos began exchanging their captives with the French for merchandise. Soon an Indian slave community grew up in northwest French Louisiana. A 1722 Natchitoches census reported eight Indian slaves. In 1726 the census listed three slaves, and a 1736 report listed fourteen: one male and thirteen female Indians. Male Indian slaves normally became servants, but the French preferred female slaves because they served as household servants and concubines. French traders often purchased female and child captives from the Caddos. A Spanish priest claimed that former French sergeant Alexis Grappe, now a Caddo trader and interpreter, kept five Indian women enslaved at his house near Fort St. Louis de Cadodacho and used them as prostitutes. Spanish officials complained that some French creoles, especially outlaws who lived on the Arkansas River, lived "in public concubinage with the captive Indian women whom for this purpose they purchase among the heathen, loaning those of whom they tire to others of less power." Apaches captured in west Texas and transported east through the Comanche-Wichita-Caddo trade network became the slaves most commonly supplied by the Caddos to the French. By the end of the eighteenth century a fairly large Apache community existed just west of Natchitoches.[51]

While the Caddos exchanged horses and slaves to the French and Spanish, just as large and important was the deerskin trade. As they had in the horse trade, the Caddos performed two roles: one as producers and the other as middlemen. In the former, Caddo hunters hunted and killed deer, their wives tanned the hides, and then they exchanged these hides to European traders for merchandise. In the latter, they received hides from other Indian peoples in exchange for European merchandise and then exchanged them with European traders for even more merchandise. No matter how they acquired the hides, the deerskin trade became the most important economic activity from the time of sustained contact with Europeans around 1700 until 1835, when the Louisiana Caddos ceded their land to the United States.

In the late 1600s Pierre Talon reported that the Caddos "have nothing to barter but buffalo and deer skins." As French traders ventured into Caddo territory in the early eighteenth century, Caddo production of animal hides increased tremendously. French traders demanded and Caddo hunters gladly provided deer hides, as well as the skins of buffalo, bear, and foxes, raccoons, and other small animals. Bear's oil also became a valuable commodity. In fact, with the Caddos supplying so many deer hides and pots of bear's oil, and because of the lack of specie in the area, Natchitoches citizens often used these two commodities in lieu of currency to pay taxes, duties, and fines.[52]

The great forests of pine and oak covering much of Caddo country provided the perfect habitat for teeming populations of white-tailed deer. With an adult doe producing two young per year, and a yearling doe producing one, the Caddos tapped into an abundant deer population that provided them with meat and hides. When stalking deer, a Caddo hunter often cloaked himself with deerskins and wore antlers. Then, catching sight of a deer, the disguised hunter made the same motions as the deer, inciting the deer to charge. When the deer got close, he shot it, sometimes with bows and arrows, later with muskets as firearms made their way into Caddo society. While a hunter might kill a deer for food at any time, as the hide trade increased in importance, bands of hunters began to go out at certain times of the year, especially in the early fall, with the express purpose of killing deer for their hides only.[53]

The Caddos also traveled west to the prairies and plains for deer and buffalo meat and hides. Prior to European contact the Caddos made seasonal hunts for meat in the late autumn and early winter, when the herds were together and their fur was the thickest. On these great hunts whole Caddo villages might venture out to the prairies and plains. There they lived in large camps of skin lodges similar to those of plains peoples. After the acquisition of horses and with the hide trade accelerating, Caddo men on horseback made longer hunts several times a year, usually after planting, in late spring/early summer, and after the second harvest, during late summer/early autumn. Sometimes all the able-bodied men of a village might head out to the prairies to hunt, leaving only women, children, and old men back at the permanent village. The main purpose was not so much to acquire meat but to take hides. While on these hunts men formed temporary hunting camps in which they might live for several weeks or months in small hide tents, and they did all the work that women normally performed: cooking, cleaning, mending pottery, and butchering and skinning deer.[54]

While the Caddos produced deer and buffalo hides themselves, they also acquired hides from other Indian peoples in exchange for goods. Kadohadacho traders often visited the communities of the Hasinai chiefdom, providing French merchandise for deer hides, buffalo hides, bear's oil, and horses. Kadohadacho and Hasinai traders also went further west, into Wichita and Comanche territory, where they provided similar goods for additional hides.[55]

Though French hunters may have produced some hides themselves, most came through the Caddos and other Indians. The hide trade attracted scores of men who wanted to participate in it. By the 1740s almost every Caddo village either had a French trader living in it or was being visited regularly by a trader who exchanged merchandise for deer and buffalo hides. These included both those traders legally licensed by the Natchitoches commandant to participate in the Indian trade and those who ignored the law and lived out among the Indians in violation of French and Spanish regulations. Whether dealing with licensed or unlicensed traders, the Caddos exchanged large quantities of hides for European merchandise.[56]

As Luis del Fierro explained in 1749 to the Spanish officials, "the traffic with the Indians friendly to [Natchitoches] is in skins, in exchange for paints, firearms, [and] munitions of war." In 1751 Pierre Mallet reported to the Marquis of Altamira that French traders regularly visited the Caddo and other Indians "to sell muskets and other things needed by the Indians, from whom they obtain annually about 100,000 pounds of furs, as well as tallow and the oil of bears, buffalos and deer." In 1761 Spanish sergeant Domingo Chirinos explained that Texas governor Jacinto de Barrios received horses, deerskins, buffalos, and other hides for the merchandise he provided the Caddos and other Indians. In 1770, after Spain took control of Louisiana, Natchitoches commandant Athanase De Mézières licensed Juan Piseros to send traders Alexis Grappe, Pierre Dupin, and Fazende Moriere to the Cadodacho, Petit Caddo, and Yatasí villages, where they would exchange various articles of merchandise, including guns, powder, musket balls, knives, beads, and copper wire for deer and buffalo hides.[57]

It is impossible to determine exactly how many deer hides the Caddos delivered to Natchitoches, or how many hides Natchitoches merchants shipped to New Orleans, but it appears to have been a considerable amount. In 1725 the Red River Caddos provided 1,000 deer hides to the French at Natchitoches. In 1751 Natchitoches merchants shipped out over 100,000 pounds of deer hides. Between March 1775 and mid-February 1776 French residents of Natchitoches exported 120 dressed buffalo skins, 36,000 deer hides, and over 10,000 quarts of bear's oil. In 1798 one merchant calculated the Caddo area could furnish about 12,000 deer hides annually. During the early 1800s Caddo hunters from the Hasinai communities provided between 1,200 and 2,500 deerskins each month to the Spanish traders at Nacogdoches, Texas. In September 1805 François Roban carried out of a Caddo village 1,100 deer hides packed on eighteen horses. When Edward Murphy, one of the area's main Indian trade merchants, died in 1808, his storehouse in Natchitoches contained 10,564 deerskins and 72 bear skins awaiting shipment to New Orleans. Even as late as 1830, 40,000 deerskins and 1,500 bear hides were coming out of the Caddo area in eastern Texas. This only increased when in 1844, 75,000 deerskins were being exported from around Waco.[58]

In the Caddo area the hide trade developed into a system of set prices and advanced credits, with the Caddo peoples manipulating both. Normally a Natchitoches merchant with access to a supply of merchandise hired a trader to make the actual trip out to the Caddo villages. The merchant furnished the goods, with the trader contracting to pay a certain amount for the merchandise by the next year, usually after the Caddos returned from their hunt and normally in deer hides that were calculated at a set price. For example, in 1770 merchant Juan Piseros advanced a large quantity of manufactured goods to Alexis Grappe, Pierre Dupin, and Fazende Moriere, the traders to the Cadodacho, Petit Caddo, and Yatasí villages, respectively. To pay off his debt for this merchandise, Piseros would accept "deer skins of good quality and marketable at thirty-five sous apiece; bear's fat at twenty-five sous a pot; buffalo hides, good and marketable, at ten livres." In 1773 Louis Rondin promised to pay back the merchandise furnished to him in deerskins valued at forty sous each. Once the traders covered their contracted debt, any deerskins remaining could be sold and counted as profit by them.[59]

As producers and consumers now within French mercantile capitalism, the Caddos quickly learned about prices, credits, and how to work the system to their advantage. Though the French and Spanish governments tried to make an official price list for goods supplied to the Caddos, it did not take the Caddos long to figure out that traders tended to mark up the price of goods until they were, in the Caddo mind, outrageously high. In 1745 the Natchitoches Caddos refused to pay the 50 percent markup the French government wanted the traders to charge. When the Caddos felt they were being gouged, they threatened to turn to other traders, such as the English or even other unlicensed traders venturing into their area. Because there were so many different traders vying for the Caddo hides, a cutthroat competition developed, which worked to the Caddos' benefit. Since traders had a debt they had to pay off within a certain amount of time or risk being sued, some found they had to undercut the official price list. In the 1782 and 1783 Bouet Laffitte gave ten musket balls and ten charges of powder for one deer hide to the Yatasís and Wichita Kichais despite the official Spanish price of only six musket balls and six charges of powder per hide. When word of this got out, the Cadodachos and Petit Caddos demanded the same prices from their traders. Much to the anger of the Natchitoches commandant and to the dismay of the traders, who complained of the low prices hides brought at that time on the international market, they could do nothing but agree to Caddo demands. As American traders made their way into the Caddo area in the early 1800s, Dehahuit, the great chief of the Kadohadacho, was much pleased to learn that they would give him a three-point blanket for five skins "and other goods as cheap."[60]

Since Caddo hunts often took long periods of time and because great quantities of hides might arrive in the village only at certain times of year, the Euro-American traders often discovered that when they arrived at a village to do business, the Caddos did not have enough skins on hand to pay for the goods they carried. Because of this the trader usually extended credit to individual Caddos with the assumption that when they returned from their hunt they would repay the debt in deer hides. The Caddos quickly accepted the credit system and ran up large debts with various traders. In 1784 the Petit Caddos owed François Morvant 154 deer hides. These credits only increased over time: in 1789 the Caddos owed Joseph Capuran 3,016 deer hides; in that same year Laffitte noted that fifty-five Caddo men owed him a total of 1,993 deer hides, with the largest single debt being 105 hides. Even the great chief of the Kadohadacho, Tinhiouen the Younger, owed him 40 hides.[61]

The hide trade and credit system created a perfect climate for misunderstandings, with Caddo and European traders often caught between the obligations of kinship and the demands of mercantile capitalism. Kinship obligated a trader to provide gifts and generous bargains to his Caddo relatives in return for hospitality and hides. At the same time the trader, faced with paying a large debt or being sued by the lending merchant, needed to acquire as many hides as he could for as few goods as possible. While sharp trading practices did not always fit with the kin-ordered mode of production, both the Caddos and Europeans used them, with the Caddos often manipulating kinships to get the best deals possible. It depended on how close a kinsperson the trader was. As anthropologist Marshall Sahlins pointed out, "close kin tend to share, to enter into generalized exchanges, and distant and non-kin to deal in equivalents or in guile." If a trader was a fictive kinsman who showed up only periodically and stingily demanded high prices for his goods, the Caddos were likely to drive a hard bargain, especially as their need for firearms and other goods increased throughout the eighteenth century. Often the Caddos shrewdly played one trader off against another. Sometimes after the hunt, when the trader fully expected the debt to be paid, he found the Caddos had already exchanged the skins with another trader for additional merchandise. Of course, the Caddos themselves could be victims as well, by having their hides taken in raids by other Indians. After suffering a raid the Caddos would appeal to their Euro-American kinsmen for more guns and ammunition, explaining that without these weapons they would never be able to pay off the debts they owed.[62]

Once a huge debt had been incurred it became almost impossible for the trader to make up the debt, as the Indians often complained about high prices and refused to pay interest on credit. In 1776, for example, the Cadodachos owed 1,400 deer hides to a Natchitoches trading partnership. When the merchants could not get the Cadodachos to pay, they tried to sell the debt to other merchants who might be more successful in collecting it. In late 1783 the Cadodachos and Petit Caddos refused to pay François Morvant for well over 3,000 *piastres'* worth of goods they had received from him during the previous year. The fifty-five individual Caddo hunters who owed Bouet Laffitte 1,993 hides in 1785 still owed him in 1789. When counting all the Indians he did business with, Laffitte declared that they owed him 14,406 *piastres'* worth of hides, which he found almost impossible to collect. He, Morvant, and other licensed traders demanded the Natchitoches commandant force the Caddos to pay their debts, but nothing came of it. As late as 1809, William Barr, whom Spain had contracted to supply goods to the Indians of northern Texas, complained that the Indians owed his trading house "more than ten thousand pelts that we have no hope of collecting." The Caddos could use these tactics because there were so many traders, both licensed and unlicensed, from Louisiana and Texas, plus a few from the English colonies and, later, American states, who competed for Caddo deer hides and horses.[63]

Though the Caddos might manipulate the system, they still depended on gifts and trade to acquire the merchandise they needed. The Spanish, who had long resented the French Louisiana traders who brazenly traveled to the Caddo villages in Texas, tried to clamp down on this wide-open trade when they took control of Louisiana. They prohibited the commandants at Natchitoches from issuing passports into Texas and instructed them to stop any unauthorized merchandise from entering the colony. Culprits would be arrested, their goods seized, and the whole lot sent to New Orleans to be prosecuted. Louisiana governor Alejandro O'Reilly knew where the real problem lay and realized that "what will contribute more that anything else to the prevention of such entries will be the vigilant care of the governor of this province in controlling the merchants of [New Orleans] who supply and give credit on these goods."[64]

While these orders sounded good on paper, the Spanish soon found it was the Caddos who dictated terms, and they did not want their supply of goods curtailed. Because of this the Spanish quickly discovered that they could not halt the supply of goods to the Caddos without serious consequences. In 1768 a Spanish troop from Texas arrested a Natchitoches trader named Du Buche while on his way to deliver a load of merchandise to the Yatasís. The Yatasís, expecting the goods, resented the Spanish interdiction. Protesting loudly to the Louisiana governor about the arrest of their trader, the Yatasís, led by Chief Guakan, decided to attack the Spanish outpost of Los Adaes in retaliation. The younger Louis de St. Denis smoothed over the insult by generously distributing presents to Guakan and the Yatasís. Louisiana governor Antonio de Ulloa explained to Texas governor Hugo O'Conor that "these nations have been accustomed for a long time past to this sort of trade and commerce, and any attempt that may be made to cut it off suddenly will have very evil consequences." Ulloa advised that the best way to prevent this sort of Indian uprising was "to give them presents, so that they never once come to talk without getting something, and to assure them that trade will be kept up in the same way as it has been carried on in the past."[65]

While Spanish vigilance might stop traders like Du Buche, the authorities never managed totally to control or regulate the Indian trade. Unlicensed French, Spanish, African, and Anglo traders flaunted Spanish law and, using the Yatasí village as a point of entry, continued to steal across the border into Spanish Texas to trade with the Hasinai communities, as well as with the Wichita and Comanche villages further west. The Spanish were helpless. The long relationship between the Caddos and the French encouraged the contraband trade. Kinships between the French and the Caddos remained strong, and many individuals, like François Morvant and the Cadodacho chief, Tinhiouen, found it impossible to uphold their reciprocal obligations within the limits of Spanish law. Also making the Spanish Texas officials worry was that Hasinai Caddos and other Indians living in eastern Texas often journeyed to Natchitoches to receive the presents they expected from the Spanish.[66]

In the end it was the Europeans' own need for hides and horses to fuel mercantile capitalism, as well as the Caddos' desire for manufactured goods, especially firearms, that made it impossible for the French and Spanish to regulate the Indian trade. The Caddos insisted that these European traders and officials become kin, uphold their reciprocal obligations, and provide their Caddo kinspeople with gifts of manufactured goods. French and Spanish authorities, wanting the Caddos as allies, and individual European traders, needing the hides and horses the Caddos provided to make profits and pay debts, found themselves bowing to Caddo demands. Spanish officials hoped to limit the quantities of firearms to the Caddos but found it difficult to break these kinship bonds. At the same time, as the Caddos' need for firearms increased during the eighteenth century, Euro-American traders found themselves being manipulated by the Caddos, who refused to pay their debts or invited outside traders to their villages. Still, the Caddos' participation in the hide trade and their close association with Europeans was not without consequences. During the eighteenth century changes over which the Caddos had no control rained down on them. The Caddos had to adapt to wholly new ways of "doing business."

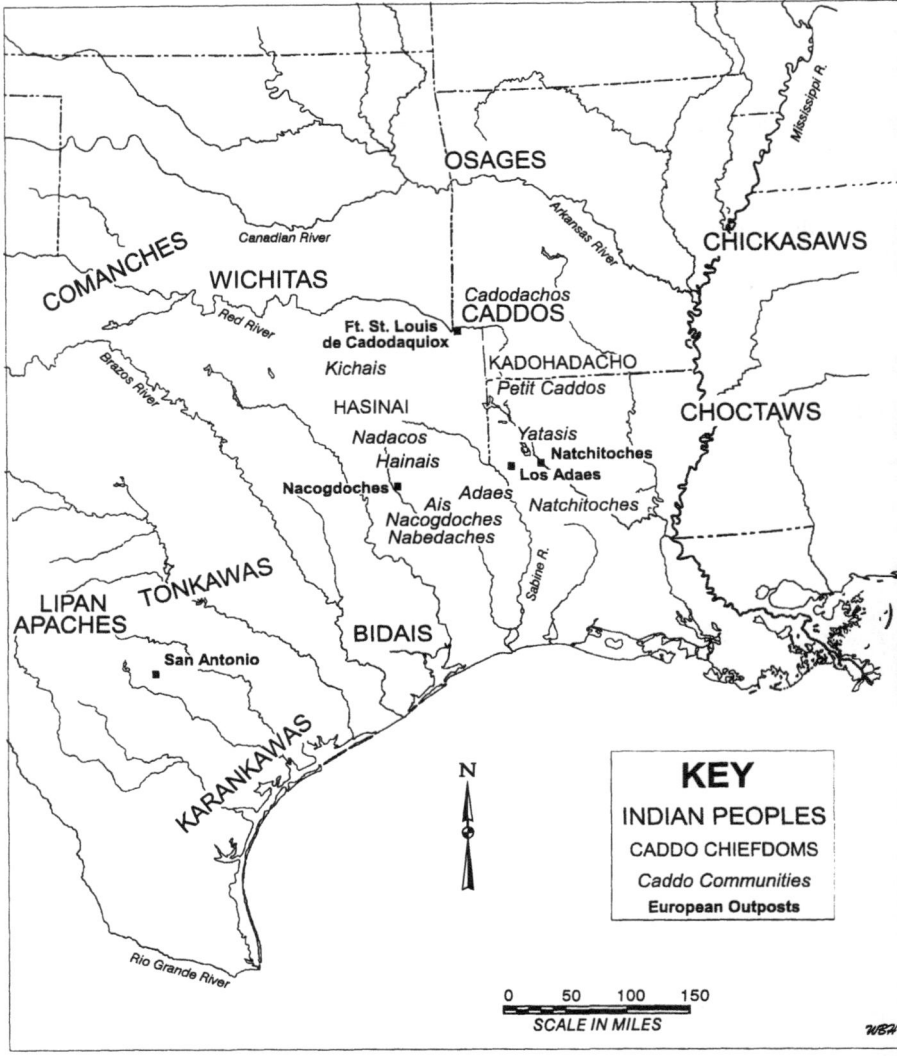

The Caddo world, ca. 1740–1790

4 // Challenges to the Chiefdoms

The French inhabitants have great respect for [the Natchitoches Indians], and a number of very decent families have a mixture of their blood in them. . . . They are gradually wasting away; the small pox has been their great destroyer.

JOHN SIBLEY, 1805,
"Historical Sketches of the Several
Indian Tribes in Louisiana," 80

WHILE the Caddos benefited greatly from the horse and hide trade, their long contact with Euro-Americans and their place as producers and consumers within a mercantile capitalist system brought many unexpected changes to Caddo society. Diseases borne by Europeans decimated Caddo populations and brought about alterations in the makeup of the chiefdoms and their governing elites. At the same time, Caddo-European intermarriage produced a large population of bicultural children, who came to play important roles as advisors and traders. The increased importance of the hide trade meant that many Caddo women spent more time tanning hides than growing corn. The influx of valuable manufactured goods brought changes in status and wealth. As goods flowed into the Caddo villages, they increasingly became the targets of Osage and Choctaw raiders needing hides, horses, and slaves because of their own connection to mercantile capitalism.

Disease brought the greatest changes. Like other Indian peoples of North America, the Caddos originally possessed no immunity to European illnesses. From a population of possibly 250,000 around A.D. 1500, the strange new maladies caused their numbers to plummet. It probably began when Luis Moscoso attempted to lead the surviving remnants of Soto's expedition through Caddo country in the 1540s. In fact, while in the Southeast, Soto's men infected much of the Indian population, and the diseases the Spanish carried shattered most of the ancient Mississippian chiefdoms. Disease so disrupted Indian cultures of the

Southeast that European colonists a century later found Indian societies much changed from those recorded by Soto's men.[1]

By the time of sustained French and Spanish contact in the late seventeenth century, about 150 years after Moscoso, the population of the two major Caddo chiefdoms and the various independent communities was considerably reduced. In 1687 La Salle's brother, Jean Cavelier, reported seeing between 500 and 600 young men at the great village of the Hasinai chiefdom, probably the main town of the Hainai community. If this was the normal village population and not inflated by a festival or ceremony, and calculating that adult males make up one-fourth of the population, then the village's total population stood between 2,000 and 2,400. If each of the ten communities that made up the Hasinai chiefdom possessed a similar population, then the Hasinai chiefdom alone had a population of about 22,000. If the Kadohadacho chiefdom and the other independent communities—Natchitoches, Yatasí, Petit Caddo, Ais, and Adaes—had similar numbers, then the Caddos had a total population of over 40,000 at French contact. On the lower end, anthropologist John Swanton believed that the Caddo population in the 1680s stood at only 8,000.[2]

No matter what was the size of the Caddo population in the 1680s, it quickly declined during the eighteenth century. An epidemic broke out at La Salle's fort on the Texas coast and killed many of the colonists. Surely this spread to the nearby Indians who had contact with the fort. La Salle himself was laid up with a "flux" for over a month. On one expedition among the Hasinais, La Salle and other members of his party came down with an illness that forced them to spend two months recuperating at a Hasinai village. Considering all the contact La Salle and his Frenchmen had with the Indian peoples of the area, and the rapid spread of European diseases afterward, this early French contact undoubtedly caused another decline in Caddo population.[3]

In 1691 Spanish priest Francisco Casañas provided the first eyewitness account of Caddo people caught in the grips a deadly plague. "About three thousand persons among all the friendly tribes of the Tejas [Hasinai] must have died during the epidemic. . . . The disease was worse in some provinces than in others. As to our own province . . . the deaths probably reached the number of three hundred—in other provinces the number was sometimes greater, sometimes less." The Hasinais blamed Casañas and the other priests for the deaths and hoped to rid themselves of the padres. Casañas refused to accept the blame. In his mind the Hasinai accusation stemmed from the "medicine men" who wanted to turn the people against the priests. In fact, Casañas believed the disease came from the medicine men themselves and that he had managed to save the Hasinais when he "hurled an exorcism against" a particularly acrimonious shaman.[4]

Even after the great 1691 epidemic, smallpox, measles, plague, diphtheria, whooping cough, trachoma, and influenza continued to batter the Caddo population. Between 1691 and 1816 eight major epidemics swept through the Caddo communities, or one about every fifteen years. While there is no doubt that Caddo population collapsed after the coming of the Euro-Americans, exact population figures and numbers of fatalities for the communities and chiefdoms are exceedingly vague and often contradictory. In 1715 the French reported that the Yatasí population had dropped to about five hundred due to disease and Chickasaw raids. In 1724 François Derbanne reported that only four hundred men could be found among all four communities of the Kadohadacho chiefdom, a far cry from the time when a single village might contain six hundred men. Bienville confirmed Derbanne's population count. He also reported in 1726 that some Caddo villages had declined to such an extent that the Wichita Kichais, Upper Nasoni, Upper Natchitoches, and Nanatsohos communities had consolidated into the Cadodacho village near the great bend of the Red River, and that together they numbered but two hundred men. Previously, he acknowledged, they had between five hundred and six hundred. Again, disease seemed the major culprit. Around the fort at Natchitoches, by 1720, there may have been fewer than seven hundred people. In 1722 Bénard de La Harpe noted how quickly disease raced through Caddo populations and pointed out that there were few old men among them. During the Spanish period officials reported similar epidemics and population decline.[5]

Accurate counts of the Caddo population during the eighteenth century are difficult to ascertain because the European observers often provided widely varying numbers. Also, they did not all observe the same peoples or make their observations at the same time of year. If a count was made during the fall, the observer usually saw a village with a small population because most residents were on hunting trips. And Caddo bands seeking refuge from raids and disease often broke away from one community and joined with another. Throughout the eighteenth century, Caddo community populations fluctuated. In early 1719 La Harpe reported that the Natchitoches, Doustionis, and Yatasís totaled only 150 people. Not long thereafter, Bienville noted that the Natchitoches, Doustionis, and Yatasís had formed one village on the Red River near the Natchitoches post and that in 1720 they had numbered altogether about 400 men, well above what La Harpe reported the previous year. Then in 1726 Bienville reported that these communities numbered only 80 men, or 320 people if we assume that adult men made up one-fourth of the population. In 1770–71 Athanase De Mézières, commandant of Spanish Natchitoches, calculated that the Cadodachos numbered 155 families; the Yatasís had 70 families; and the Petit Caddos had 63 families. In January 1778 Antonio Bonilla, Spain's commandant general of the interior provinces, reported that the Tejas [Hainai] had 300 warriors; the Kichais had 90 men; the Ais numbered only 30 men.[6]

Bonilla's figures were probably already outdated by the time he wrote them because in 1777 the Caddos experienced their worst epidemic since 1691. Hundreds, maybe thousands, of Caddos died. De Mézières wrote that the epidemic decimated the Cadodachos and almost exterminated the Adaes. During this plague the four communities of the Kadohadacho chiefdom lost their great chief, Tinhiouen. The great plague of 1777 also ripped through the Natchitoches citizenry. Church records list sixty burials between 15 October 1777 and 22 February 1778, including Louis de St. Denis, the son of the founder of Natchitoches; Maria De Mézières, daughter of Spanish commandant Athanase De Mézières; and seven unnamed Indians.[7]

The discrepancies among Caddo population counts are best seen in the numbers given by Natchitoches commandant Etienne Vaugine during the 1780s. Vaugine became commandant of Spanish Natchitoches in September 1780, and he took the opportunity to count the Indians who came to sing the calumet ceremony and make kin relations with him. According to the numbers given to him by the chiefs, Vaugine reported the Cadodachos numbered 246 men, women, and children; the Petit Caddos had 210; the Yatasís had 74; the Natchitoches, 48; the

Adaes, 33; and the Nadacos from Texas, 227. Other Indian peoples he counted included the Wichita Kichais, with 180, and the Attakapan Bidais, with 33. Three years later, in 1783, Vaugine reported 68 Hainais and Tejas Caddos together, 90 Nadacos, 368 Nacogdoches, 70 Adaes, and 236 Kichais, while the Cadodachos and Petit Caddos together could raise 150 warriors but the Natchitoches and Yatasí together had only 21 warriors. At a ratio of one warrior to four people, then, the Cadodachos and Petit Caddos had a population of 600, double what they had three years earlier. Similarly, the Kichais added almost 100 people to their numbers. This apparent population increase can be attributed to faulty counts made by the Europeans, as well as to the Caddo tendency to split up their communities, move about in band-size components, and then periodically rejoin with another community.[8]

Still, the Caddos did suffer population decline during the latter half of the eighteenth and the early nineteenth century as epidemics hammered on. John Sibley, who became the United States' Indian agent to the Caddos after the Louisiana Purchase, noted in an 1805 report on the Cadodachos that "the small pox got amongst them and destroyed nearly one half of them; it was in the winter season, and they practiced plunging into the creek on the first appearance of the eruption, and died in a few hours. Two years ago they had the measles, of which several more of them died." He calculated that only about 200 full-blood Cadodacho men and women remained.[9]

The independent Caddo community chiefdoms faced similar losses. In 1776 De Mézières announced that the Yatasís had disbanded because of disease, yet in 1805 Sibley reported that they still lived on Bayou Pierre, about forty miles northwest of Natchitoches, and totaled only 8 and 25 women and children, "but a number of men of other nations have intermarried with them and live together." The Adaes lived about forty miles due west of Natchitoches, below the Yatasís, with about 20 men and just a few more women. "They all speak Caddo, and most of them French, to whom they were always attached." The Ais, who lived about twelve miles west of the Sabine River, on the road to Nacogdoches, "are almost extinct, as a nation, not more than 25 souls remaining; four years ago the small pox destroyed the greater part of them." The Natchitoches, who were once 600 strong, now numbered only 12 men and 19 women who lived in a village about twenty-five miles north of the Natchitoches post on the Red River. They were gradually wasting away, Sibley acknowledged, because "the small-pox has been their great destroyer [but] they still preserve their Indian dress and habits."[10]

To stem this population decline the Caddos tried to replenish their numbers by intermarrying with other Indian peoples. Some of these intermarriages came with their Indian neighbors, such as the Bidais, Mayeyes, Karankawas, Apaches, Tonkawas, Orcoquisacs, Cocos, Tawakonis, Taovayas, Comanches, and Ouachitas. Other intermarriages took place with immigrant Indians from the east, who increasingly began appearing in Caddo territory in the late eighteenth century. In 1790 the Miami Indians, threatened by the Chickasaws and Arkansas Indians, sought refuge with the Caddo peoples. Other peoples moving into the area who periodically attacked and married into the Caddos included such newcomers as the Biloxis, Appalaches, Alabamas, Coushattas, Pacanas, Attakapas, Opelousas, Tunicas, Pascagoulas, Tensas, Choctaws, and Arkansas. Even acknowledged enemies of the Caddos, such as the Choctaws, could become kinspeople. By the early nineteenth century Indian agent John Sibley reported the Caddo Adaes and the Choctaws were inseparably mixed.[11]

Even as they intermarried with other Indian peoples, the Caddo population continued to decline, and they depended more and more on their European kinspeople for assistance. Fortunately, during this period the Caddos found an ever growing number of Frenchmen, Spaniards, and occasionally some Anglo-Americans who made kinships and helped replenish the Caddo population with their Caddo–Euro-American children. Some of these new kinspeople were licensed traders; some were *contrabandistas* living among the Caddos without permission of the French or Spanish authorities; others were soldiers deserting from the military or convicts escaping justice; and some were simply men who preferred the Caddo way of life to the European. Much to the annoyance of colonial officials, many Frenchmen married Caddo or other Indian women. During the French colonial period of Louisiana, official French policy discouraged European-Indian marriages, and when in 1729 the number of these marriages skyrocketed, the superior council of Louisiana promised to do everything it could to prevent them. The council even went as far as to issue two ordinances outlawing the unions.[12]

This did nothing to stop the French around Natchitoches from marrying or cohabitating with Indian women. François Derbanne, the keeper of the king's warehouse, married Jeanne de la Grand Terre, a Chitimacha woman he originally acquired as a slave during France's 1707 Chitimacha war. Jacques Guedon married Marie Therese de la Grand Terre, another Chitimacha woman and former slave. Alexis Grappe, Charles Toutin, and Joseph Duc all became brothers-in-law when they married the daughters of Jacques Guedon and Marie Therese de la Grand Terre. Soldier Jean Baptiste Brevel married a Caddo woman named Anne. Scores of these marriages, often solemnized by Catholic rites, took place in Natchitoches. Because the forts and the surrounding area were populated by both Frenchmen and Caddos, a truly bicultural population developed. In fact, Fort St. Louis de Cadodacho, on the upper Red River, eventually became almost indistinguishable from the Cadodacho villages of the Kadohadacho chiefdom, or the "ancient Caddo villages" as nineteenth-century French residents of Natchitoches came to call the area. Frenchmen like Alexis Grappe, with his bicultural wife, Louise, and their seven children, lived at the fort and established close relationships with the Cadodachos as well as a profitable Indian trade. Around Fort St. Jean Baptiste des Natchitoches, as late as 1806, U.S. Indian agent John Sibley expressed amazement at the extent to which French families had intermarried with the Natchitoches Caddos when he reported that "the French inhabitants have great respect for this nation, and a number of very decent families have a mixture of their blood in them."[13]

Naturally, force and abuse could exist among some of these intermarriages and cohabitations, but many Caddos and other Indian women willingly chose to go with European men. Caddo women often voluntarily cohabitated with European men in order to gain power and gifts that brought them prestige and status. Since status rose with the value of the gift given, it benefited a Caddo family to tie itself to a source of these new manufactured goods. As Joutel discovered in 1688, Caddo fathers and mothers' brothers, hoping to bring these rich Frenchmen into their families, tried to marry their daughters and sisters' daughters to Frenchmen. The importance the Caddos placed on making kin by marriage can be seen in their language. In the Caddo language there were no special terms for half-brothers, half-sisters, and stepfathers, so to differentiate between kin by blood and kin by marriage Caddos placed a different stress on the words.[14]

For Indian women themselves, marrying a European often brought power. Many Indian women achieved a relatively high status in both Caddo and French society. Marie Louise, the daughter of Jacques Guedon and Chitimacha woman Marie Therese de la Grand Terre, married Alexis Grappe in 1746. An incident in 1773, after her husband Alexis died, showed to what extent Marie Louise Grappe had not only risen in status but also forged new kinship ties. In that year Louis St. Denis, son of the founder of Natchitoches, filed a complaint against Marie Louise Grappe with then acting Natchitoches post commandant Baltazar De Villiers. According to St. Denis's suit the widow Grappe helped an Apache slave named Marianne escape from her master's home. Not only had Madame Grappe given the runaway Marianne refuge in her own house, but she then had provided her with passage to the Petit Caddo village and persuaded the Petit Caddos to declare Marianne one of their own people. This would prevent her from being retaken as a slave. Madame Grappe then managed, despite complaints by the slave's owner, to evade prosecution and have the matter dropped.[15]

So powerful were Caddo kinship ties that this widow managed to foil the machinations of the son of the great St. Denis, one of the most powerful men in Natchitoches. Of even greater interest is the fictive kinship involved among three different Indian peoples. Madame Grappe's mother was Chitimacha. Marianne was an Apache slave who finally wound up living among the Petit Caddos, who accepted her as one of their own. Madame Grappe probably established her kinship bonds with the Petit Caddos when her husband, Alexis, served as commandant of Fort St. Louis de Cadodacho and the king's interpreter to the Cadodachos. How Madame Grappe established her bond with Marianne is unclear. Anthropologist Dayna Lee pointed out that Madame Grappe possibly felt an affinity for Marianne because her own mother had once been a slave. Whatever the reason, Madame Grappe's bonds with the Petit Caddos must have been particularly strong for her to be able to persuade them to accept Marianne as a kinswoman and brave the ire of the powerful St. Denis family.[16]

Similar elevation in status for *mestizo* women, as the Spanish designated mixed-blood people, took place in Texas as these Indian women became increasingly immersed in the European culture. Over the years at the Spanish outpost of Nacogdoches, census takers often elevated the ethnicity, and therefore the status, of these intermarried Indian women. The 1793 census listed Trinidad Sanches Grande as a *mestiza*, but by the 1799 census she had become listed as a Spaniard. Similarly, the 1793 census listed Maria del Pilar Procela as a *loba*, a person of Indian-African mixture; by 1799 she had moved to the mulatta category, a Spanish-African mixture; then in 1805 she had advanced "up" to *mestiza*.[17]

As seen in the instance of Madame Grappe, the intermarriage between Europeans and Caddos brought about a large mixed-blood population. The survivors of La Salle's expedition left the first mixed-blood children among the Caddos. The number of mixed-bloods in the Caddo area only increased as traders visited Caddo villages and took Indian wives. Over time these mixed-blood children married French, Spanish, Indians, Africans, and, of course, other mixed-bloods, and so around Natchitoches there developed a large, highly complex multiracial population that had kinships branching out in all directions—large mixed-blood populations could be found in the town of Natchitoches itself; south of the town at Isle Brevel, named after Jean Brevel, himself a Caddo-French mixed-blood; at Bayou Pierre, northwest of Natchitoches; to the west, at Spanish Lake; and in the various Caddo villages. In 1806 Thomas Freeman and Peter Custis, while exploring the Red River, described Isle Brevel and its inhabitants as people who lived in cottages, farmed large plots of land, and were "a mixture of French, Spanish, Indian, and Negro blood."[18]

The mixed-bloods lived a bicultural existence and were often able to take advantage of both their Caddo and European heritages. In the Caddo villages around Natchitoches mixed-blood children were usually the product of unions between European men and Caddo women. In European society a child reckoned descent from both parents but took the father's last name and was the heir of the father. This meant that among the French and Spanish, mixed-blood children were normally seen as children of the father and accepted, or at least tolerated, in colonial European society. In Natchitoches, because there was so much intermarriage between Europeans, Indians, and Africans, a mixed-blood child was not uncommon and usually took the status of his or her father. Caddo society added to this tendency as sons born to higher-ranked fathers, such as European traders, took the lineage of the father. Still, matrilineality played an important role, especially in the Caddo villages, where these mixed-bloods were also seen as children of the mother, considered to be Caddos, and accorded a place in Caddo society.

This dual kinship provided mixed-bloods with a variety of options. Some remained with their Indian kin and lived an Indian life. In 1789 the Spanish complained that "the half-breed who has one blue-eye and the other one black, and his uncle called 'Pacane,' are capable of giving evil counsel to the Caddo, and have almost caused them to have a war with the Arkansas." Others lived a bicultural existence, moving back and forth between the Caddo villages and the French and Spanish towns. Because of their biculturalism, male mixed-bloods often became the perfect traders to go to the villages. Some became the official, licensed Spanish traders to some villages but many became, in Spanish eyes, *contrabandistas* dealing in guns and tafia, a potent type of rum made from sugar cane juice. The mixed-bloods gained tremendous prestige and power among their Indian kin as the Caddos came to rely on them not only for valuable manufactured merchandise but also for good advice on dealing with the Europeans and Americans. Sometimes individual mixed-bloods tried to drive hard bargains and took advantage of their Caddo kinspeople just the way some Europeans and Americans did. For the most part, however, mixed-blood people tried to uphold their reciprocal obligations and provide for the welfare of their Caddo kin.[19]

Some mixed-bloods became powerful and highly respected men. Lucas Talapoon, a Caddo mixed-blood who served as an interpreter and guide on the 1806 Freeman and Custis Red River expedition, spoke several Caddo dialects and was a master of sign language. Prior to serving with Freeman and Custis he rode with Philip Nolan, a horse herder killed by Spanish Texas authorities because they thought he was a spy.

Talapoon so impressed Daniel Clark Jr., a New Orleans merchant, that Clark proposed Talapoon be sent to Washington D.C. to meet President Thomas Jefferson. After the aborted Freeman and Custis expedition Talapoon guided several American trading expeditions to the Wichitas and Comanches.[20]

One of the most amazing examples of both fictive kinship and the assistance mixed-bloods often provided for their kin can be seen in the life of François Grappe, who grew wealthy by his close relationship with the Caddos and his ability to deal with French, Spanish, and Americans on equal footing. Grappe, who also went by the name of Touline, was a mixed-blood: three-fourths French and one-fourth Chitimacha; his mother was Marie Louise Guedon Grappe, who helped the Apache slave Marianne escape to the Petit Caddos. He was born on 4 December 1747 at Fort St. Louis de Cadodacho, which his father, Sergeant Alexis Grappe, commanded. Reared among the Cadodachos, François created strong kinship ties with them and became so closely associated with the Caddos that many believed him to be of Caddo descent. He never married into the Caddos; rather, his common-law wife was Rosette, one of his African-American slaves, whom he freed in 1796.

Grappe lived with a foot in both the Euro-American and Caddo worlds. He paid taxes in Natchitoches, owned slaves, acted as the executor of estates, possessed a large cattle ranch near Lake Bistineau, and even served as a noncommissioned officer in the Spanish Natchitoches cavalry militia. Like many mixed-bloods, he served as a guide and interpreter for both the Spanish and Americans. In 1783 he led a Natchitoches cavalry expedition to the Kichai villages in Texas when Natchitoches commandant Etienne Vaugine and Nacogdoches commandant Antonio Gil Ybarbo tried unsuccessfully to force the Kichais to deny unlicensed French creole traders access to their villages. Grappe provided the translation of the Kichai chief's refusal to bow to Vaugine's and Ybarbo's demands. In 1806 Grappe served with Lucas Talapoon as a guide for the Freeman and Custis expedition up the Red River. For the Caddos and other Indian peoples, Grappe acted as their counselor and protector; his ranch became a haven for traveling Caddos, and he became an intermediary between them and the Euro-Americans. His generosity, assistance, and good counsel earned him high esteem among the Caddos, who always referred to him as their brother. Even the

Spanish officials in Texas recognized that Grappe was an "individual possessing the confidence of the [Caddo] Nation." Grappe also acquired a Cherokee connection when one of his daughters married Richard Fields, one of the principal men of Chief Duwali's Texas Cherokees. Even after Grappe's death, in 1825, the Caddos recognized Grappe's high status when, ten years later, they demanded that a parcel of land be cut from their 1835 land cession and reserved for his heirs. According to anthropologist Dayna Lee, Grappe's fictive kin relationship remains alive in the twentieth century, as Caddo legend features a sly trickster named Tonin, sometimes called Tolin, who protects the Caddos by outwitting the whites.[21]

The melding of Caddo and French populations and cultures as a result of all this intermarriage and close contact was facilitated by the geographical isolation of Natchitoches. In fact, the French around Natchitoches soon found themselves not only adopting Caddo characteristics but dependent on their Indian kinspeople. In 1753 French Louisiana governor Louis Billouart de Kerlérec reported that because Natchitoches was so distant and difficult to reach, one of the largest expenses in the Louisiana budget was the cost of feeding the outpost. Up until the late eighteenth century the residents of Natchitoches found they could not depend on regular shipments of food from New Orleans, nor could they depend on growing enough food for their own survival. Therefore they relied on the Caddos and other peoples.[22]

Maize, squash, beans, and wild rice, as well as fruits, nuts, venison, beef, and other foods soon made their way into Natchitoches kitchens. Europeans along the Red River seasoned their foods the Caddo way, with bear's oil and filé—pounded sassafras leaves. French families even adopted Caddo- style houses: building houses by sinking logs into the ground to form a base and then making the walls with straw and wattle, the French around Natchitoches built *poteaux en terre* homes and covered the wattle with a four- inch mixture of clay, Spanish moss, and deer hair, called *bousillage*. Caddo baskets and clay pottery found their way into these French homes and became indispensable for household use.[23]

This European reliance on the Caddos was significant. The wealth of Frenchmen and Spaniards in northwestern Louisiana and eastern Texas depended almost totally on the Caddos. There were no gold or silver mines in Texas for the Europeans to exploit, and commercial agriculture in the area during the eighteenth century remained scant. While the French along the Red River cultivated some tobacco and sold it at New Orleans, it was considered to be of inferior quality to that being put on the market from the English colonies and was never economically significant. Compounding the problem of European wealth was the lack of specie. For Europeans living in Caddo territory, wealth was counted in deer and buffalo hides, pots of bear's oil, horses and cattle, land, and slaves. They depended on the Caddos to provide most of these.

The Europeans also relied on the Caddos as military allies, and the chiefs often sent contingents of warriors to help their French and Spanish kinsmen. In 1731, when a party of Natchez warriors besieged Fort St. Jean Baptiste, the Caddos sent a detachment to help their French kinsman, St. Denis. The Caddos and French broke the siege, virtually wiping out the Natchez war party. After the Spanish acquired Louisiana, Caddo warriors provided similar service. When the Xaraname Indians left their mission in Texas, Santo, chief of the Hainais, and his warriors helped search for them. In 1777, when it appeared that the American Revolution might spill over into Louisiana, De Mézières turned to the Caddos. He calculated that the Cadodachos could provide fifty warriors; the Nadacos and Nasoni, twenty-five men together; the Nabedaches, thirty warriors; the Hainai, thirty; the Kichais, twenty-five; the Tonkawas, sixty; the Tawakonis, another sixty; the Xaranames, twenty; the Taovayas, three hundred; the Pani-Mahas, or Skidi Pawnee, three hundred; and the Comanches, four hundred. All of these Indian warriors, De Mézières reported, would be riding horses and using arrows, lances, and fusils, and would be in the thick of the fighting, essential and instrumental in protecting that part of Spanish Louisiana from an English invasion. The English invasion never came, but the Euro-American residents around Natchitoches continued to rely on the Caddos to protect their homes and ranches from foreign invasion. In times of peace Caddo hunters might carry mail for the Europeans, sometimes between posts as distant as the Arkansas post and New Orleans. Individual Caddos also served as carriers and haulers of goods, rowers of canoes, guides, scouts, and general assistants.[24]

While the Caddos provided all manner of support to their European kinspeople, Caddo land was also an attraction. Not long after the coming of St. Denis to the Natchitoches Caddo villages, Frenchmen began to acquire land along both sides of the Red River. This continued throughout the later Spanish period and during the remainder of the eighteenth century. Little is known of these eighteenth-century European land negotiations with the Caddos. Some evidence indicates that Frenchmen actually purchased land from the local Caddos. La Harpe, on his trip to the Kadohadacho communities, claimed he purchased the land from the Nasoni chief on which to build Fort St. Louis de Cadodacho. In 1719 Bienville ordered François Derbanne to buy a cabin from the Natchitoches "white chief" to be used as a warehouse. In May 1778 a "free" Indian named Tsaoua Camtê, of an unidentified people, sold a large tract of land on both sides of the Red River to Manuel Trichele and Dame Veuve Alexis for three hundred *livres'* worth of merchandise.[25]

Merchandise shortages and the need for European goods often made Caddos ready to exchange land for goods or to pay off debts. In 1780 Hyamoc, the chief of the Natchitoches Indians, sold the tract of land he was living on to Jean Baptiste La Berry. The land, containing twenty *arpents* of frontage on both sides of the Red River, sold for only forty *piastres* of trade merchandise, which Hyamoc owed La Berry. Between 1776 and 1787 the Yatasís and Natchitoches Caddos, because of dwindling numbers, often did not receive some or all of their annual presents from the Spanish. By summer 1787 the shortage of gifts and trade goods forced Antoine, then the Yatasí chief, to sell a tract of land at his village to Bouet Laffitte for some cloth, a blanket, a shirt, two pounds of gunpowder, two twists of tobacco, and ten pounds of salt. Five years later, Antoine was still petitioning the Spanish for presents owed him for the past five years.[26]

Whether the Caddos perceived these land "transactions" as conveying complete property ownership to the Europeans or only usufruct rights is unknown. During most of the eighteenth century this probably made little difference to the Caddos, as there was not much pressure on their lands. During the 1780s French creoles and their slaves along the Red River numbered only 1,400, while Spaniards in eastern Texas totaled 800. The majority of these Europeans participated in some form of trade or exchange and usually limited their farming to small subsistence gardens. Most of the land was wooded and unfenced, and French herders normally allowed their cattle and hogs to roam free. It would not be until the second half of the eighteenth century that some Natchitoches residents tried their hand at tobacco, and not until the early nineteenth century that the cotton culture developed in the area. In eastern Texas Spanish farming was more sparse. Throughout the eighteenth century the Spanish commandants in eastern Texas complained of the meager harvests, and as late as 1807 they issued orders to all landowners to immediately cultivate their lands so that they and the army garrisons would not starve.[27]

With little initial pressure on Caddo land the horse and hide trade and the manufactured goods these activities drew into Caddo society brought the most obvious changes to Caddo life. During their early contact with Europeans, Caddo pottery, especially flatware such as plates and saucers, often imitated European styles, with many of these being provided to European families. Later, as larger quantities of more durable metal kettles and pots reached Natchitoches and the Caddo villages, the making of clay pottery declined. The coming of European goods to all the different Indian communities in the area helped bring about a similarity in style and material culture, especially seen in the beadwork on clothes and moccasins.[28]

Still, although European manufactured goods disrupted the ancient ways in which Caddos made things, these Indian peoples did not always use manufactured goods in the same manner as Euro-Americans. They often adapted and combined their ancient arts and technology with manufactured goods to create a uniquely Caddo tool. In 1691, when Domingo Terán led an expedition into eastern Texas to establish the Spanish missions, he found among the Hasinai communities such Spanish-made goods as a ship's anchor, several anvils, and some bells. The Caddos, he noted, did not use the bells as the Spanish did but rather as mortars for grinding corn. Always innovative, Caddos used trade scissors to cut up brass and copper kettles to make arrowheads, scrapers, and clothing ornaments, as well as to cut cloth. Mirrors, rather than for looking at one's reflection, became ornaments, arrowpoints, or excellent hide scrapers, which helped increase deerskin production. The barrels of broken guns were usually cut up into arrowheads or used as hammers. But even with the influx of manufactured goods, traditional Caddo manufactures, like pottery and cane baskets, continued to be made, used, and exchanged well into the nineteenth century. While firearms displaced bows and arrows to some degree, as late as 1830 the Caddos continued to make bows and arrows, quivers, war clubs, and saddles.[29]

Although the Caddos might still make bows and arrows, firearms, because of the psychological value in warfare, became one of the items most sought by the Caddos. Their constant need for firearms resulted mainly from an almost continuous warfare during the last half of the eighteenth century between them and the Osages and Choctaws. The Osages from the north became the great scourge of the Caddos. The Osages, Dhegian Siouan speakers, originally lived in the forests of the lower Ohio River valley. Then during the early seventeenth century they migrated west. Once across the Mississippi River they moved up the Missouri River and began breaking into smaller divisions. By the mid–seventeenth century these Dhegian-Siouan speakers comprised five autonomous groups: the Osages, Quapaws or Arkansas, Kansas, Omahas, and Poncas. Like the Caddos, they were people of the margins of the plains and prairies to the west and the woodlands to their east. They lived a semisedentary life, planting crops in the spring at their villages and spending the summer and fall hunting buffalo or deer on the prairie and plains. Just as the Caddos did, the Osages acquired horses and quickly made exchange relationships during the eighteenth century with the French and Spanish traders out of the Arkansas post located on the Arkansas River.[30]

The problem the Caddos faced was the growth of a rival northern trade network. During the early eighteenth century the relatively large number of French traders and merchants in Natchitoches and Opelousas made these two areas the most populous European communities west of the Mississippi and east of the Great Plains. Because of this, two trade networks developed from these communities: the Caddo-Wichita-Comanche network, out of Natchitoches, and the Attakapa-Tonkawa-Apache network, from Opelousas. As large profits from the hide trade sent hunters and merchants looking for fresh resources, more and more Euro-Americans moved into the area north of the Natchitoches jurisdiction along the Arkansas and Mississippi Rivers. Settlements arose, like the Arkansas post and St. Geneviève and St. Louis on the Mississippi, and traders from these communities soon ventured out to the villages of the Osages, Quapaws, Pawnees, and other Indians with gifts and trade goods. These Euro-Americans established a trade network with the Osages by supplying them with large quantities of firearms. These guns, as well as their acquisition of horses, allowed the Osages, like the Caddos, to expand their economic territory while developing a reliance on European firearms and weapons. To help feed this material need the Osages turned to raiding their Caddo trade rivals for hides, horses, and captives to exchange for more merchandise.[31]

The Osages began causing problems for the Caddos as early as 1720. When Bénard de La Harpe visited the prairies near the Kadohadacho villages on the upper Red River in May 1720, his Caddo guide nearly deserted him when they discovered some footprints considered to be made by Osages. After threatening and cajoling the man, La Harpe managed to get the guide moving, but it all fell apart when they noticed smoke on the horizon. "Then it was impossible to reassure the guide; nothing could induce him to lead [us] further." Because of this the French party returned to the Nasoni village. Throughout his short stay among the Caddos and Wichitas, La Harpe found these Indian peoples continually fearful of the Osages, so much so that even La Harpe began to feel uneasy, despite having smoked the calumet with them.[32]

Ten years later, in 1730, warfare between the Caddos and Wichitas, on one hand, and the Osages and Quapaws, on the other, became so vicious that St. Denis found the trails between Natchitoches and the Illinois country too dangerous for travel. Five or six unlucky Frenchmen who lived along the Arkansas River were killed during these attacks, and the French trade between Natchitoches and Illinois briefly shut down. As Caddo and Osage men, women, and children were killed, wounded, or captured during these attacks and counterattacks, enmity between these Indian peoples grew so great that over the next several years French attempts to arrange a peace between the Caddos and Osages failed miserably.[33]

During this time, despite the Osages believing the Wichitas were sorcerers who could control storms and make men go insane, they stepped up their attacks on the Caddos and Wichita allies. The war was so intense that between 1742 and 1757 the Grand Osage, or Big Osage, pushed the Wichitas permanently out of the Arkansas River basin. This brought the Comanches into the fray. In the early 1750s, after suffering an attack at the hands of the Osages, the Wichitas appealed to the Comanches for assistance, and together they attacked a Grand Osage village, killing twenty-two chiefs and even more warriors. Rather than snuffing out the conflict, it merely escalated the warfare between the Osages and the Caddos, Wichitas, and Comanches, which became even more severe after Spain took control of the Natchitoches jurisdiction, in 1768.[34]

Natchitoches commandant Athanase De Mézières reported in 1770 that violent episodes between the Caddos and Osages were on the increase. These two peoples had been enemies since "time immemorial," De Mézières wrote the Spanish governor of Louisiana, but because of the great distance between them and because both had been so involved in hunting hides for trade, not much conflict had occurred in recent years. At the bottom of this escalation in warfare, De Mézières said, was an increased number of Euro-American hunters and *contrabandistas* living among the Osages. According to De Mézières these hunters along the Arkansas River incited the Osages to attack the Caddos, Wichitas, and other Indians in the Natchitoches jurisdiction in order to acquire women for sex, children to sell as slaves, horses to help in hunting, and mules to carry their furs and oils back to the Arkansas post and Illinois. To assist the Osages on their raids south these hunters provided powder, balls, fusils, and other weapons. Because of this the Natchitoches district had "become a pitiful theater of outrageous robberies and bloody encounters," which forced some of the Caddo and Wichita communities to move their villages further south. De Mézières recommended that these Euro-American hunters be cleaned out of the Arkansas River valley and that the commandant at Illinois prevent these men from stirring up the Osages.[35]

Spanish authorities proved powerless to clear out these *contrabandistas,* nor could they stop the Osages from raiding the villages and ranches around Natchitoches, where they seized horses and goods from Caddos and Euro-Americans alike. Because of the ineffectiveness of the Spanish authorities, the elder Tinhiouen and the Caddos often took matters into their own hands. In 1768 a band of Osage warriors raided the main Cadodacho village and escaped north with a herd of horses. Tinhiouen and his warriors chased the Osages as far as the Arkansas

River, where they discovered two Osage chiefs in the cabin of a French creole trader. It quickly became apparent to Tinhiouen that this Frenchman supplied the weapons that the Osages were using against his people, and that he also provided asylum for returning raiders. In a rage Tinhiouen ordered his warriors to kill the Osage chiefs, and only his respect for Spanish law prevented him from killing the Frenchman.[36]

As De Mézières pointed out to the Louisiana governor, this incident brought dire repercussions for Spain's influence with her Indian allies. Tinhiouen's killing of the two Osage chiefs at the cabin of a French creole only fueled resentment toward Spain from both the Caddos and the Osages. Tinhiouen lost faith in the word of his Spanish kinsmen, who had been preaching to him that the French and the Spanish were one people. If so, here was a Spanish ally providing weapons to the Caddo's arch enemies. The Osages were no less angry at the French trader, "because he consented that his guests should be killed in his own house and before his own eyes." The Osages decided to take vengeance on the trader for not upholding his kinship obligations, but the Frenchman heard of their plans and escaped. But the Osages "did not on this account wish to fail to carry out their enterprise, and it was concluded by the killing of a poor fellow named Dauteuil, his wife, and his children."[37]

By the early 1770s revenge killings, raids, and violence between different groups of Indian peoples had become almost everyday occurrences throughout Caddo country. Red River and Texas Indian peoples sometimes banded together to attack the Osages, as did the Taovayas, Panis-Mahas [Skidi], Tawakonis, Xaranames, Tonkawa Mayeyes, and Comanches in 1770. Even the Quapaws, who lived in what today is the state of Arkansas, sometimes joined with the Caddos against the Osages. This only brought more counterattacks. Tinhiouen and his allies reminded the Spanish of their obligation to protect their Caddo kinspeople and demanded that Spanish officials halt these Osage depredations. Spanish officials in Louisiana acknowledged the justness of Caddo complaints and mouthed empty words about wiping out the Osages, but fear of losing Osage loyalty to the English, as well as a realization of the expense of such an expedition, prevented any true measures from being taken against them.[38]

During the 1770s it appeared that for every victory the Caddos won over the Osages, they also suffered a defeat. Osage raids hammered

Caddo communities and shattered villages, breaking them up and scattering bands of fearful Caddo families throughout the area in search of safety, provisions, and merchandise. Some of the smaller bands remained small and went into hiding; some merged with larger, stronger villages for safety, thereby forming composite communities; while some of the larger villages moved south and west to escape the Osages. As Natchitoches observers pointed out in January 1774, Osage pillaging of the Kichais shattered them and forced the remnants "to take refuge in some hidden spots unknown to their enemies." In fact, Osage raids split the Kichais, forcing one band to move east, closer to the protection of Tinhiouen's Cadodachos. But even the Cadodachos and Petit Caddos found themselves constantly harassed by the Osages. To put more room between themselves and Osage raiders, in 1773 Tinhiouen threatened to move his Cadodacho village further south toward the Petit Caddos and leave the upper Red River unguarded and defenseless unless the Spanish put an end to the raids.[39]

Like the Osages, the Caddos believed that it was the Euro-American hunters and traders who caused most of the problems by providing guns and ammunition to their enemies. Tinhiouen understood that if he could eliminate those traders who provided weapons to the Osages, he could eliminate much of the threat. With this in mind the Caddos began attacking Euro-American traders they found in Osage territory and whom they suspected of trading with their enemy. The Nadacos and Kichais reported that Natchitoches trader François Beaudouin was on the Arkansas River supplying the Osages with guns, powder, and musket balls, and demanded that they be allowed to kill him. De Mézières managed to prevent this as he believed that if the Caddos killed one European they would not stop there and would begin indiscriminately killing Spaniards and French creoles.[40]

No one was safe, as Osage parties killed two members of the Natchitoches militia while the men were on their way to the Taovayas. Even Qui Te Sain, chief of the Taovayas, in 1780 pointed out that he and his people could not visit Natchitoches because the roads were not safe anymore due to the Osages, who stole their horses and murdered their people. Though some Spanish officials hoped that a peace could be arranged, De Mézières knew better and explained that a peace could never be made because of the deep animosity between the two peoples.

The Caddos, he said, possessed a hatred so "imponderable that if I, who have grown up with them and in some manner naturalized with them, would come to solicit its abolition, I would immediately lose favor with them."[41]

For the Caddos, as the 1770s came to an end, the situation seemed bleak. The great chief Tinhiouen the Elder died in 1777; their kinsman and main supporter, De Mézières, died in 1779; and the merchandise shortages brought about by the American Revolution made the Caddos work harder to find a reliable supply of firearms and metal goods. During the early part of 1781 the Osages twice hit the Cadodachos, Petit Caddos, and Kichais, taking almost the entire Cadodacho herd of about 160 horses. Without horses the Caddos would be impoverished, but the number of Osage raiders in the area made it very dangerous for Caddo parties to go to the plains to capture more. Instead the Caddos turned to their Comanche trade partners, who often provided them with horses to make up for those lost in raids. To make matters worse, the raids had nearly depleted the Kadohadachos' weapons and ammunition.[42]

The Caddos counterraided as best they could, but the attacks forced them to expend valuable ammunition, which could have been better used to acquire deerskins. The frequency and severity of the Osage raids, while they did not prevent the Caddos from making their annual hunts, did make them more wary during the hunts and therefore less productive. All this led only to more severe shortages and made them turn even more to their Euro-American kinspeople. In 1782 Chief Tinhiouen the Younger informed trader François Morvant that shortages prevented him from paying back the hides Morvant had credited his people. Morvant, realizing that unless something was done the Caddos would never be able to pay the hides they owed him, interceded with Natchitoches commandant Vaugine, pleading that "the Chiefs and Warriors of the Caddo . . . beseech you for gunpowder, bullets, and some small trade items, so that they can make their summer hunt, and recover, in part, some of the damage that the Osages have occasioned them this winter in their hunts."[43]

By early 1783, as the battles depleted Caddo ammunition and goods, Tinhiouen appealed to Vaugine for their official annual gifts. Vaugine consented and told them to come to Natchitoches in April or May to receive not only their presents for 1783 but also those owed them for 1782.

When Tinhiouen and a large party of his Cadodachos arrived in Natchitoches in April 1783, he presented to Commandant Vaugine two scalps, complete with ears, that his warriors had taken in a recent raid on the Osages. He told Vaugine that the chiefs and warriors of the Kichais, Petit Caddos, and Nadacos who had also participated in the raid were on their way to receive the gifts promised them by the Spanish. Vaugine gave Tinhiouen the gifts for 1782 and 1783, which Tinhiouen then redistributed to his warriors. The Natchitoches commandant then took this opportunity to broach the idea of Tinhiouen making peace with the Osages. Tinhiouen brushed off the proposal, explaining that his people and the Osages had always been enemies and "that under the appearances of reconciliation and promises, [the Osages] had always been deceitful and liars." The actions by the Osages always put the Caddos on the defensive; Tinhiouen could not pardon all their thefts and his "intention and that of his warriors [was] to continue to make war."[44]

The meeting, for the Spanish, went from bad to worse. Not only did Tinhiouen refuse the commandant's proposal of peace, the great chief also requested that Vaugine officially raise the price of deer hides to ten balls and ten charges of powder, which they were already getting from unlicensed traders. Vaugine declined and reminded the chief he was authorized to give them only six balls and six charges of powder per skin. Vaugine also urged the great chief to pay the debts he had already run up with the trader Morvant, explaining that if he did not, Morvant would be ruined. Tinhiouen remained noncommittal. He even demanded that his people receive the same amount of gifts they had been given during the flush times before the American Revolution caused merchandise shortages, something Vaugine was incapable of doing. To make matters worse for Vaugine, the chief and his warriors remained at the fort for nine days because of rain, during which time Vaugine was forced to feed and house them out of his own pocket. The expenses almost bankrupted the commandant and forced him to appeal to merchants of the post to help cover the cost of the visit. As a final indignity, Tinhiouen drank or carried off twenty bottles of Vaugine's best wine.[45]

While Tinhiouen and his Caddos fended off the Osage attacks, they discovered just how little they could depend on the Spanish for military assistance. Though Spanish officers recommended an all-out war on the Osages, officials merely talked, remaining indecisive and fearful, and nothing came of these plans. All plans for a Spanish-Caddo campaign against the Osages ceased in the mid-1780s after the end of the American Revolution. Spanish Louisiana officials suddenly realized that a Spanish attack on the Osages might provide an opening to American encroachment into Louisiana. Rather than a punitive attack on the Osages, Louisiana governor Esteban Miró hoped to arrange a peace between the Caddos and the Osages.[46]

In spring 1785 Miró managed to get Tinhiouen and two Osage chiefs to meet in New Orleans in order to make peace. Initially, Tinhiouen refused, telling Miró that he could not trust the Osages because they did not keep their word. Miró prevailed and made a speech urging peace, to which the Osages immediately agreed. Tinhiouen remained obstinate, but then one of the Osage chiefs, Bru Caiguais, promised that his only desire was to make a permanent peace with the Caddos. Tinhiouen finally acceded, extended his hand to Bru Caiguais, and said that he had now torn all the hate from his heart. With that Tinhiouen and Bru Caiguais embraced. To recognize and ensure the peace Miró gave each a red ribbon and told them that if one of them attacked the other, the one attacked should send the ribbon back to New Orleans and the Spanish would join with the wronged party.[47]

The peace lasted about a year. In January 1786, while the Cadodachos were returning from hunting, their horses loaded with deerskins, a large party of Little Osages attacked. The battle, in which two Cadodachos were killed and two were wounded, lasted the entire day, until the Cadodachos ran out of ammunition. With their ammunition gone they waited until darkness and then managed to withdraw from the battlefield. The Little Osages next attacked a party of Kichai hunters, killing four and taking their horses and deerskins. Other Osage parties also attacked. Even Bru Caiguais, who had made peace with Tinhiouen the year previously, led a raid on the Caddos. Miró, hearing of the attacks on the Cadodachos and Kichais, feared that if something was not done the Spanish would lose the friendship of the Caddos. He threatened the Osages that he would prevent any traders from going out to them and prohibit their receiving any merchandise until they kept the peace.[48]

In disgust Tinhiouen returned the bloodstained red ribbon given to him by Miró as proof of Osage treachery. He demanded aid from the governor against the Osages. When a Spanish commandant named Judice tried to calm Tinhiouen, telling him that the Spanish really were trying to cut off trade to the Osages, Tinhiouen became so furious at the empty Spanish promises that he slapped Judice across the face. Tinhiouen's slap caused almost as much consternation with Miró as did the Osage raids. He told Natchitoches commandant Pedro Rousseau that "a white man must not ever let [the Indians] put a hand to their face and much less to a commandant." Tinhiouen's slap would give the Osages new impetus for attacks, as they could say that Tinhiouen was now an enemy of the Spanish and they were only attacking the Caddo adversaries of their Spanish brothers. Tinhiouen later explained that he had not meant to hurt Judice, but had merely been trying to touch a sick part of Judice's body. Miró urged Rousseau to make Tinhiouen see that the Spanish were doing all they could to cut off trade with the Osages.[49]

Osage attacks on the Caddo peoples continued unabated, and Tinhiouen found it impossible to stem the Osage terror. During the mid-1770s the attacks had been so fierce that his father, Tinhiouen the Elder, had planned to move the main village, and it took all the persuasive abilities of De Mézières to stop him. In 1788 Tinhiouen the Younger would not be denied, and he moved his Cadodacho village south from the great bend of the Red River into western Louisiana to escape Osage attacks. The Kichais, also hammered by Osage raids, asked to be allowed to move their main village to the Texas Gulf coast and live between the Bidais and Karankawas. The Spanish rejected the Kichais' request because it would leave a breach in the Indian defenses around Natchitoches and open the ranches and town itself to Osage attack. With the eastern band of Kichais pulled into his Kadohadacho chiefdom, Tinhiouen also urged against the Kichais' move because he depended on them as allies. Instead he proposed to settle the Kichais six leagues from the Petit Caddos, in northwestern Louisiana, and to calm them he would give the Kichais all the presents that the Spanish were to give his Cadodachos for that year. He also promised to take the Kichais to New Orleans to meet Governor Miró and have Miró select a "chief for the medal of merit, and to confer upon them annually the same presents enjoyed by the other nations."[50]

Before this could be arranged, Tinhiouen the Younger, the great chief of the Kadohadachos, died, in the summer of 1789. In 1782 he had appeared before Commandant Vaugine and asked him to recognize Bisquita, who was twenty-five years old at the time and who was the "son of the former Grand Chief of the nation," as his successor. Not much is known of Bisquita, but he did not appear to have the leadership qualities of the two Tinhiouens. Tinhiouen's death brought no relief from the Osages, and Bisquita, still trying to find a protective arrangement for his Caddos, moved the Cadodacho villages even closer to the Natchitoches post.[51]

The Texas Indians had greater success against the Osages. In late 1789 seven hundred Comanche and Wichita warriors attacked them. The Natchitoches commandant reported that the attack was so successful that these same peoples planned a larger one the following year with more warriors so that they could assault the main Osage village itself. This defeat was a turning point in the wars with the Osages, as it prevented the Osages from expanding their territory further onto the southern plains and concentrated their efforts against the Caddos.[52]

Despite periodic counterattacks by the Caddos, Wichitas, and Comanches, Osage attacks continued and grew more fierce. Trade between the Caddos and Natchitoches residents suffered from merchandise shortages and from the Osage raids. In January 1790 Natchitoches commandant Louis De Blanc wrote that the Osage attacks had just about ruined the Natchitoches economy. Just as bad, he wrote to Miró, was the suffering of the Caddos in both Louisiana and Texas because they constantly needed more guns and ammunition to defend themselves. Unfortunately, the commandant explained, the shortage of goods at Natchitoches meant the Caddos could not satisfy their needs at that post and, feeling abandoned by Spanish authorities, spent considerable time trying to locate weapons in other places. Without the guns, he continued, the Caddos were reduced to a dire necessity and would do just about anything, including raid Spanish outposts, to get the weapons they needed. The Taovayas, Yscanis, Tawakonis, Hainais, Nabedaches, and other Caddos officially in the Nacogdoches jurisdiction came to Natchitoches to ask for traders to be sent to them with merchandise, but the commandant had nothing to give them except a little merchandise to each band. De Blanc suggested what all Natchitoches officers over the years recommended: a Spanish attack on the Osages to force a peace.[53]

The Caddos had long been one of the main suppliers of hides and horses for the merchants at Natchitoches, and as Osage raids cut into Caddo productivity, it meant hard times for the Euro-Americans at Natchitoches. In 1792 De Blanc complained that while an abundance of buffalo, deer, elk, bear, beaver, otter, tallow, and lard could be found along the Red River about sixty leagues above Natchitoches, this "post and the capital are deprived of these provisions by the treacherous Osage who constantly wage the most cruel war upon us in this region as well as upon our Indian allies." Again he urged that the authorities prevent Illinois traders from providing goods to the Osages. If these traders could not be stopped, then the Osages would only continue to attack the farms and cattle ranches of Natchitoches area residents.[54]

Spain could not prevent the traders from Illinois, Arkansas, and points further east from providing goods to the Osages. And despite the supplications of the Indians in the Natchitoches jurisdiction, Osage warfare continued against the Caddos, who bore the brunt of the raids. By 1803 Daniel Clark, while making a trip through the Natchitoches area, commented that the "Cadoquias, called by the abbreviation Caddos, . . . can raise from 3 to 400 warriors, are the friends of the whites and are esteemed the bravest and most generous of all the Nations in this vast country, they are rapidly decreasing, owing to their intemperance and the numbers annually destroyed by the Osages and Choctaws."[55]

As Clark realized, the Osages were only one part of the problem facing the Caddos. Another came from the Choctaws and other Indian peoples streaming into Caddo country from the east. As early as the seventeenth century epidemics, famines, warfare, and English slave-raiding expeditions sent eastern Indian peoples fleeing west. This migration increased after France's cession of Louisiana to Spain. Now Spain looked across the Mississippi River at the aggressive Anglo-Americans and feared her new neighbors might one day reach out for Louisiana, or maybe even Texas or Mexico. In their attempts to check any

Anglo-American invasion, Spanish governors at New Orleans opened Louisiana's borders to these Indian refugees and invited some eastern Indian peoples into Louisiana in order to create a buffer against Anglo-American encroachment. By 1785 Louisiana governor Esteban Miró believed he had the makings of a good Indian defense. Between the Red and Ouachita Rivers lived "the Caddos, or Caudachos, great and small, the Yatasís, Adaes, Natchitoches, Rapidos, Pacanas, Alabamas, Choctaws, Ochanias, Biloxis, and several of less importance in the lands of the Attakapas and Opelousas." The Louisiana governor also could have added to that list parties of Chickasaws, Appalaches, Pascagoulas, Coushattas, Illinois, and Miamis.[56]

Of all these newly arriving peoples the Choctaws proved to be the most troublesome to the Caddos. For decades, bands of Mississippi Choctaws, needing to supply their own trade connections with the English and Anglo-Americans, had crossed the Mississippi River to hunt and raid in Louisiana. By the early 1790s, with more and more Anglos slipping across the Mississippi to trade with Indian peoples in Louisiana, Spain officially invited Choctaw communities to settle among the Caddos. Officials in New Orleans hoped the Caddos would cheerfully agree to this and asked the Cadodachos, Natchitoches, Yatasís, Petit Caddos, Kichais, and Yscanis, along with some of the newly arrived eastern peoples, such as the Appalaches and Pascagoulas, to invite the Choctaws to live and hunt among them. After all, the officials reasoned, Choctaw bands had often hunted in the Red River area. At the same time, they reminded the Caddos that both they and the Choctaws were all brothers under the guidance of their royal Spanish father. Ulterior motives existed, however. Along with building a buffer, Spain hoped that allowing some Choctaws into Louisiana would split these formidable peoples into two groups, one loyal to Spain, the other to England, and give Spain the opportunity to play one against the other.[57]

With the door thrown open, large bands of hundreds of Choctaws moved into the Natchitoches area and spread out along the Red River. The relocation west proved disastrous for the Caddos as the Choctaws became both invaders and trade rivals. While the Spanish managed to contain most Choctaw settlement east of Natchitoches and the Caddo lands, Choctaw parties hunted throughout Caddo territory. Caddo and Choctaw hunting parties regularly clashed in the woods between the

Ouachita and Sabine Rivers. Also wanting to tap into the Natchitoches horse and deer-hide trade, Choctaw bands raided Caddo villages, seized hides, horses, cattle, and crops, and tried to cut the Caddos out of their trade networks with the French creoles and Spanish officials at Natchitoches. The Caddos retaliated and counterraids, revenge killings, and violence flickered throughout the area. Unlike the Osages, who wanted not to expand into Caddo territory but merely to raid Caddo villages for horses, captives, and hides, the Choctaws wanted not only to raid but also to settle on Caddo lands. Other small eastern bands had settled on or near Caddo territory, but they had not been large enough to pose a threat to the Caddos. Now the Choctaws came in force and the Caddos faced a situation similar to that with the Osages: raids and revenge killings from peoples supposedly allied with their Spanish kin.[58]

At the Natchitoches post Caddo warriors and traders often came into contact with the Choctaws, Chickasaws, Miamis, Illinois, and other newcomers. According to Natchitoches commandant Louis De Blanc, when this happened, trouble usually erupted. He reported that these new Indians, especially the Choctaws and Chickasaws, wronged not only many of the Indian peoples around Natchitoches but also many European residents of Natchitoches, "robbing them of their labors, turning their horses loose in their crops, killing cattle secretly in the woods, and stealing horses in all parts in order to take them to their village." Even the Osages to the north and Indian peoples in Texas felt the lash of the Choctaws. In turn the Osages, to replace the merchandise lost to the Choctaws, stepped up their attacks on the Caddos.[59]

By 1792 the Cadodachos and other Caddo communities were already appealing to the Spanish for protection and peace. The Ais and Adaes Caddos, coming under heavy Choctaw attacks, begged the Spanish in Texas for help. Finally, in October 1792, after a devastating Choctaw raid, the Adaes and the Ais decided to counterattack, but the Spanish hoped to bring about a peace before a full-scale war could break out. The Choctaws demanded that they be allowed to hunt on Adaes land. Acting on orders from Louisiana governor Luis Hector de Carondelet, Natchitoches commandant De Blanc tried to convince the Adaes to agree to this because both peoples were subjects of the Spanish king. This proved unsuccessful, as De Blanc reported that the Choctaws had wronged too many Indians of the territory for peace to settle over the area. Commandant Jean Filhiol, at the Ouachita post in eastern Louisiana, confronted similar problems in his district. These attacks by the Choctaws, he reported, disrupted trade by forcing the district's Indians to move their villages to escape the raiders.[60]

Choctaw raids on the Caddo communities in both Louisiana and Texas continued over the next few years, despite Caddo appeals asking the Spanish to control the newcomers. Up to this time, most Choctaw raids had been conducted on the smaller Caddo communities, such as the Ais and Adaes. In fact, Spanish Texas officials became so concerned about the Ais that they considered establishing a mission for their protection, though nothing came of this. Then, in April 1795, Choctaw war parties began striking at the larger Cadodachos. According to the great chief, probably Bisquita, a large party of Choctaws from near the Ouachita post attacked their encampment in order to pillage the camp and steal their horses. In the skirmish the Choctaws killed the nephew of an allied Bidai chief who was visiting the Cadodachos and wounded the great chief with a gunshot to his thumb. Now the Caddo chief demanded justice. He had avoided taking immediate revenge out of respect for the "French" and had wanted to inform them first before he struck. He and his principal men insisted that the Spanish deliver the head of Oualabe, the Choctaw who killed their Bidai guest. If this was not done, the chief said, they would close the roads to their village to the Choctaws and kill the first Choctaws they came across.[61]

Natchitoches commandant De Blanc received the letter from the Kadohadacho great chief while visiting in New Orleans. He wrote back to Jean Filhiol, commandant at the Ouachita post, origin of the Choctaw attack, and informed him of the Kadohadacho chief's complaint. He urged Filhiol to do what the Caddos asked or war between them and the Choctaws would break out. According to De Blanc the younger warriors of the Kadohadachos were becoming impatient with the great chief's delay in taking revenge and wished to attack the Choctaws. The great chief was having difficulty containing these young warriors, De Blanc said, because "among the Indians, the chiefs do not have any authority than the gift of persuasion and nothing more." He warned Filhiol that if the Choctaws continued to raid in the Natchitoches jurisdiction, the Caddos would not wait for the response of the government, which they already considered too slow, but would take vengeance on their own. This would result, De Blanc explained, in an open war, with the Kadohadacho chiefdom and its Texas Caddo allies on one side and the Choctaws on the other. If war broke out, De Blanc warned, it "will trouble incontestably the tranquility of your post and mine and will expose the residents of the two jurisdictions to daily pillage by the war parties which will wander continuously." De Blanc then warned the Louisiana governor that he believed the winter would not pass before some hostilities erupted between the Kadohadachos and the Choctaws.[62]

While full-scale war between the Kadohadacho chiefdom and the Choctaws did not break out, Choctaw, Chickasaw, and Osage raids continued throughout 1796. Things for the Texas Caddos also looked bleak that year as bands of Choctaws and Chickasaws asked the Spanish Texas government for permission to settle in Texas. The Texas Caddo communities of the Ais, Hainai (or Tejas), and Nacogdoches, as well as the Attakapan Bidais, appealed to the Kadohadacho great chief for assistance against the Choctaws. According to Bernardo Fernández, commandant at Nacogdoches, all the tribes of his district and that of Natchitoches respected the Kadohadacho great chief, as his nation had great influence over them. The great chief visited Nacogdoches to explain the predicament of the Caddo communities and to persuade the Texas officials to prevent the Choctaws from entering that jurisdiction. While the great chief was in Nacogdoches trying to shore up Spanish support for the Texas Caddos, a large Choctaw party of about 250 warriors attacked the Cadodacho and Adaes villages near Natchitoches.[63]

The heavy attack on the great chief's own Cadodacho village spurred Spanish officials in Louisiana and Texas to try to bring about peace. In 1797 Texas officials called on Louisiana governor Carondelet to prevent the Choctaws from attacking peaceful Indians in their jurisdiction. Carondelet prevailed upon some of the Choctaw and Chickasaw chiefs to make peace with the Cadodachos. Esteban Minor, commandant at Natchez, escorted one Chickasaw and four Choctaw chiefs to the Cadodacho village for the peace talks. During the next few years, except for a few isolated attacks on individuals, the peace between the Caddos and Choctaws apparently held. Those Choctaw bands that did uphold the peace were allowed by the Spanish to hunt in Texas. This peace did not mean the Caddos were totally safe, as Osages, Chickasaws, and even Cherokees continued periodic raids on the Caddos. The new Louisiana governor, Sebastián Casa Calvo, swore to try to prevent the depredations on the Caddos in both Louisiana and Texas, but he would have no more luck in achieving this than his predecessors. Osage and Choctaw raids would lessen in severity in the early nineteenth century as all Indians in the area found themselves confronted by a common and more dangerous opponent who arrived in the guise of land-hungry American settlers.[64]

Undeniably, close contact with Europeans brought tremendous changes and challenges to the Caddos. European diseases decimated Caddo populations. Mercantile capitalism was a mixed blessing, increasing the status of some individuals and offering some relief from drudgery but introducing a shift from traditional subsistence activities to an overreliance on European manufactured goods. Competition in the hide and horse trade made the Caddos targets for raids by the Apaches, Osages, and Choctaws, and the Caddos spent much of the second half of the eighteenth century defending their villages from these enemies and counterattacking in bloody raids that expended valuable firearms and ammunition. As a result of the Caddo population loss from disease and the shattering effects of raids on their communities, Caddo communities coalesced and chiefly power increased.

5 // Restructuring the Chiefdoms

The Cados form a powerful nation, respected by all the savages. . . .
They remember with pride their antiquity and power, and pretend
to have rights superior to all other tribes, considering themselves
owners of the land.
DON MANUEL DE MIER Y TERÁN, 1828,
"Documentos Para la Historia," 264–69

W HILE firearms and metal-edged tools had the potential to
help the Caddos increase their food and deer-hide production, in reality, by the last third of the eighteenth century
Caddo agricultural production had begun to decline. The hide trade
caused the Caddos to overhunt the deer around their villages, forcing
them to go farther afield to find more. Disease brought depopulation;
exacerbating this after 1770 were raids by Osages and Choctaws that
made it more difficult for Caddos to hunt peacefully, keep crops in
their fields, and feel safe. As did the great fourteenth-century drought
and Soto's march through Caddo territory in the sixteenth century,
these pressures brought a restructuring of the Caddo communities and
chiefdoms. Their residents searched for goods, refuge, and protection,
and Caddo communities splintered, some disappearing forever, others
consolidating with larger, stronger communities. Family-oriented bands
broke away from the main towns and roamed the area. Some of these
hunted deer in the woods or prairies, others went to Natchitoches, Los
Adaes, or Nacogdoches to receive gifts or trade for goods. Others merely
tried to find a secure place, usually with a larger community headed by
a powerful caddí who could provide them with goods or protect them
from Osage or Choctaw raiders. As these changes shook the Caddos'
world, Caddo peoples in both Louisiana and Texas again looked to the
chief of the Kadohadacho chiefdom to assist them, protect them, and
intercede for them with the Europeans. Now the great chief of the Kadohadacho extended his power, played the European powers and colo-

nies against each other, and eventually became the spokesman for the Caddo people.

As raids smashed Caddo communities, between the 1770s and the 1830s a frenetic migration gripped the area between the Ouachita and Trinity Rivers as small bands of Caddos and other peoples wandered the area searching for security and supplies of needed manufactured goods. Several individual Caddo communities wholly disappeared as their people, reduced by disease or raids, left and then joined with larger, more powerful Caddo communities. But even these new multi-community towns often moved to different locations to escape the raids. Just as they had always done, once the main town had relocated, families formed hamlets and moved out away from the town to burn the forest and create their agricultural fields. As the Caddo people of these hamlets, towns, and communities mingled, they exchanged traditions and made new kin relationships. Over time, possibly under additional raids or other pressures, hamlets and towns might splinter again, with the fragmented bands moving and later remerging with other communities, only to splinter, move, and remerge again.[1]

This constant fissioning and fusing of Caddo communities and villages brought about the dissolution of some of the old Caddo communities. At European contact, the Hasinai chiefdom consisted of ten separate communities, or subchiefdoms: Hainai, Nadaco, Nasoni, Nabedache, Nacogdoche, Neches, Nacono, Nabiti, Nechauis, and Nacao. By 1791 the Spanish listed only the Hainai (Tejas), Nadaco, Nabedache, and Nacogdoche as eastern Texas Caddos. The six other communities had disappeared as separate political entities and coalesced with these remaining four Hasinai peoples. By the mid-1800s the Texas Caddos had coalesced even further into just two political entities: the Hainai, now called the Tejas, and the Nadaco, called the Anadarko. Similar coalescing took place with the old Kadohadacho chiefdom. At European contact the Kadohadacho chiefdom on the upper Red River included the Cadodacho, Nanatsoho, Upper Natchitoches, and the Upper Nasoni communities. By 1805 the people of these last three communities had been incorporated into the Cadodachos, with the names Nanatsoho and Nasoni disappearing from the records.[2]

Still closely associated with these Cadodachos were the Petit Caddos, Yatasís, and Natchitoches, along with the Wichita Kichais, who, also under pressure from the Osages, had moved further east to be under the protection of the caddí of the Cadodacho community, who was still chief of the Kadohadachos. As the chief of the Kadohadachos increased his prestige and power, the Petit Caddos, Yatasís, and Natchitoches found themselves gravitating back into the Kadohadacho orbit. Even the independent but rapidly dwindling Adaes and Ais began looking to the Kadohadacho chief for some measure of protection, while the Doustionis had long been incorporated into the Natchitoches Caddos.[3]

Warfare and disease not only caused Caddo communities to coalesce, they also forced the Caddos to physically move their villages. The great chief moved his Cadodacho village several times to escape Osage raids, eventually settling on the western edge of Caddo Lake by the late 1700s. By 1808 Samuel Davenport, Spanish Texas's official merchant to the Indians, reported that the Cadodachos lived in a fixed town east of the Sabine River and had about two hundred men with their families. The Yatasís, who once lived between the Natchitoches settlement and the old Cadodacho village, had since moved to the eastern bank of the Sabine River near present-day Logansport, Louisiana. The Natchitoches Indians moved to the west side of the Red River and settled just north of the Natchitoches post across from present-day Campti, while the remaining Adaes wound up on Bayou Pierre, northwest of the Natchitoches post.[4]

Similar movements took place in east Texas. Davenport's 1808 census reported that the Nabedaches lived on the Neches River with a population of about one hundred men and their families. The Hainais lived on the Angelina River with about sixty men and their families. The dwindling Nacogdoches lived on the Angelina north of the Nacogdoches post with about fifty men, while the Nadacos lived nearby with about one hundred men and their families. Those Kichais who remained in Texas still lived among the Wichitas, while the Kichai group attached to the Kadohadacho chiefdom had since moved further southeast to a spot on the Trinity River near the Texas Caddo communities.[5]

The stress placed on Caddo communities by disease, warfare, and intermarriage with other peoples, both Indian and Euro-American, dissolved old groups and communities and created new ones. These stresses helped the Kadohadacho chiefdom extend its power. This increased leadership role of the Kadohadacho chiefdom among the remaining Caddo communities in Louisiana and Texas, as well as community coalescing, intermarriage, and their close relationship with Euro-Americans, forced rapid social, political, and economic change among the Caddos. New peoples, new tools, new ideas all helped forge a new "Caddo" chiefdom as well as a "Caddo" identity and tribal culture that had not been in existence before.

The adoption and creation of Caddo dances reflected this change. One of the most important of the Caddo dances was the turkey dance, whose songs and movements told the history of the Caddos. The turkey dance helped link together all the Caddo peoples and communities. By the end of the eighteenth century new songs that celebrated Caddo victories over the Apaches, Osages, and Choctaws were added to the turkey dance. Dancers sang these songs in a progression, the first being sung in Cadodacho; the second, in the now extinct Ais dialect; the third, in Neche; the fourth, in Hainai; the fifth, in Yona; the sixth and seventh, in Kichai. In response to the changing conditions brought by newcomers flooding into the area, the Caddos added new dances, like the Cherokee dance and Quapaw dance.[6]

Although Caddo peoples rapidly moved toward a single Caddo nation, they continued to recognize the division of the old communities and chiefdoms. In the late twentieth century, though officially called the Caddos, among themselves they still consider themselves to be associated with the Kadohadachos, Hasinais, and Natchitoches chiefdoms. Even minor dialectical differences, such as between the Kadohadachos of Louisiana and the Hasinais of Texas, can still be found among the Caddos of Oklahoma over 150 years after they left Louisiana and Texas.

Disease and warfare also brought fundamental changes in the internal makeup of the Caddo chiefdoms and their chiefs. During the last years of the seventeenth and the early years of the eighteenth centuries, Europeans described the xinesí as a priest-chief, keeper of the eternal fire, and the intermediary between the chiefdom's people and their gods. Both the Hasinai and Kadohadacho chiefdoms had their own xinesís, but after the first few decades of the eighteenth century, all mention of the xinesí disappeared from French and Spanish records. Similarly, the titles of caddí and tamma also disappeared from the records, the Spanish and French now calling all Caddo leaders "chief." The term *tamma* appeared to be last used by Europeans in 1745.[7]

While these titles may have disappeared from European records, that did not necessarily mean the Caddos quit using them. In the late twentieth century the term *caddí,* or *cah-de,* is a title used by the Caddo people for their chief, while *tamma,* or *tuh-ma,* is used for the Caddo person who directs dances. One position that did seem to disappear was the xinesí. What happened to the xinesí is unknown. The most likely explanation relates to the population losses due to epidemics and raids. The Caddos believed that Spanish priests and their god had brought on their destruction by disease. This belief in an angry, destructive Christian god did not bring many Caddo converts, and Christianity never enjoyed much success among the Caddos until the second half of the nineteenth century. While the Caddos did not flock to Christianity, disease and disruptions may have made them lose faith in the religious power of the xinesís since Caddo gods apparently could not protect them from the wrath of the Christian god. The increased mobility of the Caddo people produced by their participation in the hide trade and their attempt to move away from raiding areas only exacerbated this. As Caddo peoples left the main villages to hunt deer or escape raiders and disease, and as more outsiders with different spiritual beliefs were incorporated into Caddo society, it became more difficult to keep the sacred fire burning. This affected the power of the xinesí, who lost both spiritual and political control of the chiefdoms. Spiritual power went to the tammas, the "town criers" who presided over and insured participation in the community's dances.[8]

Although the xinesí disappeared, there is no evidence that the Caddo people gave up their religion. Unfortunately, with the abandonment of most Spanish missions in eastern Texas during the early decades of the eighteenth century, and no establishment of missions by the French among the Caddos in Louisiana, not much information on eighteenth- and early-nineteenth-century Caddo religion was recorded. In 1726 Bienville wrote that the Caddos "possess a temple with idols that look like frogs and other insects," but other than this, French or Spanish officials and traders rarely discussed or even mentioned Caddo religion. However, a hint that Caddo religion may have continued into the late eighteenth century was provided by Spanish Natchitoches commandant Athanase De Mézières during his trips to the Wichita peoples in the 1770s. De Mézières reported that the Kichais "dedicate their chief cult and veneration to an evil spirit whom they fear and try to propitiate." In the same report he said that the Wichitas and Taovayas "recognize a creator who dwells in the highest heaven, whence, by his will and power, he directs everything, having absolute control of life, and exercising a despotic rule over mankind." Caddo and Wichita religion had perhaps changed, but they had some similarities and these two descriptions could have easily been applied to traditional Caddo religion. Furthermore, the Caddo and Wichita peoples both spoke Caddoan, and the Kichais were particularly close allies and trade partners of the Caddos, so if De Mézières found the Kichais still practicing their religion in the 1770s, it is quite likely that the Caddos were still worshiping in a similar vein.[9]

Like most Indian peoples of the Southeast, the Caddos conducted first-fruit and similar food-related ceremonies. The early Spanish missionaries among the Caddos in the late seventeenth and early eighteenth centuries had witnessed these. De Mézières, though writing of the Wichitas, also reported seeing many of these same practices in the 1770s. He wrote that the Wichitas and Taovayas had great devotion to the Creator and "offer him the first fruits of their harvests and chase; invoke his aid for success in their undertakings; prescribe rigorous fasts to secure his favor; and practice an infinite number of rites." This description could also have been applied to the Caddos. Jean Berlandier, who traveled through much of eastern Texas in 1830, reported seeing a first-fruits and black-drink ceremony among the Caddos. The black drink, a ceremonial drink common throughout the Southeast, was normally made from yaupon holly. Berlandier reported that the Caddos made it by grinding frijolillo seeds [*Calia erythrosperma Berl.*] into a paste and then mixing it with water. Once it had steeped long enough the Caddos drank it through a tube or straw, "which straightaway purges them and makes them vomit." In actuality, the drink did not make the person vomit; the vomiting was voluntary and was a purification ceremony that purged the men of pollution. It was often used with visitors as an expression of hospitality.[10]

While vestiges of Caddo religion remained, the apparent disappearance of the xinesí also did not mean an end to chiefly political power.

From the earliest times of the Mississippian cultural tradition, Caddo communities had been chiefdoms under the leadership of a caddí. At various times over the centuries, individual caddís might expand their power and prestige until they had subjugated several communities and formed them into a single major chiefdom, with themselves as xinesís and the communities, now subchiefdoms, under their political and spiritual authority. The Soto-Moscoso expedition had found this among the Caddos in 1543, with the Naguatex chief ruling over the chiefs of the Amaye and Macanac communities. By the late 1600s the Spanish and French found the two largest multicommunity Caddo chiefdoms were the Kadohadacho and Hasinai, each ruled by the xinesí priest-chief. While the xinesí, caddí, and chief possessed tremendous moral authority, they never enjoyed full autocratic power and usually called a council of elders to discuss decisions. As political anthropologist Morton Fried pointed out, "in ranked society, leaders can lead, but followers may not follow." Persuasion, rather than sanction, played the greatest role in enforcing commands.[11]

Disease, warfare, the hide trade, and village relocation during the middle years of the eighteenth century broke down the power of the xinesí and the political cohesion of the ancient Hasinai chiefdom, while allowing the caddís of the remaining communities to increase their own power. Until the early eighteenth century most Caddos followed their leaders because of the leaders' ability to harness and control supernatural powers. During the mid– and late eighteenth century, with the religious authority of the xinesí gone, the caddís of individual communities, recognized as "chiefs" by the Europeans, managed to increase their prestige and power over their much diminished people by the redistribution of the merchandise that they received as gifts from the Europeans. De Mézières, although writing of the Wichita chiefs, could just as easily have been describing the Caddo chiefs when he reported that they "pride themselves on owning nothing." The position was normally inherited, but the caddí still governed by retaining the acclamation and respect of his community's people. He maintained these by providing gifts of needed commodities, protection, and assistance. At the same time, as the numbers of governing elites dwindled, sometimes generous commoners who had managed to forge bonds of obligation through gift giving with their fellow Caddo villagers rose to fill these once hereditary positions, some acting as canahas and tammas, and were relied on as advisors by the chief. Also, mixed-blood and even fictive kin came to occupy some of these important positions.[12]

When the Spanish took over Natchitoches from the French, in the late 1760s, they found themselves dealing with several individual chiefs wielding power over separate Caddo communities. In the early 1780s Natchitoches commandant Etienne Vaugine reported that Tinhiouen the Younger was the chief of the Cadodachos, or Grand Caddos; Da Kiou was chief of the Petit Caddos; Hyamoc (sometimes spelled Yamoh) was chief of the Natchitoches; Cocay (sometimes Cocaille) was chief of the Yatasís; Ouensi was chief of the Adaes; Kyaavadouche was chief of the Nadacos; Nicotaouenanan was chief of the Wichita Kichais; and Capot was chief of a group of Bidai, normally associated with the Attakapas of southwestern Louisiana and southeastern Texas but who had established a village on Cane River about twenty-five miles from Natchitoches.[13]

The Europeans and Americans contributed to this strengthening of the community Caddo chiefs. The French and Spanish all tried to take advantage of the chief's power and prestige. They presented medals cast with a likeness of the king to the individual Caddo chiefs and designated them "medal chiefs." A large gold medal was given to the community's caddí, whom the Euro-American leaders called the big-medal chief. Smaller silver medals were given to important principal men designated by the caddí; they were called the small-medal chiefs. One of the small-medal chiefs was usually in line to become the big-medal chief. Through these medal chiefs the French and Spanish conducted diplomatic business with the community while providing gifts of merchandise to them. The European powers hoped to benefit from the reciprocal relations they made with the medal chiefs just as the medal chiefs hoped to benefit themselves and their people.[14]

While distributing medals and designating some men as medal chiefs provided an opening for the French and Spanish to dabble in Caddo politics, it would be wrong to believe that the European governments acted as kingmakers among the Caddos. Nor did the Caddos consider themselves vassals of the French or Spanish. The Caddos, though always ready to negotiate and uphold the obligations of reciprocity with their European kinsmen, never acknowledged European domination. While Natchitoches commandant De Mézières might write that the great chief Tinhiouen was a vassal of Spain, the Caddo chiefs continually insisted they were brothers and allies—equals. And the Caddos possessed enough power to make the Europeans accept their assertion of independence. Because of Caddo strength, their self-sufficiency through agriculture and hunting, and their relations with other powerful peoples such as the Wichitas and Comanches, the Europeans found themselves forced to use persuasion, gift giving, and trade rather than force to vie for and hold Caddo loyalty.[15]

While the Europeans tried to meddle in the internal affairs of Caddo community government, they usually found themselves merely accepting the Caddo community's choice of leader and providing the medal to whomever the Caddos demanded. These medals, though, increased the prestige and power of the chief by acknowledging his connection to the gift-giving Europeans and his ability to deal with them. So once a Caddo became chief he usually sought the medal to help validate his authority and position as official spokesperson for his community. A direct line could be followed from the caddís of the old Mississippian Caddo chiefdoms to these new medal chiefs. Both performed the same type of services as leaders and spokespersons for their community.[16]

Even as the authority returned to individual community medal chiefs, the Caddo propensity and need for a single, powerful leader exerted itself. Population loss made it harder for weaker communities and small family hamlets to participate in the hide and horse trade and to protect themselves from raids. This made it more difficult for them to acquire manufactured goods. Therefore these smaller bands that wandered the area depended on a single, powerful chief to protect them, provide goods, and be their spokesperson with the European powers. As the Hasinai chiefdom dissolved, the caddí of the Cadodacho community extended his power and assumed the leadership and spokesperson position among all the Caddo communities and their chiefs. In 1805 U.S. Indian agent John Sibley reported that the Cadodachos "are looked upon somewhat like the knights of Malta, or some distinguished military order." He also noted that the Cadodacho chief exerted a powerful influence over the Yatasís, Nadacos, Nabedaches, Hainai (Tejas), Nacogdoches, Adaes, Natchitoches, and Wichita Kichais, and that all these peoples "speak the Caddo language, look up to [the

Cadodachos] as their fathers, visit and intermarry among them, and join them in all their wars." In fact, Sibley explained, the Cadodachos asserted, and other Caddos believed, that the Cadodachos were the founding lineage of all Caddo peoples.[17]

The chief of the Kadohadachos came to be considered the main Caddo chief and official spokesman for the Caddos. While all Caddo communities had a chief, the caddí of the Cadodacho community was also the chief of the Kadohadacho chiefdom and was the person whom the Spanish and Americans called "grand chief," "great chief," or "great chief of the Caddos." The chief of the Kadohadacho chiefdom reasserted his ancient position and again brought under his authority the independent communities of the Natchitoches, Yatasís, and Petit Caddos. All these peoples looked to the great chief of the Kadohadacho as their leader. Even the communities of the old Hasinai chiefdom in Texas, while remaining politically distinct, came to recognize the great chief of the Kadohadacho as their leader and spokesperson. The power of these great chiefs over the other Caddo communities was not achieved by force but was accorded them by their prestige.

From the 1770s to the early 1830s the Cadodacho community of the Kadohadacho chiefdom produced several great chiefs, but three stand out: Tinhiouen the Elder, who died in 1777; his son who took his name, Tinhiouen the Younger, who was chief until his death in 1789; and Dehahuit, who appeared on the scene about 1800 and died in 1833. These three great chiefs made it a point to find ways to increase their power, often to the frustration of the Spanish and Americans.

A good example of both the making of a medal chief and the expansion of power of these great chiefs can be seen with Tinhiouen the Younger. After the death of his father in 1777, the younger Tinhiouen decided to visit New Orleans to meet with Spanish governor Bernardo de Galvez. This was an important occasion where the Kadohadacho chief and the Spanish governor would meet as brothers and recognize each other's authority. With him, the young great chief took his son, as well as a mixed-blood interpreter named Jeanot, and such important Kadohadacho principal men as Chase, La Barbue, and La Peau d'Ours.[18]

Commandant De Mézières knew that the younger Tinhiouen had inherited the position of caddí and that the Kadohadacho communities had already accepted this younger man as their leader. With one of

Spain's first priorities during the 1770s being the establishment of peace between the Comanches and the Spanish Texas settlements, De Mézières appreciated Tinhiouen's influence among the western Indians and his importance in this endeavor. With this in mind De Mézières took the liberty of instructing the governor on his new brother and how to deal with him. The Natchitoches commandant described Tinhiouen the younger as "lively and vivacious," declaring that he had "never known a man of his color more witty or keener." He reminded Galvez that Tinhiouen merited honor from the governor, of "which his father was likewise worthy," and he urged the governor to receive the great chief with all distinction and ceremony because of his importance in keeping the peace among the peoples along the Red River. He stressed just how essential it was for the governor to honor Tinhiouen and not allow such a powerful man to fall under the influence of the English on the east side of the Mississippi River. Since Tinhiouen the Younger served as the new chief, De Mézières instructed the governor to personally bestow on him the large medal as a symbol of his office and alliance with Spain. He also urged Galvez to give the smaller silver medal to Tinhiouen's son.[19]

Galvez received Tinhiouen and his advisors with all the pomp and ceremony of his office. He entertained the Kadohadacho men for several days, and when they left Galvez presented Tinhiouen with the large medal and a "present of considerable importance." He also informed De Mézières that he had planned to give the small medal to Tinhiouen's son, but the great chief believed that his son did not yet deserve it because he was young and "the people of his nation have as yet no respect for him." Tinhiouen asked Galvez to give the small medal to one of his advisors instead. Galvez did as Tinhiouen asked.[20]

The Caddo chiefs, from the earliest years of the eighteenth century, realized they possessed a certain amount of political leverage with the Europeans, and once the Spanish took actual possession of Louisiana, in 1768, they found their leverage increasing, especially in the case of powerful chiefs like the Tinhiouens. With the French out of the way and Spain controlling both Texas and Louisiana, Spanish officials hoped to bring peace to its settlements in Texas by making a treaty with the Wichitas and Comanches. These peoples, whom they designated *norteños,* or "nations of the North," had long been raiding Spanish outposts in Texas for horses and slaves for their own use and to exchange with the Caddos and French for European merchandise. To achieve this peace Spanish Natchitoches commandant De Mézières had needed to prevent unlicensed traders from supplying weapons to the *norteños*, and to prevail upon Tinhiouen the Elder, when he was alive, to use his influence to arrest these *contrabandistas* and to bring the Wichitas and Comanches to the peace table.[21]

Though De Mézières might try to rein in unauthorized Europeans living out among the Indian peoples, the Caddos had other ideas. Trade licenses and authorizations meant little to them, and many of these *contrabandistas* living in their villages were kinspeople. Where the Spanish saw French creole contraband traders, the Caddos saw wealthy kinspeople who upheld their reciprocal obligations by supplying the community with needed manufactured goods. The Caddos did not take lightly Spanish attempts to oust their kinspeople and limit the supply of goods coming into their villages. Yatasí chief Guakan's threat to attack Los Adaes in 1768 when the Spanish arrested his French trader attested to this.[22]

Though De Mézières was trying not to prevent trade but merely to regulate it in order to prevent wars between Indian peoples and violence against Spanish citizens, he found how difficult it was to break the bonds kinship had so well established between the Caddos and the old French residents. He also learned how much leverage the great chief of the Kadohadachos wielded. When De Mézières issued an order for all Europeans living among the Indians to turn themselves in at Natchitoches, one of those who showed up was François Morvant, a gunsmith who for years had been living among various Indian peoples and beyond the pale of European law. Some of that time he had run with an outlaw gang on the lower Arkansas River. In the heat of an argument, Morvant had killed the outlaw leader, a Frenchman named Brindamur. To escape outlaw vengeance, Morvant had run off to the Cadodacho village, where he had lived for nine years before turning himself in at Natchitoches, in 1770.[23]

At Natchitoches, De Mézières jailed Morvant on a charge of murder. Hearing of Morvant's incarceration, the great chief Tinhiouen the Elder, along with five of his principal men, personally visited De Mézières and demanded that he release Morvant and allow the Frenchman to live at his village. De Mézières refused and explained Spanish law, but Tinhiouen insisted. According to De Mézières, Tinhiouen reminded them of the services he and his people had provided to Spain and "insisted and persisted several times, giving us very visible knowledge of the sorrow he would feel on a refusal on our part" to release Morvant to him. De Mézières, understanding the bonds of kinship, finally relented so as to not displease such a good friend and ally of the Spanish. In return Tinhiouen promised that he would send back to Natchitoches any other unauthorized traders who appeared in his village.[24]

Not only did Tinhiouen get to keep his kinsman, a valued gunsmith, but he also managed to increase his own prestige and status with the Caddos, the *norteños,* and the Spanish. Tinhiouen, along with one of his subchiefs, Cocay, chief of the Yatasís, had met with De Mézières in April 1770 and concluded a peace between their nations and the new Spanish government of Louisiana, with each receiving the large medal from the Natchitoches commandant. Now De Mézières turned to these two chiefs for help in making peace with the Comanches and Wichitas, as he needed the high status Tinhiouen possessed with these western peoples to make it possible. Tinhiouen and his Kadohadachos held especially high status not only among all the Caddo peoples but also with the Wichitas and Comanches. This stemmed from their reputations as ancient peoples and glorious chiefs stretching back to the earliest years of the Mississippian cultural tradition and from their having been longtime providers of trade goods and merchandise.[25]

For Tinhiouen the appeal by De Mézières for his help in making peace provided an incredible opportunity. The Europeans would recognize his value as a peacemaker and his importance to their interests. This would keep European merchandise flowing to him. He could then redistribute these goods and gain increased power among his Caddo peoples. The Wichitas and Comanches would also accord him more power and prestige because they would see how the Spanish had to turn to him for help. Furthermore, the Wichitas and Comanches would see Tinhiouen as instrumental in increasing the flow of needed firearms and manufactured goods to their villages.[26]

At the urging of De Mézières, Tinhiouen sent word to the Taovayas, Tawakonis, Yscanis, Kichais, Tonkawas, and Naytane Comanches to meet De Mézières at his Cadodacho village in September 1770. Once representatives from these peoples arrived, Tinhiouen sent a party of warriors to Natchitoches in order to escort De Mézières to his village. During the peace conference Tinhiouen and Cocay, both wearing their medals with the likeness of Spain's King Charles III, and with the assistance of their old friend, Alexis Grappe, translated De Mézières's peace speech for the assembled *norteños* and made their own stands for peace.

Tinhiouen's and Cocay's diplomacy eventually paid off. In 1771, with Tinhiouen looking on, the Taovayas, the Naytane Comanches, and De Mézières signed a treaty that brought a measure of peace for Spanish Texas. Tinhiouen the Elder had more than fulfilled his reciprocal obligations to his Spanish brothers. He and the successive medal chiefs of the Kadohadachos became essential to Spain, and the Spanish knew it.[27]

Until his death in 1779, Athanase De Mézières depended on Tinhiouen and the Caddos to help defuse any Wichita and Naytane Comanche ideas of war against Texas and to protect the Natchitoches area from the southern-ranging Osages and the Choctaws coming from the east. When Tinhiouen died in the great epidemic of 1777, his son of the same name became the great chief and just as essential to the Spanish in Natchitoches. While other Indian chiefs—such as Cocay, of the Yatasís; Bigotes, of the Nabedaches; Brazo Quebrado and Nicotaouenanan, of the Kichais; Cyxnion, of the Tawakonis; and Gorgoritos, of the Bidais—exerted some authority, the great chief of the Kadohadachos eclipsed them and other chiefs in power and prestige. As they had years before, the Kadohadacho chiefs were again considered the most respected Indian leaders in the upper Red River valley, serving as spokespersons for most of the Caddo communities and as peacemaking diplomats between the Spanish and the *norteños*. In 1778 De Mézières wrote the Spanish governor at New Orleans that the younger Tinhiouen was "the best, most zealous, the most affectionate of vassals of Your Majesty, among all those of His [subjects], thus the most worthy of consideration of Your Nation." Hammering the point home to the governor, De Mézières explained that Tinhiouen the Younger "occupies one of the most important keys to the western country."[28]

Still, prestige and political power carried only so far, and during the 1770s and 1780s Tinhiouen and his Caddos found themselves facing the disadvantages of participating in European diplomacy and mercantile capitalism. With the French government of Louisiana gone, the Caddos could not play two empires against each other. Where once their intermediary position astride an international boundary provided multiple opportunities, they now found that living on the border between Spanish Texas and Spanish Louisiana could cause frustrations. The American Revolution, the wars of the French Revolution, and then the Napoleonic Wars brought shortages of goods and low hide prices, which worsened their position.

According to the Spanish the entire Kadohadacho chiefdom, now composed of the Cadodachos, Petit Caddos, Natchitoches, and Yatasís, fell under Louisiana's jurisdiction and should only receive their annual gifts from Natchitoches and only allow traders licensed in Natchitoches into their villages. The Hainai, Nabedaches (or San Pedro Indians), Nadacos, Adaes, Ais, and Nacogdoches, as well as the Wichita communities of the Kichais, Taovayas, Tawakonis, Wacos, and the various Tonkawan bands, all came under the jurisdiction of Spanish Texas and were to receive their gifts and traders out of Nacogdoches.[29]

The Caddos and other Indian peoples, as always, adamantly refused to recognize these European-made boundaries. Instead, they kept their old trade networks, which often led them to their French creole kinspeople in Louisiana and to wherever they could get the best prices for their hides and horses. For example, in September 1780, a host of Indian peoples from both Louisiana and Texas visited Natchitoches to sing the calumet ceremony when Etienne Vaugine arrived to replace De Mézières. Representatives came from the Nadacos of Texas, led by Kyaavadouch; the Yatasís, led by Cocay; the Natchitoches Indians, led by Hyamoc; the Adaes, led by Ouensi; the Bidais, who had moved into the Natchitoches jurisdiction, led by Capot; the Petit Caddos, whose medal chief had recently died; and the Kichais from Texas, led by Nicotaouenanan, their new medal chief. Tinhiouen, caddí of the Cadodachos and overall chief Kadohadacho, brought the largest contingent with him, of 246 people; the second largest group was the Nadacos, with 227. Technically, however, the Nadacos, Adaes, Bidais, and Kichais, being Indians of Texas and in the Nacogdoches jurisdiction, should not have visited Natchitoches.[30]

The arrival of these Indian peoples at Natchitoches portended the difficulties the Caddos would face during succeeding decades in acquiring manufactured goods. By 1780 the trade disruptions caused by the American Revolution produced shortages of merchandise in Natchitoches. Disinterested in such international affairs, the Caddos expected large quantities of gifts in return for their ceremony welcoming their new Spanish brother. Commandant Vaugine, trying to uphold his reciprocal obligations, and fearing to turn away such powerful and necessary allies, was forced to dig into his own supplies to provide the presents. Much to the Caddos' dismay, all the commandant could provide was a few pots of tafia and some bundles of tobacco. Angered at what he perceived as a kinsperson's stinginess, Tinhiouen warned Vaugine that the Cadodachos, Petit Caddos, Yatasís, and Natchitoches would return in May 1781 to receive their annual distribution of manufactured goods that Spain had promised them.[31]

Unfortunately, the Natchitoches commandant did not have these goods and would not be able to give them their presents when they returned. Vaugine urged Spain's interim governor of Louisiana, Pedro Piernas, to send the gifts by boat, especially some flags, canes, trade shirts, and ribbons for medals, so they could be distributed to the chiefs. Piernas scrambled for gifts and promised to send "something extraordinary." Piernas advised Vaugine to "try and entertain them as well as possible" but also warned him that "we must economize." The same situation prevailed at Nacogdoches, which also could not provide an annual distribution of gifts and merchandise. This strained relations between Spanish Texas and the Indians of that province.[32]

Whatever gifts Tinhiouen and the Caddos received in May 1781 must have been seriously inadequate because in August Tinhiouen and twenty warriors returned to Natchitoches to receive their annual gifts for 1782. They especially wanted guns and powder so they could make their winter hunt. Once again the Natchitoches commandant could not provide the quantity of gifts the Caddos expected. Vaugine told Tinhiouen that if his people wanted more goods, rather than receiving them as gifts, they could trade for them, but at an inflated price. Tinhiouen exploded in anger and told Vaugine "that his nation was already very fat and that they preferred to make a hunt with arrows rather than indebt themselves further." In a huff the great chief and his people left without their merchandise. Tinhiouen's anger and his willingness to leave Natchitoches without the gifts worried Vaugine, who wrote to the Louisiana governor requesting that at least a part of the merchandise Tinhiouen needed be sent so he could make a modest advance to the chief. As a sop to the great chief, while they waited for the annual gifts to arrive, the commandant suggested that Tinhiouen and his Caddos relieve their immediate merchandise needs by seizing the goods from any trader coming to his villages without a passport issued by him.[33]

These shortages caused problems for the Caddos as they depended on these goods for their hunts and to defend themselves against other Indians. With few gifts being provided at Natchitoches, the Caddos and their allies tried to circumvent the commandant. In 1780 the Wichita Kichais split into two bands, one remaining in Texas near the Nabedaches, the other moving closer to Tinhiouen's Kadohadacho communities in Louisiana for protection against Osage raids and to be nearer what they hoped was a surer source of guns and merchandise. In July 1782 the Kadohadacho-allied band of Kichais, led by Nicotaouenanan and at the urging of the Natchitoches Caddos, considered going to New Orleans to visit the governor and to present the Kichais' case against the shortages and high merchandise prices. Vaugine tried to persuade them not to go, finally prevailing by refusing to pay their expenses.[34] In August 1782 Hyamoc, chief of the Natchitoches, after not receiving presents for several years and then having to accept high trade prices, visited New Orleans, where he pled his case to the governor. While he received no satisfaction or presents there, he did exact a promise that his people would again receive annual gifts. It appeared that only the great chief of the Caddos could visit New Orleans and achieve some measure of success with the Spanish governor there.[35]

Tinhiouen, angered by Vaugine's suggestion that they not expect gifts but trade for them at high prices, decided to beat Vaugine at his own game. Instead of seizing the goods of unlicensed traders, as Vaugine suggested, Tinhiouen invited more unlicensed traders to his chiefdom's villages, even traders from outposts that had not normally supplied goods for the Caddos. By the early 1780s *contrabandistas*— not only from Natchitoches but also from such outposts as Pointe Coupée, Attakapas, Opelousas, and Ouachita in Louisiana, the Arkansas post in present-day southeastern Arkansas, and even Americans from east of the Mississippi River—began filtering out to the Caddo villages. From Natchitoches alone, despite laws regulating the Indian trade, scores of French creole traders, who had long kept close contacts with the Caddos, visited their villages. The hide, horse, and gun trade evolved into an intense competition in which the *contrabandistas* often undercut the prices of Spain's officially licensed traders. Increasing competition, the need for both licensed and unlicensed traders to acquire hides in order to pay off their merchandise debts, and the decreasing supply of Caddo deer hides and horses due to Osage raids forced the traders to give in to Tinhiouen's demand for lower prices. The Caddos' desperate need of firearms for hunting and protecting themselves from Osage raids meant they increasingly manipulated their kinship relations with the traders and officials. At the Caddos' insistence traders now had to give ten balls and ten charges of powder per hide rather than Spain's official price of six balls and six charges.[36]

Since the Natchitoches commandant could not stop the *contrabandistas* from undercutting the official traders, he hoped to force Tinhiouen to abide by the old six-and-six price list. Vaugine realized that if the great chief were to adhere to the old prices, then all the other Caddos would, too: "I tell you that an only means of making [Tinhiouen] understand reason is to absolutely prevent all trade until he conforms to the established price-list and he promises to not trouble the traders anymore.... When he sees the shortage [of goods], then he will be less insolent and more submissive. Before coming to extremities, he must be tempted to sweetness and accommodation."[37]

Tinhiouen had more options open to him than did Vaugine. Prior to the French cession of Louisiana, the Cadodachos, along with the Natchitoches, Petit Caddos, and Yatasís, had been aligned to the Natchitoches outpost and received their gifts and traders from there. As Tinhiouen expanded his influence among the old Hasinai communities and increasingly came to be seen as the great chief of all the Caddos, he felt perfectly justified in visiting Spanish Texas. Reacting to Vaugine's pressure for him to accept the lower prices, in July 1783 Tinhiouen called on Spanish commandant Antonio Gil Ybarbo at Nacogdoches and spent six days there in council discussing trade. During their council Tinhiouen must have made the Spaniard see the light. In his diary, Gil Ybarbo conceded that the hide and merchandise shortages, as well as Tinhiouen's insistence on more ammunition per hide, meant that the traders must give ten balls and ten shots of powder for a deerskin. The traders would bear the brunt of this.[38]

Tinhiouen also had words for Vaugine and his plan to create a shortage of goods among the Caddos to force their acceptance of fewer goods per hide. The great chief essentially gave Vaugine a lesson in Caddo economics, explaining that the annual presents the Cadodachos, Petit Caddos, Natchitoches, and Yatasís received from the Natchitoches commandant actually encouraged the commerce the officials in Texas and Louisiana wanted to establish with the Indians. The merchandise the Caddos received helped them hunt for more hides and protect their hides from raiders, which in turn allowed them to exchange more of these commodities with the licensed traders. Cutting back on merchandise for the Caddos would only hurt the Spanish themselves. If that explanation did not sink in, Tinhiouen also issued a veiled threat to Vaugine, saying that depriving them of goods would only make them unhappy with their Spanish "Father."[39]

During the last two decades of the eighteenth century Spanish officials at Natchitoches often complained about a shortage of merchandise available for gifts and trade to the Caddo and other Indians. Tinhiouen and others complained about not receiving their gifts from the officials and balked at the high prices charged by traders as they faced cycles of shortage and plenty. By the 1790s Natchitoches commandant Louis De Blanc could not find any residents with enough resources to become the officially licensed traders to the Caddo communities in Louisiana. De Blanc's own meager supply of goods was further depleted by Texas Caddos visiting Natchitoches in hopes of receiving gifts of merchandise they could not get from their near-bankrupt Texas supplier. De Blanc complained that the dearth of trade had ruined him and all the Indian peoples along the Red River and eastern Texas who depended on Spain for merchandise. He warned that the Caddos and Wichitas would revolt unless Spain provided traders and goods, especially guns, powder, and shot. De Blanc understood, as De Mézières did before him, that peace came when the Indians had a steady supply of merchandise and war came when shortages arose. To drive this point home, De Blanc described the deteriorating situation in January 1790 this way: "The worst spectacle in the world is that of poverty. These savages have forgotten the use of the arrow, and during the French domination they lacked nothing; but today they are reduced to dire necessity. They are consequently ready to commit evil actions."[40]

In reality De Blanc may have been describing his own situation more than that of the Caddos. While Spanish officials and traders may not have had as many gifts to give or goods to trade, they were bound to doing business with the Caddos. Their traditional trade partners and exchange networks were suffering from a merchandise shortage, but the Caddos tried to get around the shortages of officially provided goods from Natchitoches by shopping for more reliable sources of merchandise. The Caddos increasingly tried to play kinship and reciprocity to their advantage. There were never as many firearms supplied as the Caddos wanted, but they still periodically acquired large quantities of goods. The cargo manifests of the licensed traders sent out to their villages demonstrated this. Though the Caddos may not have paid their debts to Natchitoches or Nacogdoches merchants, Caddos still produced horses, hides, and bear's oil and exchanged them with traders from somewhere. Not only did they now allow traders from Natchitoches and Nacogdoches, licensed and unlicensed, into their villages, they also welcomed a host of traders from other Spanish posts, as well as American traders from east of the Mississippi River. When necessity dictated, Caddo traders might visit other posts, such as Fort Miro on the Ouachita River, near present-day Monroe, Louisiana.[41]

Survival was difficult for the Caddos during the late eighteenth and early nineteenth centuries as the Spanish posts of Natchitoches and Nacogdoches faced their own merchandise shortages. This forced the Caddos to find alternate sources of merchandise to help them on their hunts and to defend themselves against the Osages and Choctaws. Fortunately, the power of the Kadohadacho chief helped them during these hard times. Since the earliest years of the Mississippi cultural tradition, each individual Caddo community had been its own a political chiefdom led by its own hereditary chief who redistributed goods. Over the years some of these individual chiefdoms expanded to subjugate and control other communities. Major multicommunity chiefdoms, such as Spiro, Naguatex, Hasinai, and Kadohadacho had, over the years, risen and fallen.

By the latter half of the eighteenth century, with the large Hasinai chiefdom and many subchiefdoms shattered by disease, raids, relocation, and hide-trade activities, the old Kadohadacho chiefdom filled the power vacuum. As Caddo communities disappeared and coalesced, the chief of the Kadohadachos expanded his power, influence, and protection over the remaining communities. Rather than through claiming a connection to the sun or the ability to control the elements, or even through heroic warfare, the Kadohadacho great chief Tinhiouen and his successors led this secular chiefdom by virtue of their direct descent from the ancient Kadohadacho Mississippian chiefly lineage, by their ever growing influence with the European and American governments, by their ability to provide additional quantities of European merchandise for the subchiefdoms, and by their power to protect them from raiders and lead strikes against their enemies.

As this expanding Kadohadacho chiefdom asserted its authority in the second half of the eighteenth century, the Spanish found they still had to work with it on Caddo terms. Fearing the English and Americans aggressively pushing their boundaries further west, the Spanish had to rely more on the Caddos as a barrier against this expansion. At the same time, Tinhiouen and his successors understood they needed their Spanish allies and kin to provide ever more firearms as Osage and Choctaw raids took an increasing toll on the Caddo people. And as if Osage and Choctaw raids were not enough, the Caddos soon found themselves coming under a more insidious type of attack as Americans began to move into Caddo territory. Osages and Choctaws had raided Caddo villages for hides, horses, and captives, but now, for the first time, the Caddos found their land under attack. Now more than ever all the Caddo peoples relied on the power and prestige of the great chief of the Kadohadachos, who served as their spokesperson and leader. Fortunately, an able, talented man—Dehahuit—rose to leadership and came to be considered not only head of the Kadohadacho chiefdom but also the great chief of all the Caddos. Imposing in presence and skilled in diplomacy, Dehahuit managed to extend his power, but it would take all of his skill and abilities to protect his people and land from the United States.

6 // The Chiefdoms Shatter

Before the Americans owned Louisiana, the French, and afterward the Spaniards always treated us as friends and brothers—no white man ever settled on our lands and we were assured they never should. We were told the same things by the Americans in our first Council at Natchitoches.

TARSHAR, Head Chief of the Caddo,
1835, Caddo Agency Letters

OSAGE and Choctaw raids, while they infuriated the Caddos and forced villages to move further south, did not defeat them. What proved most disastrous for the Caddos was the same process that reduced the Osage and Choctaw raids: the coming of American traders and settlers to Louisiana and Texas. The Caddos, Osages, and Choctaws in Louisiana, Arkansas, and Texas all faced this threat and were eventually swept before it.

During the early years of the nineteenth century, great changes loomed before the Caddos. Around the turn of the century a very able Cadodacho man named Dehahuit became great chief of the Kadohada-chos. Little is known of Dehahuit's early life, but his name began to appear in Euro-American records as the great chief about this time. Under his leadership the Kadohadacho chiefdom, now consisting of the Cado-dacho, Natchitoches, Yatasí, and Petit Caddo communities, continued to exert its political power, even over the communities of the old Hasinai chiefdom. More than any of his predecessors, Dehahuit came to be seen as the great chief of all the Caddo people. Though at first the term *Caddo* was mainly applied to this expanding Kadohadacho chiefdom, the term soon came to designate all the Caddo peoples in both Louisiana and Texas, even though the Texas communities of the old Hasinai chiefdom continued to see themselves as politically and socially distinct from the Louisiana Caddo communities.

Other changes confronted the Caddos during the last years of the eighteenth and early years of the nineteenth centuries. In 1803 the

United States purchased Louisiana, and in April 1804 the American flag arose over the former French and Spanish outpost of Natchitoches. Once again the Caddos straddled an international boundary, with the Americans on the east and the Spanish to their west. President Thomas Jefferson appointed John Sibley as Indian agent to the Caddos, and soon afterward a U.S. Indian factory—a government-sponsored trading post—was built at Natchitoches.

The arrival of the Americans in Natchitoches delighted Dehahuit, as the high-quality, low-priced merchandise the Americans promised would help the Caddos in their wars against the Osages and Choctaws. Hoping to make these new strangers into kinspeople, Dehahuit eagerly sought out Sibley. According to Sibley, the "King of the Caddos" arrived in Natchitoches, found a Frenchman who could speak Caddo and English, and soon began to visit Sibley regularly in order to gain more information about the Americans. Dehahuit assured Sibley that the Caddos had "never shed white man's blood" and were very interested in acquiring American goods. Also, as Dehahuit was always on the lookout for lower trade prices, he recounted a rumor he had heard from the Chickasaws that the Americans would give a good blanket for five skins and other goods at equally cheap prices. Not only this, Dehahuit said, he also had heard that the Americans had provided the Chickasaws with cotton gins, spinning wheels, looms, and blacksmiths shops, but, Dehahuit acknowledged, he did not believe the Chickasaws. Sibley assured him it was all true.[1]

While Dehahuit scouted out the Americans, the Americans placed much hope in Dehahuit and the Caddos. Sibley concluded that the Caddos "might with proper management be made good citizens, at any rate useful on the frontier as a protection against any other Indians. I should think myself as safe in their towns as in the City of Natchez." Taking his cue from Sibley, Louisiana territorial governor William Claiborne ordered Sibley and the army commanders at Natchitoches to receive the Caddos with all "friendly attention and have a regard to their interests." By making these alliances with the Indian peoples, Claiborne, just as the French and Spanish had before him, hoped to regulate their trade and control with whom they had contact. Also like his predecessors, he tried to limit the traders who could do business with the Caddos.[2]

Unfortunately, Claiborne and the Americans seemed to have little comprehension of kinship and its obligations, and Dehahuit and his Caddos quickly became frustrated with these new peoples who did not understand the importance of gift giving and the duties of kinspeople. On one of his early visits, Dehahuit became upset that the Americans had not provided them with gifts as the Spanish and French always had done. American officials, fearful of Caddo power, which they numbered at five hundred to six hundred warriors, explained that the United States planned to establish a trading house in Natchitoches to supply "their wants on moderate terms" and protect them from the high prices charged by private traders. Claiborne reported that Dehahuit and his entourage "expressed much satisfaction; and after having received their rations retired from the post well pleased." Still, though Dehahuit might be temporarily pleased with a few rations, he expected much more from these obviously wealthy Americans. His subsequent visits always worried the Americans, as they could not supply him with the presents he demanded.[3]

Notwithstanding the small amount of gifts given to him, Dehahuit saw potential in the arrival of the Americans. Just as politically minded as his ancestors, Dehahuit believed he could now play America against Spain while increasing his prestige among his own people as well as with his Indian allies further west. To the American's pleasure Dehahuit hinted that not only the Caddos but also the Wichitas and the Comanches held the Spanish in contempt and most of the peoples of the southern plains were waiting for American traders to visit their villages. Also, he would be glad to take an American flag back to his village, and if they would give him a few extras, he would pass them out to other Indian peoples in his jurisdiction.[4]

Dehahuit now had the Americans hooked, especially as they came to understand just how much influence and power the great chief possessed. Governor Claiborne wrote Sibley that since the "Caddo nation manifested a decided influence over the various tribes of Indians with whom our frontiers can have connection," he was to devote special attention to Dehahuit and the Caddos in order to gain their friendship permanently. Even U.S. Secretary of War Henry Dearborn encouraged Dehahuit to visit Washington and sent a passport, though Dehahuit apparently never made the trip.[5]

By mid-1805 Spanish officials in Texas noticed a marked decrease in the number of Indians visiting Nacogdoches. They attributed this to Dehahuit's persuasiveness with the Indians, the gifts given by Sibley, and the trade goods provided by the U.S. Indian factory recently opened at Natchitoches. This only stiffened Spanish resolve to prevent the desertion of their Indian allies. Spanish officials begged, then threatened, the Texas Indians in an effort to stop them from visiting Natchitoches, telling the Indians they risked receiving no more gifts if they continued their visits to American Louisiana. When threats proved ineffective, Spain reminded the Caddos of the fate of such Indian nations as the Choctaws and Alabamas, who, after allying themselves with the Americans, were eventually forced from their land and pushed west by those very Americans.[6]

In their attempts to stop their Indian allies from filtering over to the Americans, the Spanish could be their own worst enemy. In August 1805 the Spanish stationed a detachment of troops at Bayou Pierre, near the old Yatasí village, about forty miles northwest of Natchitoches, where a small number of French creoles and Indian mixed-bloods lived. Their orders were to intercept Texas Indians on their way to Natchitoches. In early September 1805 the detachment seized fifteen horses loaded with 1,100 deer hides, which they believed belonged to an American trader. Eight days later Dehahuit himself appeared at Nacogdoches to complain about the seizure. According to the great chief all the skins belonged to him, and he owed them to a merchant at Natchitoches. As neither he nor any of his people had ever harmed the Spanish, why had they confiscated his hides? he asked. Nacogdoches commandant Dionisio Valle quickly returned the skins.[7]

Much to the dismay of the Spanish, the Caddos' need for firearms and ammunition, as well as obligations of reciprocity, meant they welcomed a variety of peoples to their villages. Caddos often went to Natchitoches and returned with goods for their kinspeople, sometimes guiding American traders back to the villages. A Natchitoches merchant hired a Nadaco and a Wichita to lead him to the Nadaco, Nacogdochito, Yatasí, Hasinai, and Kichai villages. There he offered excellent bargains: one hundred balls and powder for two hides, four large knives for one hide, four large mirrors for one hide, six vermillion papers for one hide, and ten strings of beads for one hide. Spanish traders could never compete with those prices, but Texas officials hoped that the Caddos would remember their loyalties to Spain and arrest these American *contrabandistas*. This hope was misplaced. Dehahuit and the Caddos would neither arrest nor turn away these merchants and wealthy potential kinsmen, and undoubtedly some American traders did make kinship relations with the Caddos. Besides, the Americans supplied more, better, and cheaper goods than did the Spanish.[8]

Still, Dehahuit played a dangerous game. In 1806 Spain and the United States inched toward war over the location of the boundary between Texas and Louisiana. Spain insisted on a line east of the Sabine River while the United States pushed for as much of Texas as possible. As war loomed both the Spanish and the Americans became reckless in their Caddo diplomacy. Spain tried to force the great chief to give up his American connection. In summer 1806 Spanish soldiers cut down the American flag flying over Dehahuit's Cadodacho village. Colonel Simon Herrera explained that the Cadodachos were on Spanish soil, and that if Dehahuit was going to fly the American flag, he should move to American territory. This only angered Dehahuit and the Americans. Tensions climbed even higher when Spanish troops turned back the Freeman and Custis expedition, which Jefferson had sent to explore the Red River and which Dehahuit had personally guided to his village on the river.[9]

The Americans also tried to bully the great chief into declaring for them in the event of war with Spain, or at least into remaining neutral. Governor Claiborne warned Dehahuit that "when white people enter into disputes, let the Red Man keep quiet, and join neither side." Dehahuit assured Claiborne of his people's friendship:

Your words resemble the words my forefathers have told me they used to receive from the French in ancient times. My ancestors, from Chief to Chief, were always well pleased with the French. They were well received and well treated by them when they met to hold talks together, and we can now say the same of you our new friends. . . . You request that our wars in the future may be against the deer only. This is what we ourselves desire, and happen what will, our hands shall never be stained with white men's blood. Your words which I have this day heard, shall be imprinted on my heart. They shall never be forgotten, but shall be communicated from one to another, till they reach the setting sun. It shall be known and remembered that the Americans are the friends to Red People.[10]

The great chief told Claiborne that he had become confused and embarrassed when he was beset on one side by the Americans and on the other by the Spanish, but now he was satisfied with the American explanation of the boundaries and would not fight. The only enemy he had and would fight were his eternal enemies, the Osages, whom it pleased God to give him.[11]

The threat of war between the United States and Spain provided an opportunity for Dehahuit to increase his prestige and power. During the war scare Sibley had hoped to draw most of the Indians of Texas into an alliance with the Americans by inviting the Texas Caddo communities, as well as the Wichitas and Comanches, to visit him in summer 1807 at Natchitoches for a peace conference. Recognizing Dehahuit's influence among all these peoples, Sibley appealed to the great chief for help. Like his ancestor Tinhiouen the Elder, Dehahuit realized that Sibley's appeal provided an opportunity to increase his status and prestige with the Americans, the Spanish, and the other Indians. The Americans would recognize how essential he was to their immediate interests. This would keep the manufactured goods flowing to him, which would help in their wars against the Osages and Choctaws, but which he could also redistribute to gain increased prestige and power among the Caddos, Comanches, and Wichitas.

At the same time, Dehahuit realized he could use Sibley to bolster his own peacemaking attempts. Choctaw raiding parties were once again striking deep into Caddo and Wichita territory. These brought counterraids and revenge killings that only escalated the violence until no Indian community could sleep peacefully or hunt without fear. Still under attack by the Osages from the north, Dehahuit hoped to arrange a peace with the Choctaws. While the Choctaws were willing, Dehahuit's Wichita allies, hot for revenge, balked. Undoubtedly Dehahuit believed that if he could get the Wichitas and Comanches to Natchitoches, where they would receive many gifts, his own status would rise and he would be able to bring about the peace his people so desperately needed. So with Sibley's invitation in hand and drawing on his considerable reputation among the western Indians, he urged the Wichitas and Comanches to come to Natchitoches, promising them all sorts of gifts.

Dehahuit's influence worked, and the Wichitas and Comanches agreed to come off the plains and into the woodlands to visit Sibley. In gratitude Sibley heaped gifts on Dehahuit, including a scarlet regimental coat trimmed in black velvet. He also provided gifts to Dehahuit's principal men, including a blue half-regimental coat and a white linen shirt to Dehahuit's son. To Big Osage, who earned the name by having been wounded in the head by an Osage musket ball, he also gave a half-regimental coat. To Cut Finger, another Caddo advisor, he gave a hat, half-regimental coat, and other goods.[12]

In August 1807 over 350 Indians visited Sibley at Natchitoches, including 119 Texas Caddos, 90 Louisiana Caddos, 80 Comanches, 26 Wichitas, 4 Chickasaws, and a mixed party of 74 Comanches and Wichitas, who arrived toward the end of the council. At the council, which lasted for two weeks, Sibley made a peace with all the Indian peoples present and distributed enormous amounts of gifts, with the chiefs receiving coats and numerous goods to give to their people. Dehahuit's prestige among the Indians skyrocketed, for they saw him being honored by the wealthy Americans and proving himself powerful enough to deliver the goods that he had promised. Even better, he received Sibley's support in his efforts to make peace with the Choctaws, to which the Wichitas finally agreed. His prestige also increased with the Americans and Spanish because they saw him as a figure who held sway over the powerful Comanche and Wichita peoples, even to the point of bringing plains peoples hundreds of miles to the piney woods of Louisiana.[13]

The number of Indians who went to Natchitoches at Dehahuit's behest surprised and alarmed the Spanish. Spanish traders and officials reported that in many villages they found only women and old men, as most of the younger men had gone to Natchitoches for the council. However, despite the gifts and promises they received in Natchitoches, the council turned out not to be as fulfilling for the Comanches and Wichitas as they had hoped. Even the Spanish realized that their allies had not actually abandoned them. When the governor of Spanish Texas later met with some of the Comanche chiefs who had gone to

Natchitoches, they told him that they had gone for no other reason than to receive the gifts offered by the American government. The chiefs complained that while they were in Natchitoches, somebody stole a large number of their horses and mules. Even worse, after they returned from Natchitoches, many members of their bands became sick and died. Because of all these calamities, the governor reported, "they have become so repentant of their act that they are disposed not to lapse again into their error."[14]

In a way, these problems only added to Dehahuit's status. The Comanches and Wichitas did not blame him for these problems, and since these plains peoples refused to come back to Natchitoches, they still relied on Dehahuit and his Caddos to supply them with guns and merchandise while allowing the old creole and new American traders to pass through the Caddo villages on the way west. This reliance only increased after 1810, when Mexico revolted against Spain and threw Texas into turmoil for the next decade. The revolution also made the Spanish see the importance of Dehahuit and his Caddos as allies against those rebels raiding into Texas from Louisiana. Over the next few years the Spanish government courted Dehahuit, giving him horses and merchandise until he promised that he would kill any rebels, or "bandits," as the Spanish termed them, found between the American border and San Antonio.[15]

Dehahuit found himself similarly approached when the War of 1812 broke out. In fall 1813 the Redstick Creeks sent emissaries to Dehahuit in hopes of persuading his Caddos to join them against the Americans. That Dehahuit might ally with the Redsticks terrified American officials. Louisiana governor Claiborne personally visited the great chief to persuade him not to join the Creeks. Claiborne laid the Creek troubles at the door of the English, whom he likened to white Osages, and begged Dehahuit not to take up arms against the United States. Whether it was due to Claiborne's speeches or was Dehahuit's own decision, he refused the Creek entreaties. A much relieved Claiborne reported to Washington that the great chief and his allies were favorably disposed toward the Americans and willing to fight on the American side if needed.[16]

When the English threatened New Orleans in late 1814, Claiborne recommended that Andrew Jackson appeal to Dehahuit to help defend the city. They would be valuable allies and, Claiborne wrote, "the Chief of the Caddos, is a man of great merit, he is brave, sensible and prudent.—You may rely on whatever he may say to you; ... he is the most influential Indian on this side of the River Grande, and his friendship, sir, will give much security to the western frontier of Louisiana." Dehahuit and his Caddo warriors agreed to help defend New Orleans, and they even gathered at Natchitoches to head downriver to support Jackson, but the battle ended before they could leave.[17]

In early 1815 Dehahuit as the great chief of the Caddos was at the height of his power. Indian peoples in Louisiana, Texas, and far out onto the plains looked to him for leadership. The Spanish wanted him to provide protection on Texas's eastern border, while the United States viewed him as a vital ally in the event of war with Indians, Spaniards, or the English. Most problems came from the Osages, with whom there had been raids, counterraids, and revenge killings for decades. But now things truly began to change for the worse. As capitalist agriculture developed along the lower Red River around the turn of the nineteenth century, it eclipsed the hide trade in economic importance and brought in a wholly different American immigrant. Rather than traders and potential kinspeople wanting hides and horses, American planters, farmers, and speculators coveted Caddo lands.

The Caddos and other Indian peoples soon found control of their territory slipping from their grasp. In 1806 Captain Burnet, from Mississippi, acquired the rights to the ancient Caddo salt works on Black Lake, north of Natchitoches, where he expected to make about forty bushels of salt per day. As early as 1810 the Natchitoches Caddos complained to Sibley that American settlers had ignored their claims and illegally appropriated their land. Sibley's solution to this encroachment was to survey and distinctly mark the Caddos' land, sell the remainder of it to Americans, and leave the Natchitoches Caddos with only "a small quantity of lands," something he was sure the Natchitoches would be "content" with.[18]

The Louisiana Caddos found themselves edged out of the Natchitoches area and pushed further northwest. They settled into an area bounded by the Red River on the east and north to its great bend, Cypress Bayou on the south, and the Texas boundary and the Sabine River on the west. To the north lived the Osages, to the east, the Americans. West was Spanish and then Mexican Texas, where their Hasinai kinspeople lived, and where they would have been welcome. In fact, in 1821 eighty-three Kadohadacho men, women, and children, at the invitation of the Mexican government, settled on lands along the Guadalupe River in Texas. Still, Dehahuit refused to relinquish Caddo claim to their lands in Louisiana.[19]

Caddos, once political equals with the Europeans, valued allies, and necessary cogs in the workings of the hide trade, now found the Americans had little need of them. With the declining hide trade, the increase in the cotton culture, and the growing realization that Spanish Texas posed little threat to national security, American settlers and officials began viewing the Caddos as a lower caste and obstacles to land acquisition and settlement. Increasingly unwelcome, more and more Caddo people began drawing away from American settlements and into more isolated areas. Ironically, this came at the time when the Caddos would have most welcomed the establishment of strong kin relations with the Americans. Population loss and their continued need for firearms and metal-edged weapons to combat the Osages and other Indian raiders, along with the pressure put on them to sell land, made the Caddos need reliable kinspeople who would remember and uphold their reciprocal obligations to give good counsel, provide assistance, and give gifts of needed merchandise. Instead, the bonds the Caddos had so long nourished with the Euro-Americans began to snap.

By 1819 the good will Dehahuit exhibited toward the Americans had dissipated in the face of encroaching settlers. To keep their hold on the land, the Caddos now began to rob and kill isolated American settlers. The U.S. government, too weak on that frontier, could do nothing, as most of the killings took place far from white settlements, and the Caddos, when confronted by John Fowler, head of the Indian factory on Sulphur Fork, blamed it on the Osages.[20]

Much to the anger of such American officials as Fowler and John Jamison, the area Indian agent, Dehahuit often visited them to complain of the continual encroachment on Caddo territory and threatened to forcibly drive out the Americans. To the Americans' dismay Dehahuit also continued to shore up his relations with the Spanish in Texas while refusing to adopt the trappings of white culture. In Fowler's opinion, the Caddos ranked far below any other Indians in the area on his civilization scale. He blamed this on Dehahuit: "He is what some call the Brute Indian—despises the habits of whitemen and is now too old to be improved. He is particularly inimical to Americans, frequently visits the Spaniards and holds the commission of Colonel from them."[21]

Fowler and Jamison became concerned about Dehahuit's hatred for the Americans, his insolence toward the government, and his potential for making trouble. They could not understand why Dehahuit did not comprehend the obligations he was under to the government for all the gifts, provisions, and services they had provided him. Fowler complained that Dehahuit had "no kind of respect for the advice given him by the agents of the government and . . . considering the length of time this tribe has had constant intercourse with the whites, they are singularly savage and far inferior to any Indians that visit this place." While Fowler did not believe Caddos could cause the Americans lasting injury, he believed the best way to deal with them was to depose Dehahuit, supplanting him with a chief more tractable and amenable to the Americans. He believed this might be done by threatening the Caddos with cutting off their rations and weapon repairs.[22]

Like the French and Spanish before them, because the Caddos exchanged their deerskins at the factory for merchandise and gun repairs, Fowler and Jamison believed the Caddos were more dependent on them than they actually were. The fear that such a powerful leader might be pushed into a total alliance with Spain, as well as government bureaucracy, prevented the two American officials from putting their plan into effect. Dehahuit's threats became more menacing, and Fowler and Jamison believed that war between the Caddos and the United States was imminent: "Although we have not much to dread from his physical force, he may nevertheless cost us both blood and treasure— He is the Chief of ten tribes, eight of whom live beyond the Sabine, in all he might raise five hundred warriors—He is vain, and with his vanity ignorant of our resources."[23]

In Washington, Commissioner of Indian Affairs Thomas McKenney took a calmer view. In his opinion the hostility of Dehahuit stemmed not so much from the factory or Americans in general but from the traders "who almost literally drown that country with whiskey." McKenney had a point. French traders had begun using liquor as an inducement to trade during the early eighteenth century and the practice had only grown and become more devastating. By this time even Fowler complained that the traders treated the Indians shamefully and plundered them of every valuable they possessed. Worse, the whiskey traders, in order to force the Indians to do business with them, tried to scare the Indians by telling them that if they did not buy whiskey, the army would come and drive them off their lands.[24]

In the face of the whiskey traders, land-hungry settlers, dispossessed Indians from the east, and continual Osage raids, Caddos living in Louisiana and the newly created Arkansas territory had two choices: move, or remain and persevere. Many Caddos, as did some eastern Indians, decided to move to Spanish Texas. Bands of Louisiana Caddos, Choctaws, Cherokees, Creeks, and Delawares petitioned the Spanish government to allow them to settle in Texas. Others, like Dehahuit, tried to stem the white tide. Under his leadership Caddo warriors, combined with warriors from smaller native and immigrant Indian peoples, continued to attack the Osages and raid the horse and hog herds of American settlers, mainly those living on what Dehahuit viewed as Caddo lands. According to one Arkansas official, the whole Arkansas territory was up in arms as these bands stole horses from the Americans; he described one raiding band as "a strolling party of Cherokees, Delawares, Shawnees, Choctaws, Creeks, and Coushattas and all backed by the Caddos, who are a very considerable tribe and their principal chief, I am told, holds a Spanish commission of colonel." Whites and other Indian bands who suffered Caddo raids hoped to retaliate but were restrained by U.S. and territorial officials.[25]

Dehahuit realized he needed more strength, and for this he devised a truly visionary plan. To stand up to the Americans Dehahuit planned to draw many of the immigrant Indian peoples into his Caddo chiefdom. Descended from the Caddo Mississippian chiefly lineage, Dehahuit was already caddí of the Cadodachos, great chief of the Kadohadacho chiefdom, and spokesman for all the Caddos; now he hoped to become the great chief of all the Indian peoples in that part of the country. Even the Spanish admitted that the "Caddo Nation is the one that commands all the nations below the Colorado [Red] River of Natchitoches." By 1820 his Kadohadacho chiefdom comprised the combined remnants of the Cadodacho, Petit Caddo, Yatasí, and Natchitoches communities with their villages located between the Sabine and

Red Rivers near the boundary of the territories of Louisiana and Arkansas. Together the chiefdom could field more or less 300 warriors. His authority was strongest among these peoples. But Dehahuit's leadership and prestige as great chief of the Caddos also extended to those Caddo peoples living in Texas, the remnants of the old Hasinai chiefdom, who lived in settled villages between the Sabine and Trinity Rivers. In addition to Kadohadacho warriors Dehahuit could call on the Nadacos (or Anadarkos, as the Americans called them) to provide 150 men; the Nabedaches, 60; the Hainais, 100; and the Kichais, 200, for a total of 800 Caddo warriors. Besides these Caddo communities Dehahuit also drew under his leadership some of the Wichita communities, such as the Tawakonis and Wacos, as well as the Attakapan Bidais. These three peoples could place an additional 850 warriors at his disposal.[26]

There was the potential for other warriors as Caddo territory now swarmed with numerous bands of Indians who originally had lived in the eastern part of the continent. By the mid-1820s even the U.S. government believed the Caddo area would be an ideal Indian territory and asked Dehahuit if it could settle eastern Indians there. Dehahuit consented to the government's relocation of Indian peoples onto his lands as it would unite even more Indian peoples under his authority. His becoming spokesperson and leader for these smaller immigrant bands, as well as ensuring them a steady supply of manufactured goods, would make his prestige grow even further, and the increase in the number of warriors in his chiefdom would give him greater leverage in dealing with whites. So as bands of Shawnees, Delawares, Pascagoulas, Kickapoos, even Choctaws and Cherokees crossed onto Caddo land, Dehahuit quickly made alliances with them.[27]

Many of these eastern immigrant bands looked to Dehahuit for leadership, but it would be wrong to conclude that the Caddos were at peace with all immigrant bands in Caddo territory. Dehahuit and his Caddos might be at peace with one Choctaw or Cherokee band, incorporate another into his expanding chiefdom, and then raid another. Dehahuit's chiefdom could not be viewed as a single, solid entity over which he exercised total, autocratic control. Caddo bands might attack Cherokee or Choctaw bands, and vice versa. The Osages still made periodic raids on Caddo villages, but now they also attacked many of the immigrant bands. All this tended to confuse many white settlers and government officials in Louisiana, Arkansas, and Texas.[28]

While Dehahuit might be spokesman for the Caddos and most immigrant bands living in his territory, he found it difficult to control all the peoples of his chiefdom. The old separation and distinctiveness between the ancient Kadohadacho and Hasinai chiefdoms remained, and the Caddo peoples identified with one or the other. Dehahuit retained strong support from the remnants of the Cadodachos, Yatasís, Petit Caddos, and Natchitoches, who all identified themselves with the old Kadohadacho chiefdom, while his power was weaker among the Texas communities of the old Hasinai chiefdom. Also, traditional limitations the Caddos had always placed on their chiefs remained in effect. While Dehahuit could authorize one hundred lashes on the Caddo man who pulled a gun on Agent George Gray, he did not exert autocratic control. He still consulted his principal men and community subchiefs for advice. Rather than force, he used persuasion, backed by the power of Kadohadacho history, to form alliances and to advance his ideas.[29]

Dehahuit found it more difficult to sustain his authority in Texas. Though the Mexican government, which won its independence from Spain in 1821, might invite him to Nacogdoches, along with the Comanches and Taovayas, for peace talks, Dehahuit's control problems in Texas stemmed from three things. First, Mexico was generally ineffective in keeping peace between the many Indian peoples in Texas. Second, the influx of American settlers to Texas perpetuated old hatreds of Indians and developed into a marked distrust of the Caddos. Third was the continual influx of large bands of eastern Indians into Texas, such as Chief Duwali's Cherokees, who became rivals of the Caddos.

In the latter half of the 1820s the Caddos found Texas to be in turmoil from almost constant warfare. Worse, Caddo numbers continually declined. By 1828 a Mexican census, which may have suffered from the same problems of Caddo movements that had earlier plagued Euro-American censuses, reported that the Kadohadacho chiefdom, comprising what remained of the old Caddo communities in Louisiana, contained 300 families, with about 400 warriors, living on the Red River near the border with the United States. In Texas, the Nabedaches, with 15 families, lived at the headwaters of the Neches River. The Hainais lived at the headwaters of the Neches and Angelina rivers with 23 families. The Nadacos lived with 29 families on the west bank of the Angelina River. The census reported an extraordinarily high popuation for the Ais—160 families—and said that they lived between the Brazos and Colorado Rivers and were constantly harassed by the Comanches and Tawakonis. The Caddos' close allies, the Kichais, were located on a branch of the Trinity River, with 37 families. According to Manuel de Mier y Terán, who took the census, Dehahuit's Kadohadachos "formed a powerful nation, respected by all the savages. . . . They remember with pride their antiquity and power, and pretend to have rights superior to all other tribes, considering themselves owners of the land. . . . They are rivals of the Cherokees; they were jealous of the influence that these were going to acquire; and in all their conversations with the Mexicans they manifest their disgust at the introduction of foreign savages." Terán noted that the Caddos did not cultivate too much land, but rather hunted buffalo and made war on the Osages. "The other savages, minus the foreigners, fear them in war."[30]

Still, the Caddos lived a life similar to that of their ancestors. Jean Berlandier, who traveled through Texas in 1830, noted that the Cadodachos, Adaes, Ais, Nabedaches, Nadacos, Hasinais, Nacogdochitos, and Kichais were all very hospitable, lived in "fixed abodes . . . devoted themselves to agriculture . . . [and] build their houses of tree trunks or thatch." They planted corn, beans, melons, and such, and continued to hold religious ceremonies and drink the black drink. Some of the things that Berlandier felt were striking about the Caddos were that they actually possessed some form of religious ceremony at marriage and were decently dressed in a somewhat European style, but he was still especially fascinated by their fashion for hanging jewels and ornaments from their noses. Some of these, Berlandier noted, were in the shapes of horses, crescents, rings, and pendants, and some wore plates of silver so long they reached the person's chest. As for hair, a Caddo man completely shaved his head except for a single strip. The shaved parts were then painted with wavy lines of vermillion, which ran down along the neck. Other Caddo peoples had similar hairstyles, although with some differences to denote that they belonged to different communities. They still hunted deer and exchanged hides in both Nacogdoches and Natchitoches for weapons, ammunition, knives, hardware, and liquor. Whiskey proved an ever growing problem, as men often traded hides for it at Nacogdoches, though Berlandier singled out the Nabedaches as being less given to drunkenness than the others.[31]

While turmoil in Texas between Indians and the burgeoning American population continued, Dehahuit's chiefdom faced other problems. White traders, and even Indians themselves, continued to provide whiskey to the Indians around the Caddo agency in Louisiana. This produced many drunken brawls and much bloodshed. The Quapaws, who had ceded their lands in Arkansas and moved to the Caddo agency, believed Dehahuit to be a tyrant; they complained to the agents about him and asked to be allowed to go back to their old lands. Bands from shattered Indian nations in the east and even from Texas continued to flock to Dehahuit's territory, making demands for food and merchandise on him and the Caddo agent. Besides these, Dehahuit and his Kadohadachos found themselves dealing, in quick succession, with three different Indian agents, two agency relocations, and a war scare with the Texas Cherokees.[32]

The United States' Caddo agency, despite occupying just about all of what is today Caddo Parish, Louisiana, and parts of southwestern Arkansas, served a population of over twenty-five hundred Indians, including some that actually lived west of the Sabine River, in Mexican Texas. Not only did such Louisiana Caddo peoples as the Cadodachos, Natchitoches, and Yatasís use the agency, but the Adaes and Ais from Texas also considered it home. Besides these Caddos, the agency also served peoples from several immigrant Indian nations. For a few years, between 1827 and 1831, the Quapaws of Arkansas also lived at the Caddo agency and received their annuities there. Frustration over late annuities and what they believed was cheating by Caddo agent Jehiel Brooks caused many Quapaws to return to Arkansas, but by 1833 the Quapaws in Arkansas, still not receiving their annuities, requested to go back among the Caddos.[33]

The agency's Indian population might suddenly decrease, such as when the Kadohadachos went on a buffalo hunt. Conversely, it also might suddenly increase. Its location next to Mexican Texas meant that Caddo peoples living in that province often crossed the border to visit and settle among their Kadohadacho kinspeople. In early 1831 some of the Nadacos and Hainais from Texas moved eastward into Louisiana and settled on lands near Bayou Pierre, where they caused problems for the Kadohadachos. Killing the cattle and hogs of Americans living in that vicinity invited retaliation. And worse, the hungry Nadacos and Hasinais raided the Kadahadacho food stores while the men were absent hunting buffalo.[34]

Kadohadachos caused the same problems when they visited their Hasinai kinspeople in Texas. Furthermore, large contingents of Louisiana Caddos crossing into Texas often frightened other Indians. In late 1830 Colonel Peter Ellis Bean, who served as superintendent of Indian affairs for Mexican Texas, reported that the Texas Cherokees believed that the Kadohadachos were coming to attack them. Bean told Brooks that if the Kadohadachos caused any more problems in Texas, he would send his Texas Cherokees to the Agency to destroy them. Nothing came of this, and three years later Bean still complained about Dehahuit's people crossing the Sabine River, stealing horses, and even settling on Texas soil without permission. He warned Brooks to advise the Louisiana Caddos not to disturb the peace in Texas or they would be considered enemies of Mexico.[35]

One reason the Kadohadachos might periodically cross into Texas was that the Caddo agency was beset with problems. Periodic droughts or floods required the agent to request emergency money to buy provisions. In February 1831 Brooks asked the war department for an extra $150 to provide food for the old men, the women, and the children who were left at the Agency while the Caddo men were out on the winter hunt. Brooks reported that the 1830 drought had killed most of the Caddos' crops, and he predicted that many of the women, children, and old men would die without the provisions. When droughts such as these hit, the Caddos and other Indians often raided the herds of nearby whites.[36]

Dehahuit, though, did not view Brooks in a friendly or sympathetic light. He complained bitterly about the agent, charging that the services Brooks provided were inadequate, and, even worse, that Brooks cheated him and his people. The major problem was the delivery of the correct amount of gifts and merchandise promised them. Up through 1830 the Kadohadachos received eight hundred dollars' worth of presents from the U.S. government per year. Dehahuit and his subchiefs received a cash annuity of twenty-five dollars, later raised to fifty dollars. Then in 1831 the government unexpectedly cut the Kadohadacho annuity in half, to four hundred dollars. Dehahuit complained to President Andrew Jackson that when George Gray ran the agency, "I was promised & did receive an annuity & my blacksmith work used to be done as I wanted it. Of late, I receive nothing & the smith refused to do my work unless I pay him for it. It is three years since I have received any thing on account of my annuity." Dehahuit believed that Brooks kept the annuities for himself. He told Jackson that he, along with all the Indian peoples in the vicinity, had lost faith in Brooks. "We all want a new agent & a new interpreter of our own choice. The agent we have is no better than none." He then asked Jackson to write him back care of his old friend John Sibley at Natchitoches so as to not have the letter fall into Brooks's hands.[37]

Relations between Dehahuit and Brooks became so strained that Brooks believed an Indian war was in the making. The Caddos, he explained, "are a primitive nation, and consider themselves objects of my particular care, but they are also a fierce, savage, and uncompromising people; have many enemies, and often threatened with war." He begged the government to detail a detachment of army troops to the agency to be placed under his command to prevent any hostilities. The army refused and Brooks continued his complaints. Many of the problems, Brooks believed, came from Mexican Texas, home to numerous angry and warlike nations, such as the Cherokees, Delawares, and Shawnees, who might cause the agency trouble. Also, much of the enmity between him and the Indians, he thought, stemmed from contraband traders doing business with the Indians about the agency, telling lies about him in order to make them distrustful.[38]

For the Caddos, their relationship with the U.S. government was a continuation of the one they had previously with the French and Spanish. The agent bestowed medals with the likeness of the president to Dehahuit and his principal men. Caddo and other Indian bands visited the agency, where they received gifts and food and had their weapons repaired—over eight hundred dollars' worth in the first half of 1832—as they had when they visited Natchitoches and Nacogdoches during the eighteenth century. They still welcomed licensed and unlicensed traders to their villages, where they exchanged hides for even more merchandise. Licensed traders pledged not to sell alcohol to the Caddos and agreed not to accept horses, guns, knives, camp equipment, or equipment the Indians used for hunting or war, nor wearing apparel, except for skins, furs, or ornaments. Unlicensed traders continued their unregulated trade, often using whiskey to acquire whatever they could from the Caddos.[39]

Like the Spanish, U.S. officials found they could not stop these illegal traders, especially the whiskey traders. Some Indians refused to partake in this traffic, while others heartily welcomed the whiskey trade, drinking away all their trade profits, staying drunk, and quarreling. Among some Indians drunkenness became so bad that Brooks called whiskey the "scourge of their race." What made the whiskey trade almost impossible to halt was that the Indians themselves, including Caddos, often participated in it. Some American smugglers recruited Caddo men to distribute whiskey to all the various bands and families. The Indians broke the whiskey down into smaller portions, which made it easier to spread it "more extensively through their villages than their incarnate tormentors like to venture; and thereby entice the Indians, far and near, to meet them for a larger supply at some agreed on but secret point on the confines of their country."[40]

Obviously, the Caddos drank whiskey, and sometimes to excess. Juan Padilla reported in 1820 that at Caddo dances, "they drink great quantities of firewater—some of them drinking until they tumble over." Though the Caddos as a whole may have drunk large quantities of whiskey, it does not appear that their society suffered the same debilitating and destructive affects that alcohol caused among the Choctaws, for example. Though little is known of early Caddo alcoholism, they seemed to have been more like their distant Caddoan-speaking Pawnee cousins, who could use liquor but not become victims of it.[41]

The major problem for the Caddos was the continual encroachment on their traditional lands by Americans. The establishment of the Caddo agency actually reduced much of what had been considered Caddo lands in Louisiana and Arkansas to an area west and south of the Red River, east of the Texas border, and north of Cypress Bayou. In reality Caddo territory did not stop at the international border but continued across the Sabine River well into Mexican eastern Texas. But by 1832 these agency borders were already under pressure from Americans. A dispute arose over just where the Caddo borders lay when a U.S. surveyor crossed the southern boundary of Cypress Bayou and placed the corner of a township a mile or two within the Caddo lands. At the same time, on the east, Americans began claiming the highly fertile lands along old channels of the Red River, which, according to the Caddos, still belonged to them. Brooks suggested the Caddo boundaries be surveyed in order to prevent these encroachments on Caddo lands.[42]

The next year, 1833, some American land speculators formulated a plan to wrest from the Caddos all their remaining land in Louisiana. A couple of speculators began taking depositions from some of the old French inhabitants of Natchitoches in order to prove that the Caddos possessed no claim to the land they occupied. If the government recognized these depositions and ruled against the Caddos, one of these speculators would have the settlement rights to the entire area that then comprised the Caddo agency. When the Caddos heard of these machinations they strongly objected and demanded that Brooks pass along their objections to the government. This plan, Brooks wrote, is "exciting unfriendly feelings among the Caddos who . . . lay the blame on me."[43]

The Caddos also faced pressure from settlers in Texas. American settlers living in Mexican Texas began surveying land on the Caddo agency in Louisiana under the impression that it belonged to Mexico. Brooks informed the Texans that they were on the American side of the border and that the land belonged to the Caddos under the jurisdiction of the United States. He ordered the surveying to cease and desist.[44]

Then disaster struck. The old great chief Dehahuit died in early 1833. He had been leader of the Kadohadacho chiefdom and the spokesman for the Caddo peoples and many other Indians in the area for some thirty years. Without Dehahuit the Caddos lost their strong man who often stood up to Brooks and the U.S. government. Tarshar, who succeeded Dehahuit, did not have the power, prestige, or charisma to make the bold stands Dehahuit had. Although chief of the Kadohadachos at the time of his ascension, Tarshar possessed little influence with the Texas Caddos. With Dehahuit gone the Caddos and their allies lost an important voice and a person who had managed to protect their lands from American settlers. Dehahuit's Caddo chiefdom began falling apart, and without him it became easier for Americans to take over Caddo territory.[45]

Now that Dehahuit was dead, the Americans were not sure how the Caddos would react to the continual pressure on their lands. Brooks grew nervous as rumors circulated around the agency that once the young men returned from their buffalo hunt on the plains they would elect a war chief who would drive the Americans out of Caddo territory. Tarshar, the new great chief, realized that he could not possibly defeat the Americans. Brooks presented the medal and other insignias to him and transferred to him the fifty-dollar annuity that had been Dehahuit's. The annuity, though, caused problems, as the government wanted to do away with it. Brooks complained that the payment to the chief was a necessity. If cutting the annuity was not bad enough, he added, the Caddos were losing their blacksmith, and no one wanted to take the job at the meager forty dollars per month the government paid.[46]

In Brooks's mind the only option available to the Caddos was for them to sell their land to the United States and move out of the country. Brooks was unmoved even when Tarshar led a party of about thirty-five Caddo warriors to help Major Henry Dodge rescue an American soldier captured by the Wichitas. In an ironic twist Brooks, because he could only find a few passports issued to the Caddos by the Spanish, claimed that the Caddos had never had title to their lands. In this he chose to ignore a guarantee by the Americans to respect Caddo lands. In a conference held in May 1805 between John Sibley and one hundred Caddo chiefs and warriors, the U.S. government had guaranteed the right of the Caddos to live on their lands in U.S. territory unless, of course, they voluntarily sold it. The conference paper stipulated that the Caddos, if they decided to sell, could only sell it to the U.S. government and that persons, including citizens of the United States, "are strictly forbidden from interrupting or disturbing you in the quiet and peaceable possession of your said lands."[47]

Caddo land, in American eyes, began looking extremely profitable, especially the rich, fertile grounds along the Red River. Work had begun in 1833 to remove the Great Red River Raft, a huge logjam of uprooted trees and debris clogging the river. Once completed, this would open even more land; anticipating this, land speculators flocked to the area in hopes of cashing in. Henry Shreve, the man in charge of removing the raft, called the lands first rate, and excellent for cotton, corn, and tobacco. In his opinion the removal of the raft would open up 71,820 additional acres of Caddo lands. If sold at the usual government price of $1.25 per acre it would bring $89,775, but Shreve believed the land was easily worth $4.00 per acre, totaling $287,280.[48]

With fantastic riches in mind, Brooks decided he wanted to profit from Caddo land. He had his eye on a piece of land called Rush Island, a long tract formed by the various channels of the Red. Not wanting to lose it and fearing the Anglo-Texans might try to grab some of the Caddos' territory, Brooks urged Tarshar and the other Caddo chiefs to sell. To speed things up and secure his title to the land, Brooks resigned his agent's position, telling the Caddos he could no longer provide them with official counsel. At the same time, he applied to Secretary of War Lewis Cass to be appointed one of the commissioners to negotiate the land-cession treaty with the Caddos. Now, at the time of greatest danger, when the Caddos most needed advice from their American kinspeople, there were few kin available to provide them with honest or correct information.[49]

In late 1834 or early 1835 Tarshar and other Caddo chiefs wrote to President Jackson. They reiterated that their claim to these lands extended back to the time when the very first Caddo had been created. They reminded Jackson that the French and the Spaniards had treated them as "friends and brothers" and that no Euro-American had ever settled on their lands, and "we were assured they never should." The Americans said the same things, the chiefs wrote, but now they did not know on whom they could rely. "Our last-named agent tells us that he is no longer our agent, and that we no longer have a gunsmith nor blacksmith, and says he does not know what will be done with us or for us." According to Tarshar the Caddos held a great council and came to the "sorrowful resolution of offering all our lands to you which lie within the boundary of the United States." The only stipulation, Tarshar insisted, was that a tract of four square leagues of land at the southeast corner along the Red River be reserved for "our friend and brother Touline (otherwise Grappe)." Though he had been dead for ten years, the Caddos had remembered the obligations owed to their old fictive kinsman François Grappe.[50]

On 25 June 1835 Tarshar and the other Kadohadacho subchiefs, along with five hundred Caddo men, women, and children, met with

Brooks and the interpreters to negotiate the land cession. Tarshar originally asked for $200 per square mile, $100 in cash, the rest in goods. The former agent insisted this was impossible. After a few days and with French creole advisors to the Caddos banned from the council, Brooks countered, and finally, on 1 July, the Caddos signed a treaty that ceded almost one million acres of their land in Louisiana for $80,000: $30,000 in goods and horses, and $10,000 per year in cash for the next five years. The Caddos also promised to move outside of U.S. territorial boundaries, "at their own expense," within one year of the treaty signing. Unfortunately, the treaty made no provision for guaranteeing the Caddos lands in the west, as other southeastern Indians received in their removal treaties with the United States. In a series of supplemental articles signed along with the treaty, the government guaranteed to the descendants of François Grappe the right to the land the Caddos left them along the Red River. They also left a tract of land to their old affinal kinsman and interpreter, Larkin Edwards. Once the Caddo chiefs and headmen signed, Brooks distributed $30,000 worth of goods and horses to the Caddos. As he described the proceedings, Brooks wrote that all the Caddos went away happy with everything they received and with the whole council in general, from start to finish. None, he guaranteed, went away dissatisfied.[51]

Brooks was wrong, as almost immediately the treaty guarantees began to unravel and over the next few years the Kadohadachos found themselves cheated out of most of the money promised to them. But even if the treaty annuity guarantees had been scrupulously upheld, the Caddos would have received far below market value for their lands. Eighty thousand dollars for one million acres of land amounted to about $0.08 per acre, far below the $1.25 a farmer paid for government land, and much below the $10.00–$20.00 per acre some speculators estimated the Caddo cession to be worth.[52]

With Dehahuit dead, his chiefdom shattered, and its Louisiana remnants forced into Texas, leadership fell back to the caddís of the individual Caddo communities. In Texas the main Caddo communities were the Hainai and the Nadaco. The Americans began referring to these as the Ioni and Anadarko respectively. The Nabedaches, Nacogdoches, and Ais also remained as distinct Caddo entities but closely allied with the Anadarko and Ioni. In Louisiana the ancient Kadohadacho chiefdom that hearkened back to Mississippian days finally splintered. A band called the White Beads joined with the Choctaws in Louisiana and eventually wound up living on the Kiamichi River in Indian territory. Another faction, led by Tarshar, moved to Texas and settled among the Texas Caddo communities there. A faction under the leadership of Mon-Won briefly went to live in Chihuahua, Mexico. About two hundred Caddos remained in Louisiana, scattered in small hamlets between Natchitoches and Shreveport. Into the early 1840s Caddos could still be seen every once in a while in Natchitoches. Silver ornaments, trade beads, and pipe tomahawks could be bought in Natchitoches stores. Store clerks in the area still spoke Mobilian in order to deal with their Indian customers. In fact, many stores in Natchitoches and Shreveport depended on the local Indian peoples for trade, and many closed their doors after these last Caddos left the area, in the early 1840s.[53]

As it had so often, the Caddo propensity and need for a single powerful leader and spokesperson exerted itself. With the shattered remnants of the Kadohadacho chiefdom needing security and supplies of manufactured goods, leadership now passed to the Nadaco community of the old Hasinai chiefdom. By the early 1840s Nadaco chief Iesh, known as José María to the Texans and Americans, began to expand his influence. Soon the chiefs of other communities and the leaders of other Caddo factions, recognizing their dependence on Iesh, began deferring to him. Until his death in 1862, Iesh remained the most influential Caddo chief and spokesman for the people.[54]

As the Caddos' political situation shook itself out after the land cession, the Caddo people themselves tried to continue their centuries-old lifestyle. They lived in villages, planted maize, hunted deer and buffalo, and traded with whomever they could. Unfortunately, in Texas, the Caddos found themselves under constant pressure and attacks from suspicious Anglo-Texans. The Report of the Standing Committee on Indian Affairs, on 12 October 1837, described the Caddo situation in these terms:

> The *Caddo, Ioni, Anadarko, Abadoche* [Nabedache] among whom are dispersed the Ais and Nacogdoches Indians speak a similar language are descended from the old Caddo nation and with the exception of the

Caddo are natives of this country—They all understand and speak the Castilian language. They are about 225 in number and previous to their late Hostilities live in the County of Nacogdoches, some have returned to their homes but most of them are still with their squaws and Children on the Prairies united with the Hostile tribes that dwell there; about one half of these Indians are good marksmen all of them Hunt for a living and are on intimate terms with all the tribes of the Prairies. They are thought to be the greatest rogues and the most treacherous Indians on our frontier.[55]

With white Texans hating and distrusting the Caddos and other Indians, peace was impossible and security for Caddo families an illusion. Even with the help and support of Robert Simpson Neighbors, a sympathetic Texas Indian agent, Texas Rangers and Indian-hating Texas citizens often attacked Caddo individuals and homesteads, blaming them for just about any nearby Indian attack or raid. At the same time, Caddo farmers faced years of successive drought that shriveled their meager crops of corn. In 1849, when Agent Neighbors counted the Indians living in Texas, he reported that the Caddos, Ionis, and Nadacos totaled 1,500 with 280 warriors.[56]

In 1854, in an attempt to protect the Caddos from Texas citizens, all the Caddo communities and bands in Texas, along with communities of Wichitas, Delawares, and Tonkawas, were placed on what was called the Brazos River Indian Reservation, located on that river near its junction with Salt Creek, in present-day Young County, Texas. Here the Caddos lived in their beehive-shaped thatched houses, farmed, and tried to live in peace with the Texans. Despite their peaceful behavior and their roles as guides and auxiliaries to Texas Rangers fighting the Comanches, the Caddos could not escape persecution by Texans. To prevent a planned massacre by Texas citizens, in August 1859 Agent Neighbors led the Caddos out of Texas and into the Indian Territory, where they remain to this day.[57]

The Caddo land cession and the actions by Texas citizens broke any of the remaining kinship bonds that the Caddos and Euro-Americans had established so long before. The Caddos, once equals and valued allies to the French and Spanish, found themselves at the mercy of the U.S.

government. In the end, as they ceded their traditional lands to the United States and marched west to Texas, Kadohadacho chief Tarshar could lament that while the French and Spanish had always treated them like brothers, they had now lost all confidence in the Americans. The problem for the Caddos was not that they adopted strangers into their families, it was when strangers refused to become family. When family members did not uphold their obligations, things fell apart. And things did fall apart for the Caddos. Maybe they were too trusting or maybe it was just impossible for a kin-ordered mode of production to stand up to capitalism. But whatever the reason, these once mighty Mississippian chiefdoms had, by 1859, declined to just a small fraction of their huge population and land base. Even then, on their reservation in Indian territory, their disappointments did not end. But like most Native Americans on reservations, the Caddos found themselves alienated and fighting to retain what traditions they could.

7 // Conclusion

THERE is some ambiguity about when the Mississippian cultural tradition ended—that tradition associated in eastern North America with an ostentatious religion called the Southern Ceremonial Complex, ranked societies, powerful priest-chiefs ruling complex chiefdoms, and large, densely populated towns complete with temple mounds. It is possible to say that it ended in the fourteenth century, when mound-building ceased throughout most of the Southeast. Another end could be the mid–sixteenth century, when the destruction and diseases brought by Soto and Moscoso shattered many of the chiefdoms and initiated a horrendous depopulation that dramatically changed Southeastern Indian life and culture. A third date could be 1730, when the French defeated the Natchez Indians and their priest-chief, called the "Great Sun."

One date cannot be decided upon because many Mississippian characteristics continued to echo down through the centuries. So it was for the Caddos, who were peoples typical of the Mississippian cultural tradition and whose early history coincides perfectly with it. The rise of their culture in the eighth century corresponds to the beginning of the tradition. They built temple mounds, but like most Indian peoples of the Southeast they had ceased this activity by about 1350. The Soto expedition of the mid-1500s brought destruction and depopulation to the Caddos, while powerful Caddo priests disappeared about the same time as the Natchez's Great Sun. Nevertheless, Mississippian beliefs and traditions continued among the Caddos well until the early decades of the nineteenth century.

Those sharing a common history can develop a sense of unity, destiny, and greatness. The Caddos of the eighteenth and early nineteenth centuries—and even to this very day—remembered their glorious Mississippian past, when their great chiefdoms dominated the area and profoundly influenced the Indian peoples of the Southeast, Plains, and Southwest politically, economically, and religiously. Their history gave the Caddos a sense of ancientness and a feeling of superiority—a perspective accepted even by their neighbors, who respected them as old ones and grandfathers.

Reinforcing this sense of their historic superiority was a specific carry-over from the Mississippian cultural tradition: a reliance upon powerful chiefs. Their powerful, hereditary chiefs united eighteenth- and early-nineteenth-century Caddos spiritually, culturally, and politically. Although these chiefs may have lost their religious importance, they still acted as protectors and spokespersons for the Caddo peoples as they came into contact with Europeans and Americans. The Caddos' strategic location between the plains and forests and astride several major river systems and trails allowed the chiefs to control much of the flow of commodities through their area and thus shore up their prestige and power.

During the eighteenth century, the ancient Kadohadacho chiefdom gained influence and power because the Caddo people saw it as the most ancient chiefdom, one linking them to their splendid pre-fourteenth-century past. Caddo communities and subchiefs throughout Louisiana and Texas looked to the Great Chief of the Kadohadachos to be their spokesperson and protector. Already possessing great prestige in the region due to his ancient lineage, the Great Chief of the Kadohadachos solidified and expanded his power through the use of gifts, reciprocity, and kinship. Eventually, other peoples joined the Caddos in looking to the Kadohadacho chief for assistance. The French and Spanish, as they came to the Caddo area, quickly recognized the power the Great Chief wielded, which included the ability to create peace with neighboring Indian peoples and to control much of the hide and horse trade upon which the local European economy depended. With many warriors at his command, the Kadohadacho chief was a valuable ally and a feared potential enemy. The European colonial powers provided him with gifts and sent traders to Caddo villages to exchange valuable manufactured goods, such as firearms, for hides and horses. The flow of manufactured goods into the Caddo chiefdoms raised the prestige of all Caddo chiefs, particularly the Great Chief. Soon other Caddos from Texas, as well some Comanche, Wichita, and Attakapa communities, looked to the Great Chief of the Kadohadachos for protection, or at least a sure supply of goods.

Since the early Mississippian years the Caddos had traded with their neighbors. The Spanish and French demand for hides and horses fit perfectly with a lifestyle the Caddos had lived for centuries. As long as the hide and horse trade remained the foundation of European mercantile capitalism in that area, Caddo chiefs could retain their power. However, as American settlers entered the Caddo area in the early nineteenth century, farming eclipsed the hide and horse trade, and Caddo chiefs lost their leverage. Still, Dehahuit, the last Great Chief of the Caddos, managed to restrain the Americans and maintain Caddo power. Hailing from the ancient Caddo chiefdoms located at the Great Bend of the Red River, he was a direct tangible link to the Mississippian cultural tradition. Only after his death in 1833 could the United States eventually pressure the Caddos into signing away their land and moving into Mexican Texas. With his death, the Kadohadacho chiefdom shattered. In a major shift, leadership of the Caddos passed from the Cadodacho community of the Kadohadacho chiefdom to the Nadaco community of the old Hasinai chiefdom. But these were weaker chiefs, and no other Caddo chief from then on would ever have the prestige or power the Kadohadacho Great Chiefs had wielded.

One might argue that the Great Chief Dehahuit's death in 1833 brought about the actual end of the Mississippian cultural tradition among the Caddos. But even this date is as slippery as the rest, because some religious ceremonies stemming from the Mississippian years, such as the Green Corn festival, continued to be practiced. Even with the Caddos' removal to Texas in 1835 and then to Indian Territory in 1859, their lifeways remained somewhat similar. Only in the latter part of the nineteenth century, while settled on a reservation in present-day southwestern Oklahoma, did Caddo society undergo fundamental changes. Protestant and Catholic missionaries exerted tremendous pressure on them to become Christians and "civilized" according to American standards. Children attended schools where they learned domestic and mechanical arts. Caddos continued farming but also raised stock and hauled freight.

Around the start of the twentieth century, the United States government broke up the reservation and allotted individual plots of land to Caddo families. Though they had traveled a long road from when their chiefdoms dominated an entire region, the Caddos remained bound together as a people. At their tribal headquarters near Binger, Oklahoma, Caddo men and women to this day celebrate their history through ceremonial drummings and dances. Caddo women still wear the traditional dush-tooh head ornament as they perform the Turkey Dance, which recounts their magnificent past. It is through this and other dances that the muffled echoes of the Caddos' Mississippian cultural tradition can still be heard.

Pronunciation Key

Amayxoya – ah-may-sho-yah
Bidai – bee-dai
Caddí – cah-dee
Cadodacho – cah-doh-da-cho
Canaha – cah-nah-ha
Chaya – chah-yah
Conna – coh-nah
Dehahuit – Day-hah-weet
Doustioni – due-stee-oh-nee
Hasinai – ha-see-nai
Kadohadacho – ka-doh-hah-da-cho
Jumano – Huu-mon-oh
Kichai – kee-chai
Nabedache – Nah-bah-dah-chee
Nacogdoches – nack-uh-doh-chess
Nadaco – nah-dah-ko
Naguatex – na-wha-tesh
Natchitoches – nack-ih-tush
Tamma – tah-mah
Taovaya – tay-oh-vah-yah
Tejas – Tay-has
Tinhiouen – ten-ee-oo-an
Xinesí – she-ne-see
Yscani – iss-kan-nee

Notes

Abbreviations

AC	Archives des Colonies, Paris, France, Record Group C13
ADM	Bolton, *Athanase De Mézières*
ASP	American State Papers, Sterling Evans Library, Texas A&M University, College Station
BA	Bexar Archives, Sterling Evans Library, Texas A&M University, College Station
BL	Louisiana Collection, Bancroft Library, University of California, Berkeley
CAL	Caddo Agency Letters
CL	Rowland, *Letterbooks of W. C. C. Claiborne*
LSU	Natchitoches Parish Records, Hill Memorial Library, Louisiana State University, Baton Rouge
MPA	Mississippi Provincial Archives, French Dominion
NPCR	Natchitoches Parish Conveyance Records
NSU	Watson Library, Northwestern State University, Natchitoches, Louisiana
PPC	Papeles Procedentes de Cuba, Archivo General de Indias, Seville, Spain
PT	*Pichardo's Treaties*
SCRT	Statistical and Census Report of Texas
SMV	Kinnaird, *Spain in the Mississippi Valley*
TP	Territorial Papers

Preface

1. Perttula, "The Caddo Nation"; F. Todd Smith, *The Caddo Indians;* Cecile Elkins Carter, *Caddo Indians.*

1 // Introduction

1. Phillips and Brown, *Pre-Columbian Shell Engravings*, 1:19–21; Peterson, "A History of Excavations," 120.

2. James A. Robertson, "True Relation," 1:142–45.

3. Wolf, *Europe and the People without History*, 88–100; Sahlins, *Stone Age Economics*, 197.

4. Holder, *The Hoe and the Horse*, 136; Rollings, *The Osage*, 2–3.

2 // The Ancient Caddo Chiefdoms

1. Dorsey, *Traditions of the Caddo*, 7–8; Newkumet and Meredith, *Hasinai*, x, 4–7.

2. Neuman, *Louisiana Archaeology*, 86–87, 216, 281; Wyckoff and Baugh, "Hasinai Elites," 231; Rogers, "Patterns of Change," 221, 224, 237; Perttula, *"The Caddo Nation,"* 13.

3. Shaffer, *Native Americans*, 76–77; Krieger, "'Gilmore Corridor,'" 176–77.

4. Rogers, "Patterns of Change," 232, 240–41.

5. Rogers, "Patterns of Change," 232–33, 239; Peterson, "Spiro Mounds Sites," 114–15, 118; Shaffer, *Native Americans*, 76–77; Baugh, "Ecology and Exchange," 107; Krieger, *Culture Complexes*, 73.

6. Perttula, *"The Caddo Nation,"* 96.

7. A single family lived on a farmstead, or *ranchito;* several linked families made up a hamlet, or *ranchería.* Several hamlets surrounded the town, which was differentiated from the hamlets only by its larger size and population and by being the political and religious seat of the community. Some towns might possess earthen temple mounds, but not all did, especially as mound building came to an end, after the fourteenth century. Together the town and hamlets created an individual community or minor chiefdom. Later, Euro-Americans often referred to the communities as tribes or nations. Among the Caddos, a band of unoccupied land and hunting territory formed a boundary between each community, as well as between the major, multicommunity chiefdoms, such as the Kadohadacho and Hasinai (Perttula, *"The Caddo Nation,"* 146–47, 155, 159–60).

8. Perttula, *"The Caddo Nation,"* 85, 96; Woodall, "Cultural Ecology," 33, 49–52, 83; Neuman, *Louisiana Archaeology*, 218–19.

9. DePratter, *Chiefdoms*, 8; Marvin T. Smith, *Aboriginal Culture Change*, 3–4.

10. Casañas letter, 215–18; Wyckoff and Baugh, "Hasinai Elites," 234, 245; DePratter, *Chiefdoms*, 77–78.

11. Wyckoff and Baugh, "Hasinai Elites," 234; Casañas letter, 290–92.

12. DePratter, *Chiefdoms*, 77–78;

13. Casañas letter, 218–19, 299–300; DePratter, *Chiefdoms*, 126, 129–30, 138, 163–64; Woodall, "Cultural Ecology," 37–51; Wyckoff and Baugh, "Hasinai Elites," 235.

14. Wyckoff and Baugh, "Hasinai Elites," 234–35, 245; Espinosa letter, 175.

15. Casañas letter, 216.

16. Casañas letter, 218.

17. Wyckoff and Baugh, "Hasinai Elites," 234–35, 245.

18. Casañas letter, 216; Espinosa letter, 175; Wyckoff and Baugh, "Hasinai Elites," 230–31; Urban, "Social Organizations," 182–83; DePratter, *Chiefdoms,* 82–84; Swanton, *Source Material,* 164–65.

19. Gaspar Solís, quoted in Swanton, *Source Material,* 173; Hudson, *Southeastern Indians,* 110.

20. Casañas letter, 216; Espinosa letter, 154–55, 171.

21. Swanton, *Source Material,* 49.

22. Espinosa letter, 175–76; Wyckoff and Baugh, "Hasinai Elites," 235.

23. Espinosa letter, 154–55; 216.

24. Casañas letter, 217; Espinosa letter, 156.

25. Holder, *The Hoe and the Horse,* 36–37.

26. Morfí, quoted in Swanton, *Source Material,* 164; Kniffen, Gregory, Stokes, *Historic Indian Tribes,* 226; Cecile Elkins Carter, *Caddo Indians,* 382 n. 40.

27. Swanton, *Source Material,* 161–65; Perttula, *"The Caddo Nation,"* 16; Stoddard, *Sketches,* 413.

28. Parsons, *Notes,* 10, 26–31; Stoddard, *Sketches,* 412.

29. Talon interrogation, in Weddle, *La Salle,* 232–33, 254–55; Joutel's journal 1:148–49; Casañas letter, 30, 215; Griffith, "Hasinai Indians," 48–51; Neuman, *Louisiana Archaeology,* 255; Rogers, "Patterns of Change," 230.

30. Joutel's Journal, 148–49; Neuman, *Louisiana Archaeology,* 247–51; Holder, *The Hoe and the Horse,* 57; Manzanet, "Carta," 281.

31. Helen Tanner, "Communication Systems," 8.

32. Rogers, "Patterns of Change," 224, 231.

33. Tanner, "Communication Systems," 12–13; Krieger, "'Gilmore Corridor,'" 172.

34. Tanner, "Communication Systems," 13; Perttula, *"The Caddo Nation,"* 26.

35. Tanner, "Communications Systems," 13.

36. Spielmann, "Nonhierarchical Societies," 4–5.

37. Peterson, "Spiro Mounds Sites," 114–20; Phillips and Brown, *Pre-Columbian Shell Engravings,* 1:9, 16–20; Rogers, "Patterns of Change," 232–33.

38. Rogers, "Patterns of Change," 234–35, 238–39, 241–42; Spielmann, "Nonhierarchical Societies," 4–5.

39. Peterson, "Spiro Mounds Sites," 118–19; Phillips and Brown, *Pre-Columbian Shell Engravings,* 1:20–21; Brose, "Ceremonial Complex," 29.

40. Hudson, *Southeastern Indians,* 84–89; Neuman, *Louisiana Archaeology,* 227; Shaffer, *Native Americans,* 55–56; Muller, "Southern Cult," 14–18.

41. Peterson, "Spiro Mounds Site," 118–19; Neuman, "Ceremonial Complex Artifacts," 122–24; Krieger, *Culture Complexes,* 73.

42. Krieger, "'Gilmore Corridor,'" 169

43. Krieger, "'Gilmore Corridor,'" 171, 176–77.

44. Jennings, "American Frontiers," 355–56, and *Founders of America,* 56–67.

45. Neuman, *Louisiana Archaeology,* 227; Hudson, *Southeastern Indians,* 88–89.

46. Wyckoff, "Adaptive Strategies," 7–12; Perttula, *"The Caddo Nation,"* 108–9.

47. Woodall, "Cultural Ecology," iv, 183; Wyckoff, "Adaptive Strategies," 515, 522, 524, 530, 533–34; Peterson, "Spiro Mounds Site," 119; Phillips and Brown, *Pre-Columbian Shell Engravings,* 1:21.

48. Krieger, *Cultural Complexes,* 255; Wilcox, "Changing Contexts," 131, 146–47; Vehik and Baugh, "Prehistoric Plains Trade," 259; Baugh, "Ecology and Exchange," 120–21.

49. Baugh, "Ecology and Exchange," 114–15, 125; Lintz, "Panhandle-Pueblo Interactions," 89–91, 94; Krieger, *Cultural Complexes,* 73; Baugh, "Southern Plains Societies," 157–59, 160–64; Spielmann, "Nonhierarchical Societies," 4–5.

50. Perttula, *"The Caddo Nation,"* 96–97; Wilcox, "Changing Contexts," 143–44, 146; Baugh, "Ecology and Exchange," 107, 114–15; Lintz, "Panhandle-Pueblo Interactions," 89–91, 94; Baugh, "Southern Plains Societies," 160; Krieger, *Cultural Complexes,* 207.

51. Krieger, *Cultural Complexes,* 193, 205; Wilcox, "Changing Contexts," 146, 152–53; Gregory, "Caddoan Archaeology," 204–5.

52. Baugh, "Ecology and Exchange," 121; Wilcox, "Changing Contexts," 144.

53. Baugh, "Ecology and Exchange," 125; Wilcox, "Changing Contexts," 131–32, 146–47, 152–53; Lintz, "Panhandle-Pueblo Interactions," 104–5.

54. James A. Robertson, "True Relation," 1:142–45; Hudson, "De Soto Expedition,", 95–96.

55. James A. Robertson, "True Relation," 1:145, 146–49; Hudson, "De Soto Expedition," 96–98; Worth, "Island of Florida," 1:244.

56. James A. Robertson, "True Relation," 1:140–41.

57. Marvin T. Smith, *Aboriginal Culture Change,* 59; Perttula, *"The Caddo Nation,"* 85–87; Hudson, *Southeastern Indians,* 41, 97–119; Swanton, *Source Material,* fig. 1, 12–13.

58. The term *Kadohadacho* will be used to designate the whole chiefdom, while *Cadodacho* will be used to designate the community of that name; Morfí, *History of Texas,* 88; ADM, 1:21–22; Hodge, *Handbook,* 1:179, 638; Woodall, "Cultural Ecology," 15–16; Perttula, *"The Caddo Nation,"* 165.

59. Hodge, *Handbook,* 1:179; Bolton, *The Hasinai,* 31, 63–64; Woodall, "Cultural Ecology," 15–16.

60. Swanton, *Source Material,* fig. 1, 12–13; Newkumet and Meredith, *Hasinai,* x; Tonty memoir, 1:72–73.

61. ADM, 1:23–24; Hodge, *Handbook,* 2:947–50.

62. Krieger, *Cultural Complexes,* 207.

63. Kelley, "Juan Sabeata," 982, 991–92; Hickerson, *The Jumanos*, xxiii–xxiv.

64. Kelley, "Juan Sabatea," 983, 988, 990; Covey, *Cabeza de Vaca's Adventures*, 71; Wilcox, "Changing Contexts," 145; Baugh, "Ecology and Exchange," 123;

65. Kelley, "Juan Sabeata," 984–88; Gregory, "Eighteenth Century Caddoan Archaeology," 236, 289; Joutel's journal, 146; W. Raymond Wood, "Plains Trade," 99, 100, 104–6; Wyckoff, "Caddoan Cultural Area, 47; Talon interrogation, in Weddle, *La Salle*, 256.

66. Kelley, "Juan Sabeata," 981–83, 988–90.

67. Kelley, "Juan Sabeata," 989, 984, 987; report of Cruzati, Oct. 1683, in PT, 1:137–39.

68. Perttula, "*The Caddo Nation,*" 117, 183, 185, 195–98; DePratter, *Chiefdoms*, 162; Marvin T. Smith, *Aboriginal Culture Change*, 97.

69. Quoted in Kelley, "Juan Sabeata," 989.

3 // The Horse, Gun, and Deerskin Trades

1. Tonty memoir, 57; on gifts and kinship, see Sahlins, *Stone Age Economics*, 186; Anderson, *Kinsmen*, xi; W. Raymond Wood, "Plains Trade," 104; Mauss, *The Gift*, 10–11; Lévi-Strauss, *Elementary Structures*, 55.

2. Vaugine to governor, 2 May 1783, *legajo* 196, doc. 469, PPC; Talon interrogation, in Weddle, *La Salle*, 251; Sahlins, *Stone Age Economics*, 193–99; Mauss, *The Gift*, 79; Lévi-Strauss, *Elementary Structures*, 60, 67.

3. Spielmann, "Nonhierarchical Societies," 4–5; Lévi-Strauss, *Elementary Structures*, 57; Swanton, *Source Materials*, 170–74, 219–21; Casañas letter, 212; Sahlins, *Stone Age Economics*, 193–99.

4. Wolf, *Europe and the People without History*, 88–100; Sahlins, *Stone Age Economics*, 197; Antoine to Mon Frere, 3 Apr. 1792, *legajo* 188C, PPC; de Blanc to Fihiol, 20 Oct. 1795, *legajo* 213, PPC.

5. Foik, "Ramón's Diary," 19–21; Woodall, "Cultural Ecology," 36.

6. Parsons, *Notes on the Caddo*, 28.

7. Joutel's journal, 162–63; Tonty memoir, 73, 76; Talon interrogation, in Weddle, *La Salle*, 231, 235–36, 238–39, 251; Parsons, *Notes on the Caddo*, 54.

8. Joutel's journal, 150, 154–55, 162–63.

9. For a discussion of power transfer and sex between Indian women and foreigners, see Gutiérrez, *When Jesus Came*, 17, 40, 50–51.

10. Jennings, "American Frontiers," 353; Foik, "Ramón's Diary," 20.

11. Joutel's journal, 171–72, 146–48.

12. Talon interrogation, in Weddle, *La Salle*, 251; Kniffen, Gregory, and Stokes, *Historic Indian Tribes*, 65; Sahlins, *Stone Age Economics*, 191–99.

13. Talon interrogation, in Weddle, *La Salle*, 251; Galloway, "'The Chief Who Is Your Father,'" 254–78.

14. Hubert to the council, 1717, MPA, 2:249–50.

15. Gregory, "Caddoan Archaeology," 190, 233–34; Wyckoff, "Adaptive Strategies," 522; McWilliams, *Penicaut Narrative*, 100–101, 145–46.

16. La Harpe, *Historical Journal*, 134; La Harpe, "Memoire of Louisiane," 8 Aug. 1763, B-1-399, AC.

17. Usner, *Indians, Settlers, and Slaves*, 258–59; Kniffen, Gregory, and Stokes, *Historic Indian Tribes*, 97; du Pratz, *History*, 311, 318.

18. Corbin, "Spanish-Indian Interaction," 269–79.

19. La Harpe, *Historical Journal*, 35–38, 134; Barrios to Count Gigedo, 30 Nov. 1754, reel 9, BA; La Harpe, "Memoire of Louisiane," 8 Aug. 1763, B-1-399, AC; De Mézières to Unzaga, 20 Feb. 1778, ADM, 2:176.

20. Secoy, *Changing Military Patterns*, 2–5, n. 3.

21. Joutel's journal, 150, 159–61.

22. Shelby, "St. Denis's Declaration," 178, 182; Foik, "Ramón's Diary," 19–21; Griffith, "Hasinai Indians," 138–39.

23. Reports of Orobio Bazterra, 1 Oct. 1745, reel 8, BA; Aguayo to Olivan Rebolledo, 27 Jan. 1724, PT, 3:411; report of Gonzalez, 17 June 1737, PT, 1:248.

24. Report of Vélez, 13 Apr. 1749, PT, 3:303; deposition of Lozoia, 20 July 1751, reel 9, BA.

25. Silva to the viceroy, 21 July 1774, ADM, 2:73–75; De Mézières to the viceroy, 20 Feb. 1778, ADM, 2:176; declaration of Grappe, 22 Sept. 1805, ASP, 2:693–94; Aubra Lee, "Fusils," 68.

26. Berlandier, *Indians of Texas*, 48, 53.

27. Tonty memoir, 1:73; La Harpe, *Historical Journal*, 137, 139– 41; letter of Derbanne, 22 Oct. 1723, C-4-102, AC; Perttula, *"The Caddo Nation,"* 192.

28. Report of Orobio Bazterra, 1 Oct. 1745, reel 8, BA; Guadiana to Muñoz, 26 Mar. 1797, reel 27, BA.

29. Deposition of Tejas Chiefs by Fr. Calahorra, 30 July 1765, reel 10, BA; Bucareli to Ripperda, 7 Oct. 1772, reel 11, BA; Bolton, *Texas*, 86–91.

30. Kerlérec to Navarette, 19 Aug. 1760, reel 9, BA.

31. Deposition of Chirinos, 31 Dec. 1761, reel 9, BA.

32. De Barrios to Count Gigedo, 30 Nov. 1754, reel 9, BA; Navarrete to Amarillas, 6 Dec. 1759, reel 9, BA; "Gifts which the Reverend Fr. J. Calahorra is taking to the Indians leaders," 1 Oct. 1762, reel 10, BA; deposition of Gallardo, 24 Oct. 1762, reel 10, BA; Cruillas to Navarrete, 18 Jan. 1764, reel 10, BA.

33. "List of the effects which should be given to the three Indian nations of the Post of Natchitoches," O'Reilly to De Mézières, 22 Jan. 1770, ADM, 1:132–34; "Lists of Gifts for Grand Caddo, Natchitoches, Petit Caddo, and Yatasí," 1783, *legajo* 2360, doc. 318, PPC.

34. Contract of Piseros with De Mézières, 3 Feb. 1770, ADM, 1:143–46; "Agreement made with the Indian Nations in Assembly," 21 Apr. 1770, *legajo* 110, doc. 220A, PPC.

35. "List of Prices of Merchandise which Bouet Laffitte traded at the Petit Caddo Village," 1 Sept. 1774, book 6, NPCR; "Account of the Load on the Barge of Sr. Pavie Going to Natchitoches," 1 Apr. 1776, book 10, doc. 1174, NPCR; Vaugine to Piernas, 20 Nov. 1781, *legajo* 194, doc. 747, PPC; interrogation of Morvant, 30 Nov. 1783, *legajo* 200, doc. 603, PPC; Filhiol to Cachou, 28 Feb. 1784, *legajo* 197, doc. 490, PPC.

36. La Harpe, *Historical Journal*, 137–41; De Mézières to Unzaga, 16 Feb. 1776, ADM, 2:120–21; Cabello to the governor of Louisiana, 15 Dec. 1783, SMV, 2:94; Cortes to Baron Carondelet, 22 Mar. 1792, SMV, 3:18–19.

37. De Mézières to the viceroy, 20 Feb. 1778, ADM, 2:174–75; De Mézières to the viceroy, 20 Feb. 1778, ADM, 2:172–86; Cabello to Piernas, 13 Jan. 1783, SMV, 2:69–70; Muñoz to Carondelet, 20 Apr. 1794, SMV, 3:274–75; Cordova to Carondelet, 26 July 1794, SMV, 3:328–29.

38. Bolton, *Texas*, 80–87.

39. Cabello to Piernas, 13 Jan. 1783, SMV, 2:69–70; Muñoz to Carondelet, 30 Apr. 1794, SMV, 3:274–75.

40. Vaugine to Miró, 28 Feb. 1783, *legajo* 196, doc. 386, PPC; Ybarbo to Vaugine, 20 Sept. 1783, *legajo* 196, doc. 578, PPC; diary of Ybarbo, 19 Oct. 1783, *legajo* 70A, doc. 182, PPC; Pacheco to de Blanc, 20 Dec. 1789, SMV, 2:303.

41. Letter of Derbanne, 22 Oct. 1723, C-4-102, AC; "Proceedings against Don Francisco Larios," 31 Dec. 1746, reel 8, BA; memoir on the services of Bienville, 1725, MPA, 3:490; Sibley, "Red River," 60; McWilliams, *Pénicaut Narrative*, 193–95; Shelby, "St. Denis's Declaration," 172; Bridges and De Ville, "Natchitoches," 257; Kniffen, Gregory, and Stokes, *Historic Indian Tribes*, 71, 110; Gregory, "Caddoan Archaeology," 267; Corbin, "Spanish-Indian Interaction," 270–71, 274; Perttula, "The Caddo Nation," 168.

42. Neuman, *Louisiana Archaeology*, 252–53; Joutel's journal, 146–47, 154; Griffith, "Hasinai Indians," 147–48.; Fox, *Traces of Texas History*, 78–79.

43. Tonty memoir, 73, 74, 77; Secoy, *Changing Military Patterns*, 22.

44. Joutel's journal, 146–47, 154; Talon interrogation, in Weddle, *La Salle*, 229–30, 256; *Pénicaut Narrative*, 139.

45. La Harpe, *Historical Journal*, 135, 148, 179; statement of Altamira, 20 June 1744, PT, 3:415; Flores, *Anthony Glass*, 8; Jackson, *Los Mesteños*, 9–11.

46. Aguayo to Rebolledo, 27 Jan. 1724, PT, 3:411; *Pénicaut Narrative*, 138; deposition of Chirinos, 31 Dec. 1761, reel 9, BA; La Harpe, *Historical Journal*, 104–6.

47. Diary of events, 1 Feb. 1725, A-8-180, AC; Bienville to Maurepas, 16 Feb. 1737, MPA, 1:333; Bienville to the minister, 31 Oct. 1738, 1-23-95, AC; De Mézières to Unzaga, 16 Feb. 1776, ADM, 2:120; Sibley to Governor Claiborne, 10 Oct. 1803, TP, 9:75.

48. Ybarbo to Vaugine, 20 Sept. 1783, *legajo* 196, doc. 577, PPC; Corbin, "Spanish-Indian Interaction," 272; Usner, *Indians, Settlers, and Slaves*, 260–61; Griffith, "Hasinai Indians," 148.

49. Statement of Barré *et al.,* 8 June 1770, *legajo* 110, doc. 131, PPC; De Mézières to the viceroy, 20 Feb. 1778, ADM, 2:172–86; trade instructions to Le Blanc, 8 Oct. 1783, *legajo* 196, doc. 650, PPC; Cabello to the governor of Louisiana, 15 Dec. 1783, SMV, 2:94.

50. Joutel's journal, 160–61; La Harpe, *Historical Journal,* 142, 145–46, 148; La Harpe, "Memoire of Louisiane," 8 Aug. 1763, B–1–399, AC.

51. "Declaration of Indian slaves owned by three Frenchmen," 17 Apr. 1770, *legajo* 188A, PPC; De Mézières to Unzaga, 20 May 1770, ADM, 1:166–68; Silva to the viceroy, 21 July 1774, ADM, 2:74–76; inventory of goods by de Blanc, 14 July 1776, book 8, doc. 1129, NPCR; Dayna Bowker Lee, "Indian Slavery," 30–33, 68–70; Mills, *Natchitoches Colonials,* 3–4, 7–8; Kniffen, Gregory, and Stokes, *Historic Indian Tribes,* 94.

52. Talon interrogation, in Weddle, *La Salle,* 233; Unzaga to De Mézières, 6 Apr. 1771, ADM, 1:247–48; inventory of goods of Marcollay, 20 Jan. 1772, book 4, doc. 719, NPCR; "Statement of Accounts of Nicolay Fourmier and Francois Doucet," 20 Apr. 1776, book 10, doc. 1165, NPCR; De Blanc to Miró, 15 Jan. 1790, SMV, 2:294.

53. *Pénicaut Narrative,* 112; Wyckoff, "Caddoan Adaptive Strategies," 519; Walter V. Robertson, "Population Dynamics," 5; Stransky, "Deer Habitat," 43.

54. "Journal of an Expedition up the Red River, 1773–1774, by J. Gaignard," 10 Nov. 1777, ADM, 2:83–100; Brooks to White, 8 July 1831, CAL; Berlandier, *Indians of Texas,* 45–46; Gregory, "Caddoan Archaeology," 238–50; diary of Fragoso, in Loomis and Nasatir, *Pedro Vial,* 55; report of Orobio Bazterra, 1 Oct. 1745, reel 8, BA; deposition of Chirinos, 31 Dec. 1761, reel 9, frame 954–55, BA; letter of Vaugine, 8 Oct. 1783, *legajo* 196, doc. 613, PPC.

56. Orobio Bazterra, 1 Oct. 1745, reel 8, BA; Pavie to Captain Bormé, 27 May 1776, book 10, doc. 1174, NPCR; De Mézières to Unzaga, 20 Feb. 1778, ADM, 2:176.

57. Cachupín's interrogation of Fierro, 13 Apr. 1749, PT, 3:303; Altamira's interrogation of Malec, 26 June 1751, PT, 3:347–48; deposition of Chirinos, 31 Dec. 1761, reel 9, BA; contract of Piseros with De Mézières, 3 Feb. 1770, ADM, 1:143–46.

58. Altamira's interrogation of Malec, 26 June 1751, PT, 3:347–48; declaration of Laffitte, 7 May 1770, book 3, doc. 640, NPCR; De Mézières to Unzaga, 16 Feb. 1776, ADM, 2:120–21; memoir of Roze, 1 Aug. 1798, DeVille Collection, folder 4, 2-E-2, NSU; declaration of Roban, 3 Oct. 1805, ASP, Foreign Relations, 2:694–695; report of the detachment of Nacogdoches, 30 June 1808, reel 38, BA; report of the detachment of Nacogdoches, 31 Aug. 1808, reel 38, BA; "Note of the merchandise belonging to the company of E. Murphy with Barr y Davenport which was found at the home of the deceased E. Murphy, Natchitoches," n.d., folder 55, box 13, 5–43, "Barr, Davenport and Murphy: 1808–1810," LSU; Surrey, *Commerce of Louisiana,* 356, 357–58; Berlandier, *Indians of Texas,* 47 n. 27; Newsom, "History of Deer," 1.

59. Officially a *livre* was worth about twenty cents, equaling one-fifth of a *piastre* or dollar. A *sol,* or *sou,* was one-twentieth of a livre, or about one cent. While

officially five *livres* equalled a dollar, due to price fluctuations and differing values between French Louisiana and the United States, a *livre* could be considered to equal a dollar (McDermott, *Glossary,* 94–95; contract of Piseros with De Mézières, 3 Feb. 1770, ADM, 1:143–46; "Engagement de Louis Rondin pour la traitte au S. Roujot," 13 July 1773, book 5, doc. 843, NPCR; partnership of Morvant and Armant, 11 Nov. 1775, book 8, doc. 1057, NPCR; outfitting of Morvant, 5 Oct. 1780, book 16, doc. 1504, NPCR.

60. Vaudreuil to Maurepas, 30 Oct. 1745, MPA, 4:248–52; Morvant to the governor, 14 Aug. 1782, *legajo* 196, doc. 566, PPC; declaration of Tessier, 18 Feb. 1783, *legajo* 196, doc. 384, PPC; statement of Fortin, 18 Feb. 1783, *legajo* 196, doc. 382, PPC; Vaugine to Miró, 23 Feb. 1783, *legajo* 196, doc. 386, PPC; diary of Ybarbo, 8 July 1783, *legajo* 70A, doc. 182, PPC; Sibley to Governor Claiborne, 10 Oct. 1803, TP, 9:75.

61. Laffitte to the governor, c. Dec. 1784, *legajo* 197, doc. 597, PPC; "Account of the hides that the Caddo Savages owe," 12 Aug. 1789, doc. 2148, book 20, NPCR; De Blanc to Carondelet, 18 Aug. 1792, *legajo* 206, PPC.

62. Morvant to Vaugine, 18 July 1781, *legajo* 194, doc. 713, PPC; Sahlins, *Stone Age Economics,* 196; Albers, "Symbiosis," 98–100.

63. Request of LeMeé, 27 June 1774, book 7, doc. 977, NPCR; "Armand's Order against Gaspard Fiole and Jean Bosquet," 14 Dec. 1775, book 5, doc. 963, NPCR; inventory of goods by De Blanc, 14 July 1776, book 8, doc. 1129, NPCR; statement of credits by De La Chaise and St. Denis, 2 Oct. 1776, book 8, doc. 1129, NPCR; letters by Morvant, 18 Oct. 1782, *legajo* 196, doc. 566, PPC; interview with Morvant, 30 Nov. 1783, *legajo* 200, doc. 603, PPC; Lamalaty et al. to Vaugine, 6 Aug. 1784, *legajo* 197, doc. 488, PPC; Vaugine to the governor, 20 Aug. 1784, *legajo* 197, doc. 507, PPC; "Account of the sale of merchandise to Monsieur Joseph Capruan," 24 Feb. 1785, book 20, doc. 214B, NPCR; Laffitte, "Account of the hides that the Caddo Savages owe," 12 Aug. 1785, book 20, doc. 214B, NPCR; Barr to Cordero, 28 Apr. 1808, reel 38, BA.

64. O'Reilly to Arriaga, 17 Oct. 1769, SMV, 1:96–99; Miró to De Blanc, 24 June 1788, SMV, 2:256; Griffith, "Hasinai Indians," 143.

65. Ulloa to O'Conor, 1768, ADM, 1:127–29.

66. Interrogation of Morvant by De Mézières, Natchitoches, 11 May 1770, *legajo* 110, doc. 164, PPC; statement of Barre et al., 8 June 1770, *legajo* 110, doc. 131, PPC; Villiers to governor, 20 July 1773, *legajo* 189A, PPC.

4 // Challenges to the Chiefdoms

1. Perttula, "*The Caddo Nation,*" 85–87.

2. Delanglez, *Journal of Jean Cavelier,* 101–2; Swanton, *Source Material,* fig. 1, 12–13.

3. Joutel's journal, 115, 129; Delanglez, *Journal of Jean Cavelier,* 73–74; Alonso de Leon, 1689, PT, 1:160–61.

4. Casañas letter, 303, 294–95.

5. La Harpe, *Historical Journal*, 223; Bienville, "Memoir on Louisiana," New Orleans, 1726, MPA, 3:429–30; De Mézières to governor general, 7 Nov. 1777, *legajo* 112, doc. 282, PPC; Bridges and De Ville, "Natchitoches," 255; Peter H. Wood, "Changing Population," 83; Ewers, "Influence of Epidemics," 107–12.

6. Ralph A. Smith, "Journey of Bénard de la Harpe," 85; Bienville, "Memoir on Louisiana," 1726, MPA, 3:429–30; report of the council at San Antonio de Béxar, 5 Jan. 1778, ADM, 2:165–66.

7. Mills, *Natchitoches 1729–1803*,146–50; De Mézières to the viceroy, 20 Feb. 1778, ADM, 2:173; De Mézières to Galvez, May 1779, ADM, 2:250 n. 303.

8. Vaugine, "Recensement des Nations Sauvages," Sept. 1780, *legajo* 193A, PPC, Holmes Collection, reel 10, NSU; Vaugine to De Croix, 13 Mar. 1783, *legajo* 196, doc. 396, PPC; Vaugine to Miró, 25 Mar. 1783, *legajo* 196, doc. 407, PPC.

9. Sibley, "Indians Tribes," 66–67; Sibley to Claiborne, 10 Oct. 1803, TP, 9:75–76.

10. Sibley, "Indian Tribes," 68–70, 79–80.

11. Filhiol to Miró, Ouachita, 16 Mar. 1790, SMV, 2:314; De Blanc to Miró, 17 Mar. 1790, SMV, 2:316; De Blanc to Miró, 4 May 1790, SMV, 2:335; "Information as to the Indian Nations of the Province of Texas," Davenport to Salcedo, 1808, reel 39, BA; Sibley, "Indian Tribes," 66–86.

12. Perrier and La Chaise to directors of the Company of the Indies, 25 Mar. 1729, MPA, 2:636–37.

13. Mills, *Natchitoches 1729–1803*, docs. 340, 342; Higginbotham, *Old Mobile*, 444–45; Lee, "Indian Slavery," 33, 108; Sibley, "Indian Tribes," 80; declaration of Grappe, 22 Sept. 1805, ASP, Foreign Relations, 2:693–94; Mills, "Mézières-Trichel-Grappe," 41–43.

14. Joutel's journal, 150, 154–56, 162–63; Parsons, *Notes on the Caddo*, 24.

15. Saint Denis *fils* complaint to De Villiers, 17 July 1773, book 5, doc. 833, NPCR; Lee, "Indian Slavery," 90–92.

16. Lee, "Indian Slavery," 90–92.

17. See 1793, 1799, 1805 Nacogdoches censuses and "Sources Documenting the Blacks in Texas, 1603–1803," in SCRT.

18. Sibley to the secretary of war, 20 Mar. 1810, TP, 9:878–79; Kniffen, Gregory, and Stokes, *Historic Indian Tribes*, 94; Dan Flores, *Jefferson*, 115–18; Mills, *Natchitoches 1729–1803*, docs. 9, 27, 40, 41, 58, 66, 74, 103, 119, 205, 207, 208, 216, 218, 235, 239, 325, 340, 342, 347, 348, 370, 371.

19. Valliere to Filhiol, 10 Sep. 1789, SMV, 2:280–81; Kniffen, Gregory, and Stokes, *Historic Indian Tribes*, 63, 89; De Mézières to Unzaga, 20 May 1770, ADM, 1:165.

20. Flores, *Jefferson*, 131, 131–32 n. 14.

21. Morvant to Vaugine, 14 Aug. 1782, *legajo* 195, doc. 615, PPC; declaration of Grappe, 22 Sept. 1805, ASP, Foreign Relations 2:693–94; declaration of Grappe, 30 July 1816, Melrose Collection, bound vol. 9, 202, NSU; Maynes to Martinez, 10 Nov.

1820, reel 65, BA; petition of the Caddo Indians, 28 Jan. 1835, CAL; Dayna Bowker Lee, "François Grappe," 53, 57, 59–65; Parsons, *Notes on the Caddo,* 68–69; Flores, *Jefferson,* 131 n. 14, 131–32, 134, 140, 140 n. 24; Mills, *Natchitoches Colonials,* 106; Dorsey, *Traditions of the Caddo,* 17; Kniffen, Gregory, and Stokes, *Historic Indian Tribes,* 63, 89. Lee, "Indian Slavery," 15; Mills, "Mézières-Trichel-Grappe," 28–34; Everett, *Texas Cherokees,* 37.

22. Michel to Rouillé, 23 Sept. 1752, MPA, 5:115–17; Kerlérec to Rouillé, 20 Aug. 1753, MPA, 5:133.

23. Memoir on the services of Bienville, 1725, MPA, 3:490; Sibley to Dearborn, 10 Apr. 1805, Melrose Collection, bound vol. 3, NSU; Kniffen, Gregory, and Stokes, *Historic Indian Tribes,* 71, 110; Gregory, "Caddoan Archaeology," 267.

24. Report by St. Denis (the Younger), 18 Aug. 1768, SMV, 1:65–69; Hackett, PT, 1:393; De Mézières to Unzaga, 21 Aug. 1770, ADM, 1:180–82; De Mézières to Unzaga, 1777, *legajo* 2358, doc. 349, PPC; Vaugine to the governor, 20 May 1781, *legajo* 192, doc. 914, PPC; Vaugine to Piernas, 24 May 1781, *legajo* 194, doc. 673, PPC; declaration of Labadia, St. Louis, 5 July 1782, SMV, 2:23; "Accounts Owed by Bouet Laffitte to Monsieur Capuran," 12 Aug. 1785, book 20, doc. 214B, NPCR.

25. Ralph A. Smith, "Journey of Bénard de la Harpe," 75; La Harpe, *Historical Journal,* 134; minutes of the Council of Commerce of Louisiana, 26 Oct. 1719, MPA, 3:267–68; "Sale of Land by Tsaoua Camtê to Manuel Trichele," 26 Mar. 1778, book 12, doc. 1279, NPCR.

26. An *arpent* was a unit of measure equal to about 180 feet. A *piastre* can be considered equal to a United States dollar. De Mézières to Unzaga, 10 Jan. 1776, *legajo* 112, doc. 237, PPC; De Mézières to Galvez, May 1779, ADM, 2:252; lists of gifts for the Grand Caddo, Natchitoches, Petit Caddo, and Yatasí, 1783, *legajo* 2360, doc. 318, PPC; "Sale of land by Hyamoc to Jean Baptiste La Berry," 13 June 1780, book 16, doc. 1491, NPCR; Rousseau and De Blanc to Miró, 20 Mar. 1787, SMV, 2:198–99; statement of Peña, 20 Aug. 1787, Juanita Henry Collection, bound vol. 167, 457, NSU; Antoine to Mon Frere, 3 Apr. 1792, *legajo* 188C, doc. 132, PPC.

27. José Ugarte, "Results at the site of Nacogdoches and Jurisdiction to the Province of Texas," 1 Aug. 1804, reel 32 BA; order of Viana, 6 Mar. 1806, reel 34, BA; Cabello, 1783 Census of Texas, SCRT; 1787 census of Natchitoches, in Mills, *Natchitoches Colonials,* 45–62.

28. Perttula, *"The Caddo Nation,"* 168, 199, 217.

29. Sandoval to St. Denis, 13 Mar. 1736, PT, 3:503; Gregory, "Caddoan Archaeology," 250–51; Griffith, "Hasinai Indians," 151; Parsons, *Notes on the Caddo,* 32; Berlandier, *Indians of Texas,* 48.

30. Rollings, *The Osage,* 5–7.

31. Miró, "A Description of Louisiana," 12 Dec. 1785, SMV, 2:159–67; Rollings, *The Osage,* 6–7, 136–39.

32. La Harpe, *Historical Journal,* 137, 142–43.

33. Périer to Maurepas, Apr. 1730, MPA, 4:33–34; letter of Leaumon, 27 May 1754, in Portre-Bobinski, *Natchitoches,* 88–91.

34. Din and Nasatir, *Imperial Osages,* 47; Holder, *The Hoe and the Horse,* 78; Rollings, *The Osage,* 7, 126–28; Bossu to Douin, 22 Feb. 1771, in *New Travels,* 81.

35. De Mézières to Unzaga, 20 May 1770, ADM, 1:166–68.

36. De Mézières to Unzaga, 29 Nov. 1770, ADM, 1:193–95.

37. De Mézières to Unzaga, 29 Nov. 1770, ADM, 1:193–95.

38. De Mézières to Unzaga, 27 June 1770, ADM, 1:202–3; De Mézières to Unzaga, 21 Aug. 1770, ADM, 1:182; De Mézières to Unzaga, 10 Feb. 1773, ADM, 2:24–25; De Mézières to the governor, 4 Mar. 1777, *legajo* 112, doc. 257, PPC; Din and Nasatir, *Imperial Osages,* 81–82 n. 51.

39. De Villiers to the governor, 26 Jan. 1774, *legajo* 189A, doc. 760, PPC; De Mézières to the governor general, 4 Mar. 1777, *legajo* 112, doc. 257, PPC; statement of Vaugine, 4 Aug. 1784, *legajo* 197, doc. 482, PPC; Din and Nasatir, *Imperial Osages,* 88–89, 92–93; Rollings, *The Osage,* 142–43.

40. De Villiers to the governor, 26 Jan. 1774, *legajo* 189A, doc. 760, PPC; ADM 2:130 n. 150.

41. De Mézières to the governor, 1779, *legajo* 91, PPC; Que Te Sain to Galvez, 4 Nov. 1780, BL; Din and Nasatir, *Imperial Osages,* 105–6.

42. De Mézières to the viceroy, 20 Feb. 1778, ADM, 2:175; Vaugine to Piernas, 20 May 1781, *legajo* 94, doc. 665, PPC; Din and Nasatir, *Imperial Osages,* 137–38.

43. Vaugine to Piernas, 20 May 1781, *legajo* 94, doc. 665, PPC; Vaugine to Miró, 6 June 1781, *legajo* 14, doc. 471, PPC; Vaugine to Miró, 14 June 1781, *legajo* 94, doc. 682, PPC; Vaugine to Miró, 25 June 1781, *legajo* 94, doc. 697, PPC; Vaugine to Miró, 2 July 1781, *legajo* 94, doc. 703, PPC; Morvant to Vaugine, 18 July 1781, *legajo* 94, doc. 713, PPC; Vaugine to Piernas, 15 Sept. 1781, *legajo* 94, doc. 729, PPC; Vaugine to Piernas, 21 Sept. 1781, *legajo* 94, doc. 734, PPC; Vaugine to Piernas, 20 Nov. 1781, *legajo* 94, doc. 753, PPC; testimony of Morvant, 1 July 1782, *legajo* 96, doc. 509, PPC.

44. Vaugine to Miró, 28 Jan. 1783, *legajo* 96, doc. 371, PPC; Vaugine to Miró, 2 May 1783, *legajo* 96, doc. 469, PPC.

45. Vaugine to Miró, 2 May 1783, *legajo* 96, doc. 469, PPC.

46. Vaugine to Miró, 15 Jan. 1784, *legajo* 97, doc. 395, PPC; statement of Vaugine, 4 Aug. 1784, *legajo* 97, doc. 482, PPC; Din and Nasatir, *Imperial Osages,* 150–51.

47. Miró to DuBreuil, 24 Mar. 1786, doc. 335, PPC; Din and Nasatir, *Imperial Osages,* 154–60; Rollings, *The Osage,* 165–66.

48. Rousseau to Miró, 3 Mar. 1786, *legajo* 98A, doc. 819, PPC; Miró to DeBreuil, 24 Mar. 1786, doc. 335, PPC; Miró to Cruzat, 24 Mar. 1786, SMV 2:171–73; Rollings, *The Osage,* 166–67.

49. Rousseau to Miró, 18 Apr. 1786, *legajo* 99, doc. 371, PPC; Miró to Rousseau, 5 May 1786, doc. 409, PPC; Miró to Galvez, 1 Aug. 1786, SMV, 2:182–84.

50. De Mézières to Galvez, May 1779, ADM, 2:249–50; De Blanc to Miró, 17 June

1788, SMV, 2:256; De Blanc to Miró, 5 Aug. 1788, SMV, 2:259.

51. Vaugine to Miró, 8 Nov. 1782, *legajo* 95, doc. 623, PPC; Filhiol to the governor, 25 June 1789, *legajo* 02, doc. 477, PPC; De Blanc to Miró, 17 Mar. 1790, SMV, 2:316; De Blanc to Miró, 30 Mar. 1791, SMV, 2:407; De Blanc to Carondelet, 18 Aug. 1792, *legajo* 06, PPC.

52. De Blanc to Miró, 30 Sept. 1789, SMV, 2:281; De Blanc to Miró, 27 Mar. 1790, SMV, 2:316; De Blanc to Carondelet, 18 Feb. 1792, SMV, 3:9–11; Din and Nasatir, *Imperial Osages,* 192.

53. De Blanc to Miró, 20 Jan. 1790, SMV, 2:295–97; De Blanc to Miró, 2 Sept. 1790, SMV, 2:377.

54. De Blanc to Miró, 30 Sept. 1789, SMV, 2:281; De Blanc to Miró, 20 Jan. 1790, SMV, 2:295–97; De Blanc to Carondelet, 18 Feb. 1792, SMV, 3:9–11.

55. Trudeau to Carondelet, 14 May 1796, *legajo* 3, PPC, Holmes Collection, microfilm 381, reel 9, NSU; Clark to Madison, 29 Sept. 1803, TP, 9:63.

56. The Ochanias appear to have been a Shawnee band, while the Pacana were a small Alabama–Koasati people originally from the Coosa River; Hodge, *Handbook,* 2:104, 182; Miró, "Location of Indians around Natchitoches," 12 Dec. 1785, SMV, 2:160; Layssard to Miró, 1 June 1787, *legajo* 18, PPC, Holmes Collection, microfilm 381, reel 1, NSU; De Blanc to Carondelet, 16 Apr. 1792, SMV, 3:25–27; O'Callaghan, "Removal Policy," 281.

57. De Mézières to Croix, 18 Apr. 1778, ADM, 2:201–4; Miró to Choctaw chief Coté Ambé, 9 Dec. 1790, reel 20, BA; Kniffen, Gregory, and Stokes, *Historic Indian Tribes,* 84–85; O'Callaghan, "Removal Policy," 288.

58. Kniffen, Gregory, and Stokes, *Historic Indian Tribes,* 84–85, 91.

59. De Blanc to Miró, 27 Mar. 1790, SMV, 2:316; De Blanc to Carondelet, 16 Apr. 1792, SMV, 3:25–27; De Blanc to Cordova, 27 June 1792, reel 22, BA; Carondelet to De Blanc, 18 Oct. 1792, SMV, 3:92; De Blanc to Carondelet, 1 Dec. 1792, SMV, 3:99–100; O'Callaghan, "Removal Policy," 288; Kniffen, Gregory, and Stokes, *Historic Indian Tribes,* 84–85, 91.

60. De Blanc to Cordova, 27 June 1792, reel 22, BA; Cordova to Muñoz, 26 July 1792, reel 22, BA; Filhiol to the governor, 3 Aug. 1792, *legajo* 362, PPC, Holmes Collection, microfilm 381, reel 1, NSU; Carondelet to De Blanc, 18 Oct. 1792, SMV, 3:92; De Blanc to Carondelet, 1 Dec. 1792, SMV, 3:99–100.

61. Villebueve, 12 Aug. 1794, *legajo* 636, PPC, Holmes Collection II, microfilm 381, reel 3, NSU; Nava to Muñoz, 26 Feb. 1795, reel 25, BA; letter of Caddo Chief, 28 Apr. 1795, BL; Nava to the governor of Texas, 15 July 1795, reel 25, BA; Nava to the governor of Texas, 26 Aug. 1795, reel 25, BA.

62. De Blanc to Filhiol, 20 Oct. 1795, *legajo* 13, PPC; De Blanc to Carondelet, 7 Nov. 1795, *legajo* 11A, PPC.

63. De Blanc to Carondelet, 15 Feb. 1796, *legajo* 3, PPC, Holmes Collection, microfilm 381, reel 9, NSU; Sotechaux to Fernández, 25 Aug. 1796, reel 26, BA; Fernán-

dez to Muñoz, 25 Sept. 1796, reel 26, BA; Fernández to Muñoz, 23 Oct. 1796, reel 26, BA; Guadiana to Muñoz, 25 Nov. 1796, reel 26, BA.

64. Guadiana to Carondelet, 2 Mar. 1797, reel 27, BA; Minor to Gayoso, 16 Nov. 1797, *legajo* 8, PPC, Holmes Collection II, microfilm 381, reel 3, NSU; Calvo to Elguezábal, 26 Apr. 1800, reel 29, BA; Moral to Elguezábal, 26 June 1800, reel 29, BA; Nava to Elguezábal, 10 Nov. 1800, reel 29, BA.

5 // Restructuring the Chiefdoms

1. Salcedo, "Nations of the Province of Texas," 24 Apr. 1809, reel 41, BA. On the fissioning and fusing of different peoples and their effects, see Service, *Primitive Social Organization,* 77.

2. Davenport to Salcedo, "Information as to Indian Nations of the Province of Texas," 1808, reel 39, BA.

3. Peña to Miró, 22 Sept. 1787, SMV, 2:234–35; De Blanc to Carondelet, 18 Feb. 1792, SMV, 3:9–11; Sibley, "Indian Tribes," 41–53; Salcedo, "Information as to the Indian Nations of the Province of Texas," 24 Apr. 1809, BA.

4. Trudeau to Salcedo, 30 Oct. 1802, *legajo* 19, doc. 201, PPC; Davenport to Salcedo, "Information as to Indian Nations of the Province of Texas," 1808, reel 39, BA; Williams, "Aboriginal Location," 550–55.

5. Rousseau and De Blanc, 20 Mar. 1787, SMV, 2:198–99; "Relation of Andres Benito Courbiere," 29 Aug. 1791, reel 21, BA; Rodriguez, "Report of the Cost of Maintenance and Presents for Four Hundred Twelve Indians from the Friendly Tribes of the North who visited this Town," 1 Jan. 1806, reel 34, BA; Barr and Davenport to Viana, 1 Jan. 1808, reel 37, BA; Davenport to Salcedo, "Information as to the Indian Nations of the Province of Texas, 1809, reel 39, BA.

6. Newkumet and Meredith, *Hasinai,* 69, 72, 79, 88–89, 102–3; Heflin, "Oashuns," 39–42.

7. Espinosa letter, 156, 160; report of Orobio Bazterra, 1 Oct. 1745, reel 8, BA.

8. De Mézières to Ripperda, 4 July 1772, ADM, 1:284–306; Newkumet and Meredith, *Hasinai,* 54–56; Griffith, "Hasinai Indians," 151.

9. Bienville, "Memoir on Louisiana," 1726, MPA, 3:429–30; De Mézières to Ripperda, 4 July 1772, ADM, 1:286, 295.

10. De Mézières to Ripperda, 4 July 1772, ADM, 1:295; Berlandier, *Indians of Texas,* 94, 95 n. 102.

11. Fried, *Evolution,* 133; Service, *Primitive Social Organization,* 133–34; De Blanc to Filhiol, 20 Oct. 1795, *legajo* 13, PPC.

12. De Mézières to Ripperda, 4 July 1772, ADM, 1:295; Newkumet and Meredith, *Hasinai,* 56.

13. 1780 census of Indian allies, Natchitoches jurisdiction, in Mills, *Natchitoches Colonials,* 40–41; Vaugine to Miró, 8 Nov. 1782, *legajo* 95, doc. 623, PPC.

14. Vaugine to Miró, 8 Nov. 1782, *legajo* 95, doc. 623, PPC; Kniffen, Gregory, and

Stokes, *Historic Indian Tribes*, 64–66; Dumont de Montigny, "History of Louisiana," 5:96–97.

15. De Mézières to the governor, 1778, *legajo* 91, doc. 639, PPC; "Agreement made with the Indian Nations in Assembly," 21 Apr. 1770, ADM, 1:157–58; Griffith, "Hasinai Indians," 137–38.

16. Vaugine to Miró, 8 Nov. 1782, *legajo* 95, doc. 623, PPC; Caddo Chief to Galvez, 28 Apr. 1795, BL.

17. Sibley to Dearborn, 10 Apr. 1805, Melrose Collection, bound vol. 3, NSU; Sibley, "Indian Tribes," 66–68.

18. De Mézières to Galvez, May 1779, *legajo* 92, doc. 779, PPC; De Mézières to Galvez, May 1779, *legajo* 92, doc. 916, PPC; De Mézières to Galvez, May 1779, *legajo* 92, doc. 919, PPC.; De Mézières to Galvez, May 1779, ADM, 2:249–52, 205 n. 303.

19. De Mézières to Galvez, May 1779, *legajo* 92, doc. 916, PPC; De Mézières to Galvez, May 1779, ADM, 2:248–53; Galvez to De Mézières, 1 June 1779, ADM, 2:253–54.

20. Galvez to De Mézières, 1 June 1779, ADM, 2:253–54.

21. Gil Ybarbo to Gálvez, 1 Nov. 1780, SMV, 2:390; ADM, 1:88–110; "Declaration of Three Indian Slaves owned by Three Frenchmen," 17 Apr. 1770, *legajo* 88A, PPC; Bucareli to Ripperdá, 7 Oct. 1772, reel 11, BA; Chipman, *Spanish Texas*, 183; John, *Storms*, 383–86.

22. Ulloa to O'Conor, 1768, ADM, 1:127–30.

23. Interrogation of Morvant by De Mézières, 11 May 1770, *legajo* 10, doc. 164, PPC.

24. Report of De Mézières, 11 May 1770, book 3, doc. 642, NPCR; De Mézières to Unzaga, 15 May 1770, ADM, 1:160–63.

25. "Agreement made with the Indian Nations in Assembly," 21 Apr. 1770, ADM, 1:157–58; "Report by De Mézières of the Expedition to the Cadodachos," 29 Oct. 1770, ADM, 1:206–20; Sibley, "Indian Tribes," 67.

26. De Mézières to Unzaga, 1 Feb. 1770, ADM, 1:140–42; "Report by De Mézières of the Expedition to Cadodachos," 29 Oct. 1770, ADM, 1:208.

27. De Mézières to Unzaga, 20 May 1770, ADM, 1:199–200; De Mézières to Unzaga, 20 May 1770, ADM, 1:200–202; De Mézières to Unzaga, 27 June 1770, ADM, 1:202–3; De Mézières to Unzaga, 27 Sept. 1770, ADM, 1:204–6; "Report by De Mézières of the Expedition to the Cadodachos," 29 Oct. 1770, ADM, 1:206–20; "Treaty of Peace made with the Taovaya, Pani-Piques, and Naytane Comanche Indians," 1 Nov. 1771, *legajo* 357, PPC, Holmes Collection, microfilm 381, reel 5, NSU; John, *Storms*, 402.

28. De Mézières to the governor, 1778, *legajo* 91, doc. 639, PPC; De Mézières to Galvez, 3 July 1778, *legajo* 92, doc. 786, PPC; De Mézières to Galvez, May 1779, *legajo* 92, doc. 779, PPC; De Mézières to Galvez, May 1779, *legajo* 92, doc. 916, PPC; De Mézières to Galvez, May 1779, *legajo* 92, doc. 919, PPC; De Mézières to Galvez,

May 1779, ADM, 2:248 n. 300, 250 n. 303; ADM, 1:74; De Mézières to Unzaga, 10 June 1770, ADM, 1:175.

29. Vaugine, "List of Trade Goods for Annual Gifts given to the Four Different Nations," 1 Oct. 1780, *legajo* 94, doc. 610, PPC; Vaugine to Piernas, 23 Jan. 1781, *legajo* 94, doc. 627, PPC; Vaugine to Croix, 13 Mar. 1783, *legajo* 96, doc. 396, PPC.

30. Vaugine, "Recensement des Nations Sauvages," 1780, *legajo* 93A, PPC, Holmes Collections, reel 10, NSU.

31. Vaugine, statement of accounts, 3 Sept. 1780, *legajo* 94, doc. 629, PPC.

32. Ourné to Piernas, 8 Jan. 1781, *legajo* 94, doc. 622, PPC; Vaugine to Piernas, 23 Jan. 1781, *legajo* 94, doc. 626, PPC; interim governor to Vaugine, 26 Jan. 1781, *legajo* 94, doc. 632, PPC; interim governor to Vaugine, 27 Jan. 1781, *legajo* 94, doc. 635, PPC; Vaugine to Piernas, 21 May 1781, *legajo* 94, doc. 669, PPC.

33. Vaugine to Piernas, 21 Sept. 1781, *legajo* 94, doc. 734, PPC; statement of Grappe, Brevel, and Mulon, 4 Oct. 1781, *legajo* 94, doc. 737, PPC.

34. Bormé to Vaugine, 16 July 1782, *legajo* 95, PPC, Holmes Collection, microfilm 381, reel 5, NSU; Vaugine to Ybarbo, 5 Jan. 1784, *legajo* 97, doc. 380, PPC.

35. Governor to Bormé, 14 Aug. 1782, *legajo* 95, doc. 614, PPC; Vaugine to Miró, 25 Mar. 1783, *legajo* 96, doc. 410, PPC; report of Vaugine, 30 Apr. 1783, *legajo* 196, doc. 463, PPC.

36. Order of De Villiers, 4 Dec. 1773, *legajo* 89A, doc. 753, PPC; instructions to Vaugine from the governor, 15 July 1780, *legajo* 94, doc. 708, PPC; Vaugine to Piernas, 20 May 1781, *legajo* 94, PPC; Vaugine to Piernas, 24 May 1781, *legajo* 94, doc. 673, PPC; Vaugine to the governor, 26 July 1781, *legajo* 94, doc. 713, PPC; Vaugine to Piernas, 20 Nov. 1781, *legajo* 94, doc. 747, PPC; Vaugine to Piernas, 20 Nov. 1781, *legajo* 94, doc. 753, PPC; De Blanc to the governor, 22 Dec. 1781, *legajo* 94, doc. 780, PPC; Bormé to Vaugine, 16 July 1782, *legajo* 95, PPC; statement of Louis Fortin, 18 Feb. 1783, *legajo* 96, doc. 382, PPC.

37. Memoir of Vaugine, 28 May 1783, *legajo* 96, doc. 484, PPC.

38. Ybarbo to Vaugine, 8 July 1783, *legajo* 0A, doc. 183, PPC; diary of Ybarbo, 8 July 1783, *legajo* 0A, doc. 182, PPC.

39. Vaugine to Miró, 19 July 1783, *legajo* 96, doc. 554, PPC.

40. De Blanc to Miró, 20 Mar. 1787, *legajo* 3, doc. 143, PPC; De Blanc to Miró, 20 Jan. 1790, SMV, 2:295–97; De Blanc to Miró, 2 Sept. 1790, SMV, 2:377; De Blanc to Miró, 30 Mar. 1791, SMV, 2:407; De Blanc to Carondelet, 18 Feb. 1792, SMV, 3:10–11.

41. Vaugine to Miró, 10 Oct. 1783, *legajo* 96, doc. 615, PPC; Filhiol to the governor, 25 June 1783, *legajo* 96, doc. 696, PPC; Filhiol to Cachou, 28 Feb. 1784, 7 Aug. 1784, *legajo* 96, doc. 490, PPC; Filhiol to Miró, 1 Aug. 1787, *legajo* 88C, doc. 189, PPC; Peña to Miró, 17 Aug. 1787, SMV, 2:232–33; Peña to Miró, 22 Sept. 1787, SMV, 2:235; lists of expenses for entertaining friendly Indians, 14 May 1788, reel 19, BA; De Blanc to Filhiol, 14 Nov. 1788, *legajo* 13, doc. 642, PPC; Filhiol to the governor, 20

Aug. 1789, *legajo* 02, doc. 485, PPC; Villebeuvre to Carondelet, 7 July 1794, SMV, 3:317; Guadíana to Muñoz, 26 Mar. 1797, reel 27, BA.

6 // The Chiefdoms Shatter

1. Sibley to Claiborne, 10 Oct. 1803, TP, 9:75–76.

2. Sibley to Claiborne, 10 Oct. 1803, TP, 9:75–76; Claiborne to Turner, 25 Feb. 1804, CL, 1:385–86.

3. Claiborne to Madison, 4 Aug. 1804, CL, 2:292–93; Claiborne to the president, 30 Aug. 1804, TP, 9:287; Turner to Claiborne, 13 Oct. 1804, CL, 2:385; Claiborne to Turner, 3 Nov. 1804, CL, 2:390.

4. Claiborne to the president, 4 Nov. 1804, TP, 9:318–19; Turner to Claiborne, 21 Nov. 1804, TP, 9:335–36.

5. Claiborne to Sibley, 10 June 1805, CL, 3:87; secretary of war to Sibley, 17 Oct. 1805, TP, 9:514–15.

6. Elguezábal to Salcedo, 20 June 1804, reel 32, BA; Salcedo to Yturrigaray, 23 Jan. 1805, reel 32, BA; Amangual to Elguezábal, 23 Feb. 1805, reel 33, BA; Salcedo to the governor of Texas, 20 May 1805, reel 33, BA; Valle to Elguezábal, 11 June 1805, reel 33, BA; Valle to Elguezábal, 10 Aug. 1805, reel 33, BA.

7. Salcedo to acting governor of Texas (Cordero), 13 Aug. 1805, reel 33, BA; Salcedo to Cordero, 26 July 1805, reel 33, BA; Valle to the Texas governor, 3 Oct. 1805, reel 33, BA; declaration of Roban, 3 Oct. 1805, ASP, Foreign Relations, 2:694–95; statement of Cadodacho contraband, 16 Oct. 1805, reel 33, BA.

8. Valle to Elguezábal, 4 May 1805, reel 33, BA; Guadiana to Viana, 31 May 1806, reel 34, BA; Viana to Cordero, 7 June 1806, reel 34, BA; Viana to Cordero, 9 July 1807, reel 36, BA.

9. Guadiana to Viana, 20 June 1806, reel 34, BA; Claiborne to Herrera, 26 Aug. 1806, CL, 3:384; note of Herrera, 28 Aug. 1806, CL, 3:392. For a complete examination of the Freeman and Custis Expedition and Dehahuit's role in it, see Flores, *Jefferson.*

10. *Mississippi Messenger.*

11. *Mississippi Messenger.*

12. Sibley, *Report,* 12–13, 20–21, 63–64.

13. Sibley, *Report,* 48–67.

14. Viana to Cordero, 18 Aug. 1807, reel 36, BA; Cordero to the commandant general, 1 Feb. 1808, reel 37, BA.

15. Corbelo, lists of gifts for the Indians, 31 Aug. 1810, reel 46, BA; Salcedo to Soto, 11 Aug. 1812, reel 52, BA; Soto to Varela, 23 July 1816, reel 56, BA; Arredondo to the commandante general, 7 Nov. 1816, reel 57, BA; Flores to Perez, 16 Nov. 1816, reel 57, BA.

16. Claiborne to Macarty, 16 Oct. 1813, CL, 6:274; speech by Claiborne to the great chief of the Caddo Nation, 18 Oct. 1813, CL, 6:275–77.

17. Claiborne to Jackson, 28 Oct. 1814, CL, 6:293–94; Claiborne to Monroe, 20 Dec. 1814, CL, 6:327–28.

18. Sibley to Dearborn, 10 Apr. 1805, bound vol. 3, Melrose Collection, NSU; Sibley to secretary of war, 20 Mar. 1810, TP, 9:878–79; Kniffen, Gregory, and Stokes, *Historic Indian Tribes,* 89.

19. J. F. [John Fowler] to McKenney, 25 June 1818, *Letterbooks of the Natchitoches-Sulphur Fork Factory, 1809–1821;* Dehahuit to president, 28 May 1831, CAL; Kniffen, Gregory, and Stokes, *Historic Indian Tribes,* 7; testimony of Lattier, 9 Dec. 1840, U.S. House of Representatives, *Caddo Indian Treaty.*

20. Fowler to McKenney, 14 June 1819, TP, 19:73–75.

21. Fowler to Jamison, 16 Apr. 1819, TP, 19:70–71; Fowler to McKenney, 14 June 1819, TP, 19:73–75.

22. Fowler to Jamison, 16 Apr. 1819, TP, 19:70–71.

23. Jamison to the secretary of war, 26 May 1819, TP, 19:69–70; McClellan to McKenney, 10 May 1821, TP, 19:293.

24. Fowler to McKenney, 14 June 1819, TP, 19:73–75; McKenney to the secretary of war, 16 July 1819, TP, 19:86.

25. Fowler to McKenney, 2 July 1819, TP, 19:96; Miller to the secretary of war, 20 June 1820, TP, 19:194; grand jury presentment in Hempstead County, Arkansas Territory, Apr. 1820, TP, 19:196; petition of the Caddo, 10 Nov. 1820, reel 65, BA; Vivero to Martinez, 28 Mar. 1821, reel 67, BA; Brearley to the secretary of war, 26 Apr. 1821, TP, 19:285; Gray to the secretary of war, 30 Sept. 1821, TP, 19:306 n. 80; secretary of war to Gray, 17 Nov. 1821, TP, 19:354.

26. Grand jury presentment in Hempstead County, Apr. 1820, TP, 19:197–98; Gov. Miller to the secretary of war, 20 June 1820, TP, 19:193; Maynes to Martinez, 10 Nov. 1820, reel 65, BA; Conway to Gaines, 25 June 1822, TP, 19:445.

27. Gray to the secretary of war, 28 Feb. 1824, TP, 19:611–12; Gray to the secretary of war, 26 May 1825, TP, 20:52; McKenney to Gray, 9 July 1825, TP, 20:90–92; McKenney to Gray, 16 Nov. 1825, TP, 20:152–53; Gray to Barbour, 29 Nov. 1825, CAL; Gray to the secretary of war, 30 Apr. 1826, TP, 20:237–38; Gray to the secretary of war, 30 Aug. 1828, TP, 20:742.

28. Sibley to the secretary of war, 20 Mar. 1810, TP, 9:878–79; Gray to Brent, 15 Dec. 1823, TP, 19:578; Gray to the secretary of war, 1 Mar. 1823, TP, 19:497, 497 n. 41.

29. Letters of Arciniega, 1 Feb. 1826, reel 89, BA; Gray to the secretary of war, 6 Apr. 1826, TP, 20:225–26.

30. Terán, "Documentos," 264–69.

31. Berlandier, *Indians of Texas,* 35, 39, 43–44, 46, 48, 52, 89, 103–5, 141–42.

32. Dillard to the secretary of war, 12 Aug. 1828, TP, 20:728–29; Tar Ra Sin et al. to the great war chief, 28 Jan 1827, CAL; Gray to the secretary of war, 13 June 1827, TP, 20:479–81; Gray to the secretary of war, 1 Sept. 1828, TP, 20:744; Brooks to Ea-

ton, 16 Aug. 1830, CAL; Brooks to Lt. Col. Maury, 15 Sept. 1830, CAL; Brooks to Eaton, 18 Sept. 1830, CAL.

33. Tar Ra Sin to the great war chief, 28 Jan. 1827, CAL; Latham et al. to Brooks, 21 Dec. 1830, CAL; Brooks to Eaton, 29 Dec. 1830, CAL; Brooks to Eaton, 25 Feb. 1831, CAL; Brooks to White, 8 July 1831, CAL; Brooks to Herring, 15 May 1833, CAL; Tononzekah to the secretary of war, 31 Aug. 1833, CAL.

34. Brooks to Eaton, 14 Jan. 1831, CAL.

35. Brooks to Lt. Col. Maury, 15 Sept. 1830, CAL; Brooks to Eaton, 18 Sept. 1830, CAL; Col. Bean to Brooks, 25 Feb. 1833, CAL.

36. Brooks to Eaton, 16 Feb. 1831, CAL.

37. Brooks to White, 8 July 1831, CAL; Dehahuit to the president, 28 May 1831, CAL; Brooks to Herring, 13 Feb. 1832, CAL; Brooks to Herring, 25 Nov. 1833, CAL.

38. Brooks to Eaton, 14 Jan. 1831, CAL; Brooks to White, 8 July 1831, CAL; Brooks to Herring, 13 Feb. 1832, CAL.

39. Brooks to Herring, 26 Feb. 1832, CAL; receipt of medals by Brooks, 11 June 1832, CAL; pledge of Norriss, Poiriere, Irwin, and Wallace, 13 May 1833, CAL.

40. Gray to the secretary of war, 30 Dec. 1824, TP, 19:739–40; Brooks to Robb, 15 Sept. 1832, CAL; Brooks to Herring, 4 Apr. 1833, CAL; Brooks to Herring, 25 Nov. 1833, CAL.

41. Padilla, "Texas in 1820," 48. For information on Choctaw and Pawnee attitudes toward whiskey, see White, *Roots of Dependency,* 85–87, 190–92.

42. Brooks to Herring, 13 Feb. 1832, CAL.

43. Brooks to Herring, 9 Apr. 1833, CAL; Brooks to Herring, 8 June 1833, CAL.

44. Brooks to Aldridge, 31 Aug. 1833, CAL.

45. Brooks to Herring, 4 Apr. 1833, CAL.

46. Brooks to Herring, 4 Apr. 1833, CAL; Brooks to Herring, 25 Nov. 1833, CAL.

47. Brooks to Herring, 10 July 1833, CAL; Gen. Leavenworth to Brooks, 11 May 1834, CAL; Brooks to Herring, 30 June 1834, CAL; Brooks to Cass, 21 Feb. 1835, CAL.

48. Shreve to Herring, 30 Apr. 1834, CAL.

49. Brooks to Herring, 1 July 1834, CAL; Brooks to Herring, 9 Feb. 1835, CAL; Brooks to Cass, 25 Feb. 1835, CAL; Lange, "Caddo Treaty," 253–54, 262.

50. Tarshar to the president, CAL (this piece of correspondence is undated but there is an endorsement with it written by President Andrew Jackson dated 28 Jan. 1835 that asks the secretary of war whether a commissioner could be appointed to "obtain a complete cession of their lands to the United States").

51. U.S. Bureau of Indian Affairs, "Documents Relating"; Lange, "Caddo Treaty," 272–81.

52. Testimony of Edwards, in Lange, "The Caddo Treaty," 300–302; Lee, "François Grappe," 61–65.

53. Kniffen, Gregory, and Stokes, *Historic Indian Tribes,* 96; Newkumet and Meredith, *Hasinai,* 76; F. Todd Smith, *Caddo Indians,* 131.

54. F. Todd Smith, *Caddo Indians,* 143–44; Neighbours, "Jose Maria," 254–74; Newkumet and Meredith, *Hasinai,* 76; Everett, *Texas Cherokees,* 115.

55. "Report of Standing Committee on Indian Affairs, 12 Oct. 1837, in Winfrey and Day, *Texas Indian Papers,* 1:23.

56. Neighbours, *Robert Simpson Neighbors,* 39, 42, 49.

57. Neighbours, *Robert Simpson Neighbors,* 111, 158, 279–83; Lange, "Caddo Treaty," 304–15; Newkumet and Meredith, *Hasinai,* 76–77.

Bibliography

Albers, Patricia C. "Symbiosis, Merger, and War: Contrasting Forms of Intertribal Relationship Among Historic Plains Indians." In *The Political Economy of North American Indians*. Ed. John H. Moore. Norman: University of Oklahoma Press, 1993.

American State Papers. Microfiche, microtext department, Sterling Evans Library, Texas A&M University, College Station.

Anderson, Gary Clayton. *Kinsmen of Another Kind: Dakota-White Relations in the Upper Mississippi Valley, 1650–1862*. Lincoln: University of Nebraska Press, 1984.

Archives des Colonies. Microfilm, series C13A, 54 vols., Paris.

Bolton, Herbert E., trans. and ed. *Athanase De Mézières and the Louisiana-Texas Frontier, 1768–1780*. 2 vols. Cleveland: Arthur H. Clark, 1914; New York: Kraus Reprint, 1970.

Baugh, Timothy G. "Ecology and Exchange: The Dynamics of Plains-Pueblo Interaction." In *Farmers, Hunters, and Colonists: Interaction between the Southwest and the Southern Plains*. Ed. Katherine A. Spielmann, 107–27. Tucson: University of Arizona Press, 1991.

———. "Southern Plains Societies and Eastern Frontier Pueblo Exchange During the Protohistoric Period." *Papers of the Archaeological Society of New Mexico* 9 (1984): 157–67.

Berlandier, Jean Louis. *The Indians of Texas in 1830*. Ed. John Ewers. Washington DC: Smithsonian Institution Press, 1969.

Béxar Archives. Microfilm, microtext department, Sterling Evans Library, Texas A&M University, College Station.

Bolton, Herbert E. *The Hasinai: Southern Caddoans as Seen by the Earliest Europeans*. Norman: University of Oklahoma Press, 1987.

———. *Texas in the Middle Eighteenth Century: Studies in Spanish Colonial History and Administration.* Berkeley: University of California Press, 1915; Austin: Texas History Paperbacks, 1970.

Bossu, Jean-Bernard. *Travels in the Interior of North America, 1751– 1762.* Trans. and ed. Seymour Feiler. Norman: University of Oklahoma Press, 1962.

Bridges, Katherine, and Winston De Ville. "Natchitoches and the Trail to the Rio Grande: Two Early Eighteenth-Century Accounts by the Sieur Derbanne." *Louisiana History* 8 (summer 1967): 239–59.

Brose, David S. "From the Southeastern Ceremonial Complex to the Southern Cult: 'You Can't Tell the Players without a Program.'" In *Southeastern Ceremonial Complex: Artifacts and Analysis, The Cottonlandia Conference.* Ed. Patricia Galloway, 27–37. Lincoln: University of Nebraska Press, 1989.

Caddo Agency Letters. Microfilm, microtext department, Sterling Evans Library, Texas A&M University, College Station.

Carter, Cecile Elkins. *Caddo Indians: Where We Come From.* Norman: University of Oklahoma Press, 1995.

Carter, Clarence E., ed. *The Territorial Papers of the United States.* 26 vols. Washington DC: U.S. Government Printing Office, 1940.

Casañas de Jesus Maria, Francisco. Letter to the Viceroy of Mexico, Mission Santíssima Nombre de Maria, 15 August 1691. In "Descriptions of the Tejas or Asinai Indians, 1691–1722." Trans. Mattie Austin Hatcher. *Southwestern Historical Quarterly* 30 (Jan. 1927): 206–18, 283–304.

Chipman, Donald E. *Spanish Texas: 1519–1821.* Austin: University of Texas Press, 1992.

Conveyance Records. Clerk of Court's Office, Natchitoches Parish Courthouse, Natchitoches LA.

Corbin, James E. "Spanish-Indian Interaction on the Eastern Frontier of Texas." In *Columbian Consequences: Archaeological and Historical Perspectives on the Spanish Borderlands West.* 3 vols. Ed. David Hurst Thomas, 269–79. Washington DC: Smithsonian Institution Press, 1989.

Covey, Cyclone, trans. and ed. *Cabeza de Vaca's Adventures in the Unknown Interior of America.* Albuquerque: University of New Mexico Press, 1961.

Delanglez, Jean, ed. *The Journal of Jean Cavelier: The Account of a Survivor of La Salle's Texas Expedition, 1684–1688.* Chicago: Institute of Jesuit History, 1938.

DePratter, Chester B. *Late Prehistoric and Early Historic Chiefdoms in the Southeastern United States.* New York: Garland, 1991.

DeVille Collection. Watson Library, Northwestern State University, Natchitoches LA.

Din, Gilbert C., and Abraham P. Nasatir. *The Imperial Osages: Spanish-Indian Diplomacy in the Mississippi Valley.* Norman: University of Oklahoma Press, 1983.

Dorsey, George A. *Traditions of the Caddo*. Washington DC: Carnegie Institution, 1905.

Du Pratz, Le Page. *The History of Louisiana*. Ed. Joseph G. Tregle Jr. 1774; Baton Rouge: Louisiana State University Press, 1975.

Dumont de Montigny, Jean Francois. "History of Louisiana." *Historical Collections of Louisiana, Embracing Many Rare and Valuable Documents Relating to the Natural, Civil and Political History of that State*. Vol. 5. Ed. B. F. French. New York: Wiley and Putnam, 1846; New York: AMS Press, 1976.

Espinosa, Isidro Felis de. Letter on the Asinai and Their Allies, 1722. In "Descriptions of the Tejas or Asinai Indians, 1691–1722." Trans. Mattie Austin Hatcher. *Southwestern Historical Quarterly* 31 (Oct. 1927): 151–80.

Everett, Dianna. *The Texas Cherokees: A People Between Two Fires, 1819–1840*. Norman: University of Oklahoma Press, 1990.

Ewers, John C. "The Influence of Epidemics on the Indian Populations and Cultures of Texas." *Plains Anthropologist* 18 (May 1973): 104–15.

Flores, Dan, ed. *Jefferson and Southwestern Exploration: The Freeman and Custis Accounts of the Red River Expedition of 1806*. Norman: University of Oklahoma Press, 1984.

————. *Journal of an Indian Trader: Anthony Glass and the Texas Trading Frontier, 1790–1810*. College Station: Texas A&M University, 1985.

Foik, Paul J., trans. "Captain Don Domingo Ramón's Diary of His Expedition into Texas in 1716." *Preliminary Studies of the Texas Catholic Historical Society* 2 (Apr. 1933): 3–23.

Fox, Daniel E. *Traces of Texas History: Archeological Evidence of the Past 450 Years*. San Antonio: Corona, 1983.

Fried, Morton H. *The Evolution of Political Society: An Essay in Political Anthropology*. New York: Random House, 1967.

Galloway, Patricia. "'The Chief Who Is Your Father': Choctaw and French Views of the Diplomatic Relation." In *Powhatan's Mantle: Indians in the Colonial Southeast*. Ed. Peter H. Wood, Gregory A. Waselkov, and M. Thomas Hatley, 254–278. Lincoln: University of Nebraska Press, 1989.

Gregory, H. F. "Eighteenth Century Caddoan Archaeology: A Study in Models and Interpretation." Ph. D. diss., Southern Methodist University, 1973.

Griffith, William. "The Hasinai Indians of East Texas as Seen by Europeans, 1687–1772." *Philological and Documentary Studies* 2. New Orleans: Tulane University Press, 1977.

Gutiérrez, Ramón A. *When Jesus Came, the Corn Mothers Went Away: Marriage, Sexuality, and Power in New Mexico, 1500–1846*. Stanford CA: Stanford University Press, 1991.

Hackett, Charles W., trans. and ed. *Pichardo's Treatise on the Limits of Louisiana and Texas.* 4 vols. Austin: University of Texas Press, 1931–46.

Heflin, Eugene. "The Oashuns or Dances of the Caddo." *Bulletin of the Oklahoma Anthropological Society* 1 (1953): 39–42.

Hickerson, Nancy. *The Jumanos: Hunters and Traders of the South Plains.* Austin: University of Texas Press, 1994.

Higginbotham, Jay. *Old Mobile: Fort Louis de la Louisiane, 1702–1711.* Mobile, AL: Museum of the City of Mobile, 1977.

Hodge, Frederick W. *Handbook of American Indians North of Mexico.* 2 vols. Washington DC: U.S. Government Printing Office, 1907.

Holder, Preston. *The Hoe and the Horse on the Plains.* Lincoln: University of Nebraska Press, 1970.

Hudson, Charles. "The Hernando de Soto Expedition, 1539–1543." *The Forgotten Centuries: Indians and Europeans in the American South, 1521–1704.* Athens: University of Georgia Press, 1994.

———. *The Southeastern Indians.* Knoxville: University of Tennessee Press, 1976.

Jackson, Jack. *Los Mesteños: Spanish Ranching in Texas, 1721–1821.* College Station: Texas A&M University Press, 1986.

Jennings, Francis. "American Frontiers." *America in 1492: The World of the Indian Peoples before the Arrival of Columbus.* Ed. Alvin M. Josephy Jr., 339–67. New York: Vintage Books, 1993.

———. *The Founders of America: From the Earliest Migration to the Present.* New York: W. W. Norton, 1993.

John, Elizabeth A. H. *Storms Brewed in Other Men's Worlds: The Confrontation of Indians, Spanish, and French in the Southwest, 1540–1795.* Lincoln: University of Nebraska Press, 1975.

Joutel, Henri. "Joutel's Historical Journal of Monsieur de La Salle's Last Voyage to Discover the River Mississippi." *Historical Collections of Louisiana, Embracing Many Rare and Valuable Documents Relating to the Natural, Civil and Political History of that State.* Vol. 1. Ed. B. F. French. New York: Wiley and Putnam, 1846; New York: AMS Press, 1976.

Kelley, J. Charles. "Juan Sabeata and Diffusion in Aboriginal Texas." *American Anthropologists* 57 (Oct. 1955): 981–95.

Kinnaird, Lawrence, ed. *Spain in the Mississippi Valley, 1765–1794: Post War Decade, 1782–1792.* 3 vols. *Annual Report of the American Historical Association for the Year 1945.* Washington DC: U.S. Government Printing Office, 1946.

Kniffen, Fred B., Hiram F. Gregory, and George A. Stokes. *The Historic Indian Tribes of Louisiana from 1542 to the Present.* Baton Rouge: Louisiana State University Press, 1987.

Krieger, Alex D. *Cultural Complexes and Chronology in Northern Texas.* Austin: University of Texas Press, 1946.

———. "Importance of the 'Gilmore Corridor' in Culture Contacts between Middle America and the Eastern United States." *Bulletin of the Texas Archeological and Paleontological Society* 19 (1949): 155–78.

La Harpe, Jean-Baptiste Bénard de, *The Historical Journal of the Establishment of the French in Louisiana.* Trans. Joan Cain and Virginia Koenig, ed. Glenn R. Conrad. Lafayette: University of Southwestern Louisiana, 1971.

Lange, Charles H. *The Caddo Treaty of July 1, 1835.* In *Caddoan Indians II.* New York: Garland, 1974.

Lee, Aubra. "Fusils, Paint, and Pelts: An Examination of Natchitoches-Based Indian Trade in the Spanish Period, 1766–1791." Master's thesis, Northwestern State University, 1990.

Lee, Dayna Bowker. "François Grappe and the Caddo Land Cession." *North Louisiana Historical Association Journal* 20 (spring/summer 1989): 53–69.

———. "Indian Slavery in Lower Louisiana during the Colonial Period: 1699–1803." Master's thesis, Northwestern State University, 1989.

Letterbooks of the Natchitoches-Sulphur Fork Factory, 1809–21. Microfilm, microtext department, Sterling Evans Library, Texas A&M University, College Station.

Lévi-Strauss, Claude. *The Elementary Structures of Kinship.* Trans. James Harle Bell, ed. John Richard Von Sturmer and Rodney Needham. Boston: Beacon Press, 1969.

Lintz, Christopher. "Texas Panhandle-Pueblo Interactions from the Thirteenth through the Sixteenth Century." In *Farmers, Hunters, and Colonists: Interaction between the Southwest and the Southern Plains.* Ed. Katherine A. Spielmann, 89–106. Tucson: University of Arizona Press, 1991.

Loomis, Noel M., and Abraham P. Nasatir, eds. *Pedro Vial and the Roads to Santa Fe.* Norman: University of Oklahoma Press, 1967.

Manzanet, Damian. "Carta de Don Damian Manzanet á Don Carlos de Siguenza sobre el descubrimiento de la Bahía del Espíritu Santo." Trans and ed. Lilia M. Casis. *Texas State Historical Association Quarterly* 2 (Apr. 1899): 253–312.

Mauss, Marcel. *The Gift: Forms and Functions of Exchange in Archaic Societies.* Trans. Ian Cunnison. London: Cohen and West, 1969.

McDermott, John Francis. *A Glossary of Mississippi Valley French: 1673–1850.* St. Louis: Washington University Press, 1941.

McWilliams, Richebourg Gaillaird, trans. and ed. *Fleur de Lys and Calumet: Being the Pénicaut Narrative of French Adventure in Louisiana.* Baton Rouge: Louisiana State University Press, 1941.

Mills, Elizabeth Shown. *Natchitoches 1729–1803: Abstracts of the Catholic Church Registers of the French and Spanish Post of St. Jean Baptiste des Natchitoches in Louisiana.* New Orleans: Polyanthos, 1977.

———. *Natchitoches Colonials: Censuses, Military Rolls and Tax Lists, 1722–1803.* Chicago: Adams Press, 1981.

———. "(De) Mézières-Trichel-Grappe: A Study of a Tri-Caste Lineage in the Old South." *The Genealogist* 6 (spring 1985): 4–84.

Mississippi Messenger, vol. 3, no. 109, 30 Sept. 1806.

Morfí, Juan Agustín, *History of Texas, 1673–1779.* Trans. Carlos Eduardo Castaneda. Albuquerque: Quivira Society Publication, 1935; rpt. New York: Arno Press, 1967.

Muller, Jon. "The Southern Cult." *The Southeastern Ceremonial Complex: Artifacts and Analysis–The Cottonlandia Conference.* Ed. Patricia Galloway, 11–26. Lincoln: University of Nebraska Press, 1989.

Natchitoches Parish Records. Special Collections, Hill Memorial Library, Louisiana State University, Baton Rouge.

Neighbours, Kenneth F. "Jose Maria: Anadarko Chief," *Chronicles of Oklahoma* 44 (autumn 1966): 254–74.

———. *Robert Simpson Neighbors and the Texas Frontier, 1836–1859.* Waco TX: Texian Press, 1975.

Neuman, Robert W. *An Introduction to Louisiana Archaeology.* Baton Rouge: Louisiana State University Press, 1984.

———. "A Note on Southeastern Ceremonial Complex Artifacts from the Central Great Plains." *The Southeastern Ceremonial Complex: Artifacts and Analysis–The Cottonlandia Conference.* Ed. Patricia Galloway, 122–24. Lincoln: University of Nebraska Press, 1989.

Newkumet, Vynola Beaver, and Howard L. Meredith. *Hasinai: A Traditional History of the Caddo Confederacy.* College Station: Texas A&M University Press, 1988.

Newsom, John D. "History of Deer and Their Habitat in the South." *White-Tailed Deer in the Southern Forest Habitat.* Proceedings of a symposium at Nacogdoches TX, 25–26 Mar. 1969, Southern Forest Experiment Station, U.S. Forest Service, U.S. Department of Agriculture and School of Forestry, Stephen F. Austin State University, Nacogdoches, 1969.

O'Callaghan, Mary A. "An Indian Removal Policy in Spanish Louisiana." *Greater America: Essays in Honor of Eugene Herbert Bolton.* Berkeley: University of California Press, 1945; Freeport NY: Books for Libraries Press, 1968.

Padilla, Juan Antonio, "Texas in 1820." Trans. Mattie Austin Hatcher. *Southwestern Historical Quarterly* 23 (July 1919): 47–68.

Parsons, Elsie Clews. *Notes on the Caddo.* Memoirs of the American Anthropological Association, no. 57. Menasha WI: American Anthropological Association, 1941; New York: Kraus Reprint, 1969.

Perttula, Timothy K. *"The Caddo Nation": Archaeological and Ethnohistoric Perspectives.* Austin: University of Texas Press, 1992.

Peterson, Dennis A. "A History of Excavations and Interpretations of Artifacts from the Spiro Mounds Sites." *The Southeastern Ceremonial Complex: Artifacts and Analysis–The Cottonlandia Conference.* Ed. Patricia Galloway, 114–21. Lincoln: University of Nebraska Press, 1989.

Phillips, Philip, and James A. Brown, *Pre-Columbian Shell Engravings from the Craig Mound at Spiro, Oklahoma.* 2 vols. Cambridge MA: Peabody Museum, 1978.

Portre-Bobinski, Germaine, ed. *Natchitoches: Translation of Old French and Spanish Documents.* Natchitoches LA, private publication, 1928.

Robertson, James A., trans. and ed. "The True Relation of the Harships Suffered by Governor Hernando de Soto by a Gentleman of Elvas." *The De Soto Chronicles: The Expedition of Hernando De Soto to North America in 1539–1543.* Ed. Lawrence A. Clayton, Vernon James Knight Jr., and Edward C. Moore. 2 vols. Tuscaloosa: University of Alabama Press, 1993.

Robertson, Walter V. "Population Dynamics of White-Tailed Deer." *White-Tailed Deer in the Southern Forest Habitat.* Proceedings of a symposium at Nacogdoches TX, 25–26 Mar. 1969. Southern Forest Experiment Station, U.S. Forest Service, U.S. Department of Agriculture and School of Forestry, Stephen F. Austin State University, Nacogdoches, 1969.

Rogers, J. Daniel. "Patterns of Change on the Western Margin of the Southeast, A.D. 600–900." In *Stability, Transformation, and Variation: The Late Woodland Southeast.* Ed. Michael S. Nassaney and Charlers R. Cobb. New York: Plenum Press, 1991.

Rollings, Willard H. *The Osage: An Ethnohistorical Study of Hegemony on the Praire-Plains.* Columbia: University of Missouri Press, 1992.

Rowland, Dunbar, ed. *Official Letterbooks of W. C. C. Claiborne.* 6 vols. Jackson MS: Mississippi State Department of Archives and History, 1917.

Rowland, Dunbar, and A. G. Sanders, eds. *Mississippi Provincial Archives: French Dominion.* 3 vols. Jackson MS: Press of the Mississippi Department of Archives and History, 1927–32.

———, trans. and eds. *Mississippi Provincial Archives: French Dominion,* vols. 4 and 5. Rev. ed. Patricia Kay Galloway. Baton Rouge: Louisiana State Univesity Press, 1984.

Sahlins, Marshall. *Stone Age Economics.* Chicago: Aldine-Atherton, 1972.

Secoy, Frank Raymond. *Changing Military Patterns of the Great Plains Indians.* Seattle: University of Washington Press, 1953; Lincoln: University of Nebraska Press, 1992.

Service, Elman R. *Primitive Social Organization: An Evolutionary Perspective*. New York: Random House, 1962.

Shaffer, Lynda Norene, *Native Americans before 1492: The Moundbuilding Centers of the Eastern Woodlands*. Armonk NY: M. E. Sharpe, 1992.

Shelby, Charmion Clair. "St. Denis's Declaration Concerning Texas in 1717." *The Southwestern Historical Quarterly* 26 (Jan. 1923): 165–83.

Sibley, John. "Account of the Red River." In *Travels in the Interior Parts of America*. Ed. Thomas Jefferson. London: J. G. Barnard, 1807.

——. "Historical Sketches of the Several Indian Tribes in Louisiana, Aouth of the Arkansa River, and between the Mississippi and River Grand." In *Travels in the Interior Parts of America*. Ed. Thomas Jefferson. London: J. G. Barnard, 1807.

——. *A Report from Natchitoches in 1807*. Ed. Annie Heloise Abel. Ville Platte LA: Evangeline Genealogical and Historical Society, 1987.

Smith, F. Todd. *The Caddo Indians: Tribes as the Convergence of Empires, 1542–1854*. College Station: Texas A&M University Press, 1995.

Smith, Marvin T. *Archaeology of Aboriginal Culture Change in the Interior Southeast: Depopulation during the Early Historic Period* Gainesville: University Press of Florida, 1987.

Smith, Ralph A., trans. and ed. "Account of the Journey of Bénard de La Harpe: Discovery Made by Him of Several Nations Situated in the West." *The Southwestern Historical Quarterly* 62 (July 1958): 75–86; (Oct. 1958): 246–59; (Jan. 1959): 371–85; (Apr. 1959): 525–41.

Spielmann, Katherine A. "Interaction among Nonhierarchical Societies." In *Farmers, Hunters, and Colonists: Interaction between the Southwest and the Southern Plains*. Ed. Katherine A. Spielmann, 1–17. Tucson: University of Arizona Press, 1991.

Stoddard, Amos. *Sketches, Historical and Descriptive of Louisiana*. Philadelphia: Mathew Carey, 1812.

Stransky, J. J. "Deer Habitat Quality of Major Forest Types in the South." *White-Tailed Deer in the Southern Forest Habitat*. Proceedings of a symposium at Nacogdoches TX, 25–26 Mar. 1969. Southern Forest Experiment Station, U.S. Forest Service, U.S. Department of Agriculture and School of Forestry, Stephen F. Austin State University, Nacogdoches, 1969.

Surrey, N. M. Miller. *The Commerce of Louisiana during the French Régime, 1699–1763*. New York: Columbia University Press, 1916.

Swanton, John R. *Source Material on the History and Ethnology of the Caddo Indians*. Washington DC: Smithsonian Institution, U.S. Bureau of American Ethnology, bulletin 132, 1942.

Tanner, Helen. "The Land and Water Communication Systems of the Southeastern Indians." In *Powhatan's Mantle: Indians in the Colonial Southeast*. Ed. Peter

H. Wood, Gregory A. Waselkov, and M. Thomas Hatley, 6–20. Lincoln: University of Nebraska Press, 1989.

Terán, Don Manuel de Mier y. "Documentos Para la Historia, año de 1828: Noticia de las tribus de salvajes conocidos que habitan en el Departamento de Tejas, y del número de familias de que consta cada tribu, puntos en que habitan y terrenos en que acampan." Boletin de la Sociedad Mexicana de Geografia y Estadistica 1870, 264–69.

Tonty, Henri de. "Memoir by the Sieur de la Tonty." *Historical Collections of Louisiana, Embracing Many Rare and Valuable Documents Relating to the Natural, Civil and Political History of that State*. Vol. 1. Ed. B. F. French, New York: Wiley and Putnam, 1846; New York: AMS Press, 1976.

Translations of Statistical and Census Reports of Texas, 1782–1826, and Sources Documenting the Black in Texas, 1603–1803. Microfilm A207 (3 reels), Sterling C. Evans Library, Texas A&M University, College Station.

Urban, Greg. "The Social Organizations of the Southeast." In *North American Indian Anthropology: Essays on Society and Culture*. Ed. Raymond J. DeMallie and Alfonso Ortiz, 172–93. Norman: University of Oklahoma Press, 1994.

U.S. Bureau of Indian Affairs. "Documents Relating to the Negotiation of the Treaty of July 1, 1835 with the Caddo Indians, Ratified Treaty No. 197." *Documents Relating to the Negotiation of Ratified and Unratified Treaties with Various Tribes of Indians, 1801–69*. Record group 75, Ratified Treaties, 1833–37, roll 3, National Archives, Washington DC.

U.S. House of Representatives. Executive Documents, 27th Congress, 2d Session, 1841–42, House doc. 25.

Usner, Daniel H., Jr. *Indians, Settlers, and Slaves in a Frontier Exchange Economy: The Lower Mississippi Valley Before 1783*. Chapel Hill: University of North Carolina Press, 1992.

Vehik, Susan C., and Timothy G. Baugh, "Prehistoric Plains Trade." In *Prehistoric Exchange Systems in North American*. Ed. Timothy G. Baugh and Jonathon E. Ericson, 249–74. New York: Plenum Press, 1994.

Weddle, Robert, ed. *La Salle, the Mississippi, and the Gulf: Three Primary Documents*. Trans. Ann Linda Bell. College Station: Texas A&M University Press, 1987.

White, Richard. *The Roots of Dependency: Subsistence, Environment, and Social Change among the Choctaws, Pawnees, and Navajos*. Lincoln: University of Nebraska Press, 1983.

Wilcox, David R. "Changing Contexts of Pueblo Adaptions, A.D. 1250–1600." In *Farmers, Hunters, and Colonists: Interaction between the Southwest and the Southern Plains*. Ed. Katherine A. Spielmann, 128–54. Tucson: University of Arizona Press, 1991.

Williams, Stephen. "The Aboriginal Location of the Kadohadacho and Related Tribes." In *Explorations in Cultural Anthropology*. Ed. Ward Goodenough, 545–70. New York: McGraw Hill, 1964.

Winfrey, Dorman, and James M. Day. *The Texas Indian Papers, 1825–1843*. 5 vols. Austin: Texas State Library, 1959.

Wolf, Eric R. *Europe and the People without History*. Berkeley: University of California Press, 1982.

Wood, Peter H. "The Changing Population of the Colonial South: An Overview by Race and Region, 1685–1790." In *Powhatan's Mantle: Indians in the Colonial Southeast*. Ed. Peter H. Wood, Gregory A. Waselkov, and M. Thomas Hatley, 35–103. Lincoln: University of Nebraska Press, 1989.

Wood, W. Raymond. "Plains Trade in Prehistoric and Protohistoric Intertribal Relations." *Anthropology on the Great Plains*. Ed. W. Raymond Wood and Margot Liberty, 98–109. Lincoln: University of Nebraska Press, 1980.

Woodall, Joe Ned. "Cultural Ecology of the Caddo." Ph. D. diss., Southern Methodist University, 1969.

Worth, John E., trans. and ed. "Relation of the Island of Florida by Luys Hernández de Biedma." *The De Soto Chronicles: The Expedition of Hernando De Soto to North America in 1539–1543*. 2 vols. Ed. Lawrence A. Clayton, Vernon James Knight Jr., and Edward C. Moore, 1:221–46. Tuscaloosa: University of Alabama Press, 1993.

Wyckoff, Donald G. "Caddoan Adaptive Strategies in the Arkansas Basin, Eastern Oklahoma." Ph. D. diss., Washington State University, 1980.

———. *The Caddoan Cultural Area*. In *Caddoan Indians I*. New York: Garland, 1974.

Wyckoff, Donald G., and Timothy G. Baugh. "Early Historic Hasinai Elites: A Model for the Material Culture of Governing Elites." *Midcontinental Journal of Archaeology* 5 (1980): 225–88.

Index

In the Indians of the Southeast series

---

*William Bartram on the
Southeastern Indians*
Edited and annotated by Gregory A.
Waselkov and Kathryn E. Holland
Braund

Deerskins and Duffels
*The Creek Indian Trade with Anglo-
America, 1685–1815*
By Kathryn E. Holland Braund

Cherokee Americans
*The Eastern Band of Cherokees in
the Twentieth Century*
By John R. Finger

Choctaw Genesis 1500–1700
By Patricia Galloway

*The Southeastern Ceremonial
Complex Artifacts and Analysis*
The Cottonlandia Conference
Edited by Patricia Galloway
Exhibition Catalog by David H. Dye
and Camille Wharey

An Assumption of Sovereignty
*Social and Political Transformation
among the Florida Seminoles,
1953–1979*
By Harry A. Kersey Jr.

The Caddo Chiefdoms
*Caddo Economics and Politics,
700–1835*
By David La Vere

Cherokee Women
*Gender and Culture Change,
1700–1835*
By Theda Perdue

The Brainerd Journal
A Mission to the Cherokees, 1817–1823
Edited and introduced by Joyce B.
Phillips and Paul Gary Phillips

The Cherokees
A Population History
By Russell Thornton

*American Indians in the Lower
Mississippi Valley*
Social and Economic Histories
By Daniel H. Usner Jr.

Powhatan's Mantle
Indians in the Colonial Southeast
Edited by Peter H. Wood, Gregory A.
Waselkov, and M. Thomas Hatley

Creeks and Seminoles
*The Destruction and Regeneration
of the Muscogulge People*
By J. Leitch Wright Jr.

www.ingramcontent.com/pod-product-compliance
Lightning Source LLC
Chambersburg PA
CBHW031533260326
41914CB00032B/1790/J